The Power of Many

How the Living Web Is Transforming Politics, Business, and Everyday Life

The Power of Many

*How the Living Web Is Transforming
Politics, Business, and Everyday Life*

Christian Crumlish

SYBEX San Francisco London

Library of Congress Card Number: 2004109414

ISBN: 0-7821-4346-6

SYBEX and the SYBEX logo are either registered trademarks or trademarks of SYBEX Inc. in the United States and/or other countries.

TRADEMARKS: SYBEX has attempted throughout this book to distinguish proprietary trademarks from descriptive terms by following the capitalization style used by the manufacturer.

The author and publisher have made their best efforts to prepare this book, and the content is based upon final release software whenever possible. Portions of the manuscript may be based upon pre-release versions supplied by software manufacturer(s). The author and the publisher make no representation or warranties of any kind with regard to the completeness or accuracy of the contents herein and accept no liability of any kind including but not limited to performance, merchantability, fitness for any particular purpose, or any losses or damages of any kind caused or alleged to be caused directly or indirectly from this book.

Manufactured in the United States of America

10 9 8 7 6 5 4 3 2 1

To Briggs, my one and only

Contents

Acknowledgments

Since the early 1990s, when I started writing full time and began relying on Internet access to connect me with employers and colleagues, I've experimented with many different approaches to collaboration, often working in multidisciplinary teams with the various members spread out all over the globe. Today it's hard to accomplish anything, in the workplace or outside of it, without the help of others whom you may rarely see or even speak to.

This book involved the efforts and support of over a hundred people, and I'm desperately afraid of forgetting to thank someone. If I have left out your name, I apologize!

My circle of acquaintances, friends, and colleagues expanded dramatically after I wrote some Internet primers in the mid '90s. I watched the Net become adopted more widely around the globe. My books were sold abroad and translated into scores of languages, and I received email from places farther and farther afield. By the late '90s, I was getting messages from readers in places like China and the Kurdish protectorate in northern Iraq and living more and more of my social life online.

I'd like to thank Delshad Fakhreddin in Erbil, Iraq, who started out as one of my readers and who has become, through the agency of the Web, a close friend of mine whom I hope to meet someday.

My experiments with web publishing and content strategy eventually led to the new media formats powered by instant gratification: blogs and wikis. (More about these two oddly named concepts later.) Indirectly, that led to this book.

Pete Gaughan, my editor, and Dan Brodnitz, my publisher, conceived of this project and asked me to write it. Without the opportunity they gave me, this book wouldn't have come into being. They made the whole thing possible and shepherded it through my publishing house, Sybex, with the support of

Rodnay Zaks, Sybex's founder and president, and Alan Hanrahan, vice president of sales and marketing. Rodnay, in fact, had inspired some of my original thinking along these lines in a talk he gave at a Waterside conference a few years ago on the subject of an always-on Internet that he refers to as the Evernet. Alan also steered my thinking in several fruitful directions, helping me find the topics and themes that would be of value to sales, marcom, and customer-relationship professionals. Everyone at Sybex was remarkably supportive throughout this effort despite a very high-pressure schedule. In fact, the enthusiasm for the book at Sybex certainly buoyed me through the most difficult stretches of writing, interviewing, and rewriting.

Beyond Pete and Dan and Rodnay and Alan, the other publishing professionals without whose help I couldn't have ever written this book include marketing specialist Cammie Allen, publicist Susannah Greenberg, copyeditor Sarah Lemaire, production editor Mae Lum, compositor Maureen Forys at Happenstance Type-O-Rama, proofreaders Laurie O'Connell and Nancy Riddiough, and indexer Ted Laux. Photographer Robert Birnbach took the author photo. Mary Hodder contributed an invaluable peer review.

As I noted, Pete and Dan thought up the idea for the book, but why did they ask me to write it? I am not a sociologist, nor am I a computer scientist, nor a scholar of social networks for that matter. I majored in philosophy at Princeton and entered the workforce during a recession in the late 1980s. But I grew up reading about computerized fictional futures and messed around with computers from grade school on. I built a computer in a cigar box in 1974, "designed" another computer that doubled as a fortune telling machine, and started learning BASIC on a Digital PDP 11/30 running RSTS around the same time—we shared the computer with other New York schools and dialed in from a thermal printer over an acoustic coupler modem running at about two baud, I should imagine. So I wasn't computerphobic and quickly found that the workplace would reward me for fiddling around with DOS, Lotus 1-2-3, and so on.

I got my start in publishing with Sybex, hired by David Kolodney, a mentor who now contributes to my political weblog Edgewise, and Joanne Cuthbertson, who also gave me some of my other key opportunities coming up. Others I'd like to thank from my computer-book publishing days include Eric Stone, Bob Myren, Richard Mills, Jim Compton, Dave Clark, and Cheryl Applewood.

I'd like to thank the people at Netcom, who provided me with my first Unix shell account and my first Internet email address; the members of the first online community I became attached to, Usenet's rec.music.gdead; as well as the merry punsters (never trust a punster), the Bay Area taper's group, antiweb, and the many remarkable people I've met on The WELL.

I thank all the contributors to Enterzone, Coffeehouse, Telegraph, and Mediajunkie; Boris Khadinov at Edgewise; Andrew Bayer at Radio Free Blogistan; and Elizabeth Spiers from The Kicker.

Thank you to weblog software entrepreneurs and leaders, including Ben and Mena Trott and Anil Dash of Six Apart; Evan Williams, Meg Hourihan, Paul Bausch, and others from Pyra; and Dave Winer of UserLand and Scripting News fame. In addition, I'd like to thank Joshua Schachter of Delicious and Memepool, whose relentless inventiveness astounds me, as well as Matt Haughey, Nick Denton, Duncan Riley, and others pushing out the boundaries of the blogosphere.

Thanks to my favorite pundit bloggers as well, including Atrios, Kos, David Neiwert, Taegan Goddard, Kevin Drum, Adam Felbers, Brad DeLong, Daniel Drezner, Oliver Willis, and Joshua Micah Marshall. I am no doubt forgetting many here, but I mustn't forget Ward Cunningham!

I'd like to acknowledge the inspiration of Governor Howard Dean and Joe Trippi, the campaign manager who turned conventional wisdom on its head.

The many experts, wise folks, and online veterans who offered their time to me; answered interview questions via phone, email, IM, and blog; reviewed chapters; or otherwise offered suggestions and feedback include: Jerome Armstrong, Nick Arnett, Levi Asher, Gene Austin, The One True b!X, Matt Bailey, Andrew Baio, Vinay Bhagat, Joan Blades, Felicia Borrego, danah boyd, Justin Burke, Mal Burnstein, Marc Canter, Ed Cone, Vicki Cosgrove, Laramie Crocker, Brian Dear, Neil Drumm, Julie Eddy, Mary Fifield, Christopher Filkins, Erica Fox, Richard Frankel, Seth Godin, Jeff Green, Gwen Harlow, Scott Heiferman, Mary Hodder, Taylor House, Aldon Hynes, Joichi Ito, Eden James, Paul Jene, Clay Johnson, Steven Berlin Johnson, Peter Kamali, Roger Karraker, George Kelly, Rick Klau, Josh Koenig, Elizabeth Lane Lawley, Jon Lebkowsky, Om Malik, Matt Margolis, Ross Mayfield, Susan Mernit, Judith Meskill, Markos Moulitsas Zuniga, Craig Newmark, Freeman Ng, Christine

O'Connell, Chuck Olsen, David Pollard, Derek Powazek, Howard Rheingold, Zack Rosen, Liza Sabater, Jon Shemitz, Clay Shirky, David Sifry, Yaniv Soha, Paul Spitz, Matt Stoller, Nigel Strafford, Janet Stromberg, Zephyr Teachout, Jeff Tiedrich, Rayne Today, Robert Vogel, Cecil Vortex, Gabe Wachob, David Weinberger, Nancy White, and Phil Wolff.

In some ways, this book can be read as a guided, distributed conversation among the above-named people, with me merely conducting the discussion. While reviewing the galleys, I realized that one way to skim the book is simply to read the numerous epigraphs; they serve as a kind of executive summary of the (for the most part) pithy sound bites of webloggers. Each chapter also ends with a set of links to further resources online for those who wish to read the source materials in full. And in fact, I'll be publishing some complete interviews with some of the contributors listed above as well as with additional guests at the book's website (http://www.thepowerofmany.com).

I'd like to thank my former agent Danielle Jatlow, who did this deal for me and always believed I could write this type of book, and my current agent Margot Maley at Waterside Productions, who's one of the best. I also want to thank Matt Wagner and Bill Gladstone who represented me ably in the past, as well as David Fugate, Kimberly Valentini, and Maureen Maloney at Waterside, who have helped me in numerous ways.

Thanks to friends who have inspired me, including David Gans, Rita Hurault, Nicholas Meriwether, Ted Nadeau, and Martha Conway, and my family members, especially Mom and Dad, Jennifer, Arthur, Peter, Sara, Caleb, and Sam. I'd like to also thank my extended Crumlish family, some of whom I reconnected with in researching this book, as well as T.J. Spitznas and the whole Spitznas side of my family.

Most of all, dedication notwithstanding, please allow me to thank Briggs Nisbet, who proofread all the galleys to protect me from my own worst excesses, who has given me the kind of support that most writers only dream of, and who made room for me to go a little crazy in order to get this thing done in time.

Foreword

Ten years ago, a handful of people were using the Internet, convinced that some-day, people would use the Net to change everything—business, social relation-ships, and eventually, governing. It would be everyone's printing press.

Ten years ago, I was evangelizing the Internet at Charles Schwab, telling folks that the brokerage business would someday rely on it. I was one of those suggesting that it would change everything.

We all kept at it for a few years while technological and economic cycles converged. More people saw the potential of the Net and got really excited. The Internet, and the "new economy," got badly overhyped. A lot of money was invested, people got a lot of good jobs, and a lot of people made a lot of money…much of which existed only on paper.

If you believe that the Net could be everyone's printing press, this was pretty good. Lots of technology got developed and then deployed, resulting in relatively low-cost systems and Net connections. This happened fairly fast, at least in historical terms.

However, the focus on making lots of money fast was a distraction. The industry forgot that the Internet must serve real human needs.

People started to realize that the "new economy" was a bit of a mass hallucination—that it wasn't fulfilling its promise, relative to the hype. The bubble burst; a lot of people lost jobs; a lot of people lost savings.

On the other hand, the infrastructure remained intact, and a lot of people trained in new technologies moved across the world.

People who believe in the use of the Net have kept on plugging away, using it to change the way we address everyday needs, to tell people what con-ventional media neglects, and to change the nature of governance, possibly everywhere.

This is a slow, organic process that is now occasionally erupting into the press, the Dean campaign being the best example.

In *The Power of Many*, Christian Crumlish describes a lot of the ways people are using the Net to change the world right now—small efforts, large efforts—showing what we all can do with everyone's printing press. Take a look. Find something that works for you and do it, change it, fix it now.

—Craig Newmark
Founder, craigslist.org
June 2004

Introduction

The living part of the Web—the constantly-being-updated part—is reaching a critical mass. Sure, it's early days yet when it comes to the Internet and society. We are still living through the dawn of electronic internetworking, still learning the rules of the game. Across the planet, a small proportion of people—roughly 10 percent—are active users of the Internet, but that fraction keeps growing. More and more people know people in their own personal networks of friends and family, acquaintances and trusted colleagues, who are involved in some sort of social network with an online component, or who are getting some of their news or some of their civic engagement through digitally organized groups.

The living Web changes every day. It is not the static web of billboards and brochures but a dynamic web of people's voices. It is born from the same group-building impulses that we evolved on the savannas, translated via the magic of remote and electronic communications formats such as mailing lists and instant messaging and persistent archived discussion boards and forwarded petitions and peer-to-peer networks and software and weblogs into a living, changing, growing, evolving web of people working together to improve a neighborhood or change the world.

We are at another major turning point in the way people are using the online world to organize their human relationships and their involvement in society. In the run-up to this year's presidential election, it became clear that new ways of using the Web were becoming de rigueur among political candidacies and with activists, but the trend far outstrips politics and neighborhood causes; once you start looking, it shows signs of entering into nearly every aspect of community life.

Is this really any different? People were discussing things online with the PLATO system in the 1970s. The first what's-new-on-the-Web websites around 1991 were already functioning as weblogs. There have been mailing lists as long as there has been email. This is all true.

What's different now is the increasing adoption of online communication by wider circles of, for the lack of a better word, ordinary people—as opposed to the academics, computer adepts, and military people who populated Arpanet and the early days of the Internet. The proverbial grandparent is using ofoto.com to share family photographs.

The living Web is scaling up, and it's accelerating. You may safely ignore it today, but in a few months to a year you are going to find this topic inescapable.

My goal with this book is to identify the trends and some of the new methods and techniques that people are using to connect with each other online and accomplish real effects in the world, so that you can take the pattern to heart and start seeing where it applies in your own life: in your own work, at your job, in your network, with your customers or suppliers or colleagues (or students, or relatives, or your motorcycle club, and so on).

I've been studying, analyzing, and experimenting with online media for over a decade, writing about technology and consulting with business and nonprofits (and now political campaigns). I keep up with emerging technology, and I'm not afraid of jargon, but I'm much more interested in how people end up making use of technology than in the whys and wherefores of the engineering involved.

With this book, I try to help you get a handle on what's changing and what's new and how it's going to affect you.

Tech startups have popularized a number of vivid slang-y expressions that have crossed over into the regular business world, such as "we drank the Kool-Aid" (meaning we've become believers in this new technology or business idea) or "we have to eat our own dog food" (meaning we need to use our own technology or our customers won't trust it). In writing this book, I drank the Kool-Aid and I've been eating the dog food. The research, writing, editing, and review of the material in this book has largely taken place over the Internet—in email, on weblogs, on social network software systems, in instant messages—and with the help of more than 50 people who sat for interviews, reviewed chapters, offered suggestions, and otherwise helped me sift through my pile of half-baked ideas and helped with the baking. In the final week, I was passing the manuscript of Chapter 2 around many of the key players for and against Howard

Dean's primary campaign, getting last-minute corrections of chronology and other important minutiae.

I'm assuming that you have some passing familiarity with the Internet, especially email but also at least with the World Wide Web. I don't assume that you follow politics closely or that you are an expert in any of the topics discussed in the book (activism, neighborhood community activities, self-help, art, online dating, or business networking) but I do expect that you'll be able to recognize the patterns I'm talking about and see where they apply in your own life. I've included a glossary of technical terms at the end of the book so anytime you see a three-letter acronym (such as RSS) or any unfamiliar jargon, you can flip to the back to get a brief definition, some basic grounding in the concept, or pointers to more information on the Web.

The book has an online presence (of course, at http://www.thepowerofmany.com) and a weblog for collecting links and commentary that extends back to 2003 and should continue until the topic has become second nature to us all. A collaborative "wiki" (whiteboard) website will enable us to collect corrections, requests for glossary entries, and further elaborations and commentary from readers and colleagues.

You can also keep up with further developments related to the living Web and its impact in the real world, discuss the book with other readers, contribute to the glossary or request new definitions, suggest areas of research that we should be aware of, and discuss social networking online. I'd like to extend the same invitation to you as I did to Mary Hodder (who became this book's key peer reviewer) in a Berkeley café at the conclusion of a three-hour interview about the focus of this book: "I hope we continue this conversation for the rest of our lives."

Chapter 1   People Get Ready

So, anyway, dinner. It was a great reminder of the real-world
rewards of this new electronic community I've become a part
of. Allan and I had a great time talking, laughing, eating, and
sharing a bottle of wine. That kind of experience cements a
friendship in a way that instant messenger just can't do. I don't
use technology for the sake of using technology—at least, I try
not to. I use it to enhance the things that I care about in my
life—friends, family, my research. Yesterday afternoon I spoke
to my kids over iChat audio. I arranged to meet Allan using
email and IM. And I participated in great discussions about
my areas of research interest during presentations. But all of
those spill over into the real world, and I use them to enhance
the real world, not replace it.

—ELIZABETH LANE LAWLEY, "Step Away
from the Laptop"

The phone rang; it was Catherine Saint Louis, who introduced herself as calling from the Sunday *New York Times Magazine* and asked to speak to my partner, Briggs Nisbet. Great, I thought, another solicitation; at least they didn't call
her "Mr. Briggs Nisbet." But, no, Catherine told me that she edits the Lives column, that they were doing a special issue on landscaping in two weeks, that
she'd been reading Briggs' gardening blog, *True Dirt,* and did I think Briggs
would be interested in writing a piece for her column in the magazine?

I nearly passed out from shock and stammered that I suspected that she would indeed be interested and here's her work number, her work email, her personal email, and my email address. Oh, you don't need my address? Of course you don't, sorry about that. No, that's fine, bye.

Over the next five days, Catherine and Briggs collaborated via email and cell phone on three different versions of the column until it was just so.

What does this have to do with the power of many or the living Web? I asked Briggs to ask Catherine how she found *True Dirt*. Catherine had wanted a personal insight for the Lives column. She thought that searching the Internet for weblogs on gardening might help her find a suitable columnist.

She googled for something like "gardening blogs" to find a writer for the Sunday ever-lovin' *New York Times Magazine*? She trusted the Internet to help her find a suitable writer? Interestingly, the chain that led to the call went through a web-archived article from the *Boston Globe* (owned by the same company that owns the *Times*) on garden blogs that listed *True Dirt* in its short list of recommended sites at the end of the article.

How did that author find *True Dirt*? Perhaps because of some of the other people who publish their thoughts about gardening or nature or food or related topics on the Web, some of whom sometimes link to *True Dirt*. How did *they* find it? Because of promotional efforts online and word of mouth from *True Dirt*'s publisher: a tiny web operation that consists mainly of me and whoever else is helping out with the current front-burner projects. Which means mostly me.

True Dirt, written by Briggs and Richard Frankel, is part of a network of sites presented as a group site at Telegraph.nu. It is an example of niche journalism in the old-fashioned sense of journal writing and an example of what is sometimes semi-facetiously called "nanopublishing." Nanopublishing is niche publishing managed with lightweight content-handling systems that users like using, including blogs and wikis, but usually at the moment blogs.

The quality of the writing at our sites and the pertinence of the material to its subject matter is apt enough to attract the sort of people who notice stuff on the Web, link to it, and keep running logs (or blogs) of links, insights, interesting thoughts, and notes—that is, people who take note of their surroundings and sometimes remark on it soon after making observations, usually in the form of a sequential log. Those people have at least occasionally linked to us, and we point to each other, and we are thus in some ways like the bogus "link farms" used to try to game Google's page rank system. But in our case, the sites are real, the domains are distinct, and the authors are many.

By hosting *True Dirt* on Mediajunkie, I helped ensure that Briggs' writing would have a better chance of being noticed by the larger network through which certain bridge nodes connect my various small cliques to the wider Internet culture of early adopters. It also helps connect to what are sometimes called the influentials, the people whose sites offer trend-tracking clues to mainstream media (and other sales, advertising, marketing, publicity, and communications professionals), the freelance meme watchers of the living Web: the independent bloggers.

In My Day, We Shared Music via Snail

When I first got on the Internet more than a decade ago, I did so by using my modem to dial up to a service called Netcom. Once connected, I found myself at a command line. A few geeky friends taught me how to use the mail programs ("elm" and "Pine" were my options, or the even more bare-bones "mail") and how to use the "man" command to read manuals and learn about other command-line options.

This was before the Web had a graphically driven interface available (Mosaic and later Netscape were still more than a year away). Somehow I managed to stumble onto Usenet, a worldwide distributed network of networks hosting discussions on any topic imaginable. I was a fan of the Grateful Dead but had few nearby friends with whom I could discuss the band, so I quickly discovered the rec.music.gdead newsgroup, which became my first online community "hangout."

It was great to be able to connect to people all over the world who shared my interests and to ask questions and share information that otherwise would have maundered unaired in the back of our minds or on someone's shelves. But what truly amazed me was the first time I opened my mailbox to find a package containing cassette tapes. The tapes featured a recording of my first

Dead concert—a show in Saratoga, New York in 1984. As I stood there with a physical artifact in my hand, it dawned on me that throughout this Internet cloud—sitting in front of their own computers and typing messages to the same forums—were in fact real flesh-and-blood people. It took something happening in the real world, an actual object being sent through the so-called snail mail, and my chance to hear once again music that I'd heard for the first time twenty years ago to bring this point home to me. I immediately got online and posted something silly to the effect of "Wow, I just found out you all are real!"

Over time, I started running into people at Dead concerts in the Bay Area, whom I knew only from being online and that was another revelation. Some people were *exactly* like they seemed online. Others were very different from the personas they projected. In each case, I had to expand my mental file to add new information about these people: what their faces looked like, how they stood, what they did with their hands while talking, and the timbre of their voices. In each case, a virtual person became a real person.

These were my first clues that the true power of the Internet would be unleashed only when online interaction crossed over into the so-called real world.

By the way, I realize it doesn't help my credibility much to talk about this love of Grateful Dead music, but I'm told by researchers such as danah boyd that the online world frequently caters to otherwise marginalized parts of one's public identity. When I interviewed boyd, I told her about my involvement in the DeadHead Usenet group when I would ordinarily not mention that aspect of my online experience around hip younger Bay Area folks, for fear of being stereotyped as dope-smoking hippie with flowery aesthetics and half-assed politics. I think I did this deliberately to expose my own vulnerability, my own marginalized identity, even as I risked a stereotype of me clicking into shape in her mind.

The other reason I mentioned it was because I had just been through the second meaningful online community experience of my life—this time with the Dean campaign—and I wasn't the only person to remark on the Dead-show atmosphere at some of the big Dean rallies and events in California last year.

Who Was Howard Dean and How Did He Go So Far?

Before I get too far into this, I should probably get my biases out on the table. This book isn't about my political opinions or my ideology. The lessons I am discovering about how the living Web works, how it's changing group behavior and organizing techniques and politics, have nothing to do with the political spectrum of left to right (and perhaps a bit to do with the spectrum of decentralization vs. hierarchy). Nonetheless, my own experience is relevant both because it informs my ideas about what is changing, and because it will enable readers who don't share my political leanings to factor out any bias that I am unable to eliminate from my point-of-view.

I volunteered for the local grassroots group working to support Howard Dean in the Democratic primary in 2003 and early 2004. (I live in Oakland, California, so for me that meant East Bay for Dean.) Through the course of my involvement, I performed a wide range of political organizing and activism roles and ended up on the local organizing committee. After Dean lost the nomination, the group that I belong to changed its name to East Bay for Democracy, and its work continues with goals that still include electoral activities but will continue beyond the upcoming November election.

One of the hats I wore in the thick of the campaign was "giver of the fundraising pitch" at houseparties. (Because of a loophole in FEC regulations, it's easier to host a fundraiser in a person's house than it is in a public accommodation, so houseparties proliferated to raise the insane amount of money required to keep a national campaign in the game.) This involved attending houseparties, answering guests' questions about the Dean candidacy, and giving a speech making the case for supporting Dean financially and evangelizing the idea of a $100 revolution (more about that in Chapter 2, "All Politics Is Personal").

At one such party, my host told me how he got involved in volunteering in the primary. He attended a meetup in San Francisco to learn more about the candidate in March 2003, twenty months before the election and a full year before the California primary. He noted that by the next meetup he attended, a month later, twice as many people were present, and that the growth continued exponentially all that summer.

Once the meeting had been called to order, the attendees were given a chance to introduce themselves and discuss the political issues that most affected them. (This was something called "The Great American Conversation," because a large part of the effort involved getting people to meet in person in coffeehouses and living rooms, meet their neighbors, and start rebuilding the American community one block at a time.) After the introductions, though, came the most striking activity of the event, from my host's point-of-view. The meeting organizers—who had obtained their materials to run the meeting by downloading position papers from the DeanforAmerica.com website, by participating in a conference call, and by signing up and receiving packages in the mail—handed out packages to each of the attendees who were willing. Each package contained the names and addresses of two undecided Democratic voters in Iowa who were eligible to participate in the January 2004 Iowa caucuses. Also in the packages were stationery, envelopes, and stamps.

Participants were asked to write personal letters to their two assigned recipients, telling them in their own words why they supported Howard Dean for president and why they hoped that the Iowan would brave the cold and snow, attend the caucus, and stand for Dean. My host was impressed not merely that the campaign wasn't scripting or controlling or reviewing the contents of these letters before they were sealed and sent. (Yes, they provided some suggested "talking points," but each participant was free to send whatever message they deemed worthy of committing to paper.) What blew him away was that the campaign had leveraged the Internet—that famous disembodied tool of virtual connections and anonymous interaction—to get a group of local people together in the same room and to motivate them to hand-write *snail mail* to send to people in another state, one with a much more crucial early nominating event than California's March primary.

"My hand was cramping up," he told me. "I can't remember the last time I wrote one letter, let alone two. Plus, I was sort of worried about what the other people were writing. There was this one guy next to me who looked horrendous. I couldn't imagine he was going to convince an Iowa farmer to support Dean, but I was struck by the *trust* the campaign was showing in us volunteers."

The Internet is finally starting to become an integrated tool for face-to-face communication and directed, intentional, "real-world" actions. That combination of virtual organizing and physical activity, of structured top-down direction and fringe-driven, self-organized, spontaneous organization, that marriage of order and chaos, began to be recognized as Dean rocketed from an obscure dark horse insurgent to the presumptive frontrunner before a single primary vote had been cast. His was a revolutionary new story about how people could use these technologies to connect to each other, take action, and effect change in these media-driven, TV-anesthetized times.

This book, then, is an examination of the lessons that can be learned from what has worked and what has not worked. It's an attempt to tease out the intertwining sinews of networked telecommunications with real minds and bodies, and an attempt to look ahead at how these enabling technologies might be leveraged most effectively as they become ever more embedded in our day-to-day lives.

Usenet traditionally scheduled "burgermunches" as a way for their participants to meet in person; the pioneering online service The Well learned that its community coalesced best after parties where people had a chance to meet face to face. This lesson continues to trickle out to others trying to take advantage of the unprecedented reach of the Internet. Without embodied action, without face-to-face interaction, and without people meeting up together in place and time, the Internet might as well be a dream world. As the interconnectedness of the Web reaches into the mundane details of ordinary reality and causes actual bodies to share space, real conversations to take place using lips and tongues, heard by ears and processed by auditory apparatus in brains—that's when the magic starts to happen.

The Dean nomination run failed in its principal goal—but, as craigslist founder Craig Newmark said at a recent conference, "We're still talking about it." In the aftermath of that campaign, a thousand flowers are blooming or dying back in the form of new organizations—from skeletal websites to large functioning networks of people—that have emerged in the wake of the Dean for America (DFA) project to emulate those parts that worked so well to get people up off their couches and out into the streets.

When Did Everyone Get a Blog?

So why has it taken so long for these lessons to be applied in the real worlds of politics, civic communities, activism, and other forms of real-world organizing?

For one thing, in the long scheme of things, the Internet is still young, still new. In time, a generation will grow up for whom the Internet has always been there. These people will be natives of the Internet, and they will be intimate with its folkways and fluent in its protocols. For now, many of us are still grasping at these new models of interaction and still trying to draw analogies from our earlier lives and imagine and invent ways to connect up the virtual world with the real world.

And to be perfectly honest, the Internet and computers are still too difficult for many people to use. There are still multiple, overlapping digital divides. There's the matter of generation, as well as economic class and other factors as well. My parents are still not sure what they're looking at when they're looking at the monitor of their Apple Macintosh. What to me is naturally a modal dialog box is to them just another rectangle among many on a screenful of confusing metaphors.

So we still have a long way to go just to make the basic tools of online interaction accessible to everyone. A perfect case in point is blogging. Blogging has been around in one form or another as long as the Web has been around (and the Web was invented in 1991). But the strange new word "blog" wasn't coined until 1999, the buzz didn't start till 2000, and the first big wave of political bloggers didn't get traction until late 2001 in the aftermath of the terrorist attacks on the World Trade Center. Blogging didn't come into its own as a political communications tool until 2003 with the run-up to the 2004 presidential election. The hype continues to expand outward concentrically, yet blogging still isn't easy or intuitive enough for everyone's grandmother to do (or to care about or want to get involved with).

Rebecca Blood, who writes a long-running weblog called Rebecca's Pocket and published a guide to blogging called *The Weblog Handbook,* coined a "law" to describe the way the blog "revolution" perpetually seems to have just hit the mainstream to whomever has just discovered it:

> Blood's Law of Weblog History: The year you discovered weblogs and/or started your own is 'The Year Blogs Exploded.' Corollary: The year after you started your blog is the beginning of 'Weblog Permanent September.'

> Anil's Corollary: The first weblog you read is the one that invented the medium.

But the power of blogging lies in its ease. Since the Web arrived, it was theoretically possible for just about anybody to create their own website and publish their own writing freely online. The Web has been heralded as a potential communications revolution, possibly unequaled since Gutenberg and the movable type printing press. But the promise of online self-publishing has fallen short of the hype, because of the technical barriers. I had to learn Unix command-line hieroglyphics to send my first email messages. Email didn't catch on in a big way until there were nice graphical point-and-click interfaces and seamless Internet connections backing everything up. In the same way, personal online self-publishing didn't reach its full potential until the advent of easy, forms-driven, push-button publishing interfaces and, perhaps more importantly, easy automatic publish-and-subscribe syndication formats that enable a global conversation to emerge.

The presidential election of 2004 will be the first in which every major candidate's website had a weblog and in which bloggers played the traditional Washington-based pundit driving the debate and determined what topics of discussion were on the table.

Perhaps more importantly, the next presidency, regardless of who wins this November, will be the first to be blogged by thousands of ordinary people from Day One. Bloggers will scrutinize cabinet choices and transition-team appointments and start organizing to support or oppose the president's policies even before the inauguration.

By themselves, blogs don't create communities any more than Usenet did or email would. They represent, however, a great leap forward in the ease of people expressing themselves, communicating, and meeting each other online. As a result, they are a critical enabling technology for the kind of real-world impact that concerns me in this book.

In fact, blogs are just the best current tool that supports freer personal expression. "Disintermediating" the mass-broadcast middleman that has dominated global communication in the previous century and supplementing (if not replacing) it with people-to-people communications channels that will eventually yield their own media forms, perhaps more collaborative or more granularly nuanced.

This new form already does a better job of incorporating multiple viewpoints than one-size-fits-all broadcast media, and blogging also favors participatory reading and writing of news and analysis instead of passive reception of information monopolized by experts, pundits, and people who can afford to make a career or a hobby of covering one particular beat in endless detail. Many-to-many communication on the living Web is a moving target if there ever was one. More and more, books and even weblog entries begin to look like snapshots of waterfalls. Frozen for an instant, the picture gives much valuable insight into the dynamics of that moment, but it's the unending flow of water that conveys the full story.

There's Something Happening Here— What It Is Ain't Exactly Clear

We shouldn't overlook the importance of music and other media and filesharing. They have proven the concept for the emergent, cellular ways that people are organizing themselves. Back in my online Deadhead days, when we wanted to exchange music, we posted offers or requests to newsgroups, we exchanged email messages agreeing on trades, and we sent each other tapes filled with music. That way the concentric circles expanded.

Even then, we had some inkling that this was going to change. Digital audio tapes (DATs) were already popular and the prospect of recordable CDs was known to be in the offing. To anyone who thought hard about it for a little while, it was clear that some combination of fatter pipes (more bandwidth) and better compression formats was eventually going to create a circumstance where it would be possible to send or distribute music directly online, without the intervening analog media of tape cassettes, stamped mailers, and U.S. Postal Service employees.

If anything, that day came sooner than we expected, with MP3 as a "good enough" digital format, and the advent of broadband Internet connections. By now, anyone plugged into the Net is aware of how Napster revolutionized music distribution, not simply because of the digital media technologies (there had already been websites like mp3.com and etree.com where the music was downloaded from centralized repositories), but because of the revolutionary peer-to-peer model by which people could find each other's music and share it freely without any intervening authority. Yes, Napster was stopped by the record companies, who, like the film companies today, saw a serious threat to their copyrights and their monopoly on distribution. But the filesharing model has continued in the form of endless variations such as Gnutella, KaZaA, and many others. And now an application called Bit-Torrent has taken the shared-download phenomenon a step further. There will be no stopping this revolution.

Mary Hodder writes a weblog and maintains a website called The Napsterization of Everything, in which she argues that this peer-to-peer revolution will extend far beyond music and other media sharing, and that it actually represents a new paradigm of person-to-person communication and networking. This is yet another of the ingredients in this ongoing revolution in self-organizing human communities.

Television Not Meeting Our Needs

"Television…Teacher, mother…secret lover."

—Homer Simpson, *The Simpsons*

So there is starting to be a critical mass of people online, and the tools are gradually becoming human-friendly enough to make it easy for people to join groups, write their thoughts, and connect to virtual communities. The question is, what needs are these new resources meeting?

We are leaving behind a century of mass media for which Americans (and, slowly, the rest of the world) have been trained to sit passively and consume entertainment as an audience. The fundamental difference between the Internet and older media networks is that the Internet is interactive. Everyone can be a producer just as everyone can be a consumer. This is not some utopian ideal that posits that everyone will become famous or make a living in entertainment or art or media, or that everyone's soapbox or megaphone is just as big and loud and effective as everybody else's. We will not see inequality erased in our lifetimes, if ever. There will always be people of differing means and abilities, those who see and grasp and manipulate the possibilities offered by new technologies and those who are alienated by them and shun them.

The point is not that everyone gets to be famous so much as everyone is permitted a voice, can talk back, and speak truth to power.

In the last century, participation in public life in the United States has withered. There are fewer common spaces, fewer public areas, fewer town halls. Outside of intentional communities, it has become harder and harder for people to find each other as we lock ourselves away in our homes and turn on our television sets.

Internet analyst Clay Shirky wrote about the unmet promise of the Dean campaign in a seminal essay called "Exiting Deanspace." In it, he noted that voting remains one of the human activities that is still explicitly tied to geography. In most other realms of human behavior, "culture matters, and since the 1970s, anyone who has looked at the cultural effects of the Internet has picked the same key element: the victory of affinity over geography. The like-minded can now gather from all corners and bask in the warmth of knowing you are not alone."

But the Internet doesn't destroy geography. There is nothing inherent in the Net's freeing from the details of our physical location that prevents us from organizing along geographical lines as well. Shirky noted to me in a phone conversation that in the earlier days of the Net, when the population was sparser, it was more salient that one could find commonalities with people from farther away. If you were the only ostrich fancier in your small town, good luck finding people to come to your meeting. But get online and you could find a Usenet group, a web page, or a mailing list where you might be able to meet ostrich fanciers from around the globe.

This hasn't changed. What has changed is that now there are large communities of neighbors who are all online. In some neighborhoods, it's not unreasonable to expect many of the people who live up the street from you are also online. It turns out that online organizational tools and behaviors can supplement real-world networking, even when physical proximity is available.

By itself, the Internet doesn't eliminate passivity. It is just as easy to turn on a computer and ignore your neighbor or your loved ones as it is to zone out in front of a TV. The one critical difference, however, is that operating the computer and connecting to the Internet requires a degree of involvement that goes beyond reaching out with a remote control and changing the volume or the channel.

Furthermore, broadcasting functions on a one-to-many model, in which each individual station sends out a signal and the people within range have only two choices: to tune in or not. However, the Internet fundamentally facilitates an entirely different many-to-many model in which choices multiply and smaller groups of people—even smaller audiences—can coalesce around the performers, the issues, or the topics that interest them. Instead of ever-widening circles emanating from a single point, there are endless interlocking circles of various sizes, some of which connect with other circles and others which float freely.

The human urge to connect and form communities is as strong as ever, even as the public infrastructure that enables it has withered from disuse. All by themselves, Internet groups (mailing lists, Yahoo! Groups, newsgroups, websites, and so on) do not replace real-life community; they merely present what's possible. They enable our minds to connect while our bodies are sedentary and uninvolved.

The online facilitated communities are created only when actions are involved. They are created when people rise up from their easy chairs, leave their homes, inconvenience themselves, discover the church basement or the community center, enter a stranger's living room or fight City Hall.

It's a commonplace online that unbridled arguments (sometimes called *flame wars*) arise more easily than in face-to-face conversation. The semi-anonymity of sitting behind a computer screen makes it easier to post denuded ASCII text calling someone a jerk or an idiot (or an "idiotarian"). It's often said that people will insult each more readily this way, when in person they would be more likely to seek comity and behave like a mature human being. The detachment of a pure online existence permits us to evade the consequences of our bad behavior. It allows us to hit and run, to harm others verbally and then get up from the computer, make a sandwich, turn on the television, and forget what we said and who we hurt. If we know we will be seeing someone at church, on the playing field, or at a face-to-face meeting, we're reminded of what being part of a human community really entails. We're also reminded of the sensible self-imposed limits of free expression in a world, where we are all shoulder to shoulder, breathing the same air and laboring under the same—or equivalent—challenges and difficulties. Compassion is necessary when we are embodied.

Ridiculously Easy Group Formation

The challenge for community leaders, politicians, clueful entrepreneurs, and anyone who seeks to take advantage of the enormous potential of Internet-mediated communities is to harness the spontaneity of emergent organizations. Social software tools must be designed to promote ease of use and to guide people into productive interaction. While the trend we are seeing is that people are spontaneously forming their own communities of self-interest, there is still a role for leaders and for the people who seek to host or provide services to these groupings.

The trick involves

- Balanced order and chaos

- Finding the proper role for direction

- Structure

- Leadership on the one hand and freedom, spontaneity, and emergent self-organization on the other

Nigel Strafford, a trustee of the Chaordic Commons, explained to me that human beings are not entirely comfortable with too much structure or with too much freedom. Both order and chaos in the extreme make us anxious and push us toward the other pole. It is somewhere in the gray area between them that the power of both combine to create something uniquely effective. It is as easy to squelch creativity with a heavy hand as it is to fritter away effective action in undirected spasms of always starting and never following through.

On the one hand, we're seeing leaderless group formation; on the other hand, we're really seeing a new form of leadership. These new kinds of leaders have to find the right balance between giving direction and giving up control. Joe Trippi, Howard Dean's original campaign manager, had to unlearn all of his past campaign experience, with its military model of command-and-control. He realized, partly because he had spent some time in Silicon Valley consulting with Internet businesses during and after the dotcom boom, that the only way to unleash the creativity at the fringes was to permit the grassroots to set their own agendas and to take actions without explicit direction or even permission from the center.

The risks involved in this are huge and in fact, are terrifying to traditional organizers. What if someone out there on the fringes says or does something stupid? How will that reflect back on the center? It's not an easy question, and there isn't a simple answer. Somehow, though, Trippi understood that the risk was worth it, that the reward of unleashing spontaneous creative energy would outweigh the potential harm of an operative doing something that would harm the campaign or reflect badly on the candidate. Not only that, Trippi understood that this emergent form of community organization was in fact *the only way* that an insurgent presidential candidate from a small state would have any chance at all to challenge the Washington-based presumptive frontrunners for his party's nomination.

So we are seeing the emergence of new forms of laterally organized, network-driven groups that represent a challenge to the hierarchical, corporate-style organizations that we are all familiar with. Mind you, there is nothing inherently positive or progressive about this structure. Just as order and chaos do not equate to good and evil, this new cellular form of structure does not map up to any kind of inherent good or evil. Al-Qaida uses the Internet. Terrorists can create their own chaordic entities.

If anything, the challenge to people who wish to create a better world, whether their vision is informed by traditionally left- or right-wing politics, is to adopt and embrace these tactics and technologies now, and master them quickly. Those who do not have our best interests at hearts will surely do so, and we can't let them win.

The Smart Mob

Although I'm most interested in the people in the trenches and in examining efforts that have succeeded or are succeeding and those that have failed, in an attempt to tease out the secrets of leveraging online technology to create effective action in the real world, I do not wish to ignore the enormous amount of theoretical thinking that informs the activities we're seeing sprout up around us.

Yes, theories go only so far, and actual real-world empirical examples are always more informative, but a lot of very smart people have put some real effort into understanding, analyzing, and predicting how these things can and do work. You will see quotations from some of these people as well as excerpts from interviews, commentaries, and essays throughout this book. Some names may pop up just once in context, and others will appear throughout the book. These include people such as

- Knowledge management expert David Pollard, who writes a weblog called How to Change the World

- Howard Rheingold, who has been examining virtual communities since his early days on the Well and recently wrote the bestselling book *Smart Mobs*

- Jim Moore, whose essay "The Second Superpower Rears Its Beautiful Head" brought the idea of semi-coordinated, online-mediated political action to wide attention

- danah boyd, a researcher at University of California at Berkeley, a consultant to social software companies, and a hands-on participant in the online communities she studies

Throughout the book, as is appropriate, I credit insights to the people who identified them or supplied them to me. As I told more than one participant, there's a reason this book isn't called *Christian Crumlish Is a Guru Who Knows Everything*. Any insight or skill that I bring to this project has to do with asking the right questions and getting hold of the people who can supply the answers. My approach in this book is to live out the credo within it: If I work with many people, I produce much more powerful effective work than if I limit myself to only what I can do alone.

We have new tools for working together and collaborating to create communities that are infinitely more than the sum of their disconnected parts.

The Web Comes Alive

This is not a book about technology and not a how-to book, but many Internet and web-related technologies figure into the story. In an influential essay titled "Ten Tips for Writing the Living Web," literary hypertext publisher and software entrepreneur Mark Bernstein provides a good working definition of the living Web:

> Some parts of the Web are finished, unchanging creations—as polished and as fixed as books or posters. But many parts change all the time:
>
> - news sites bring up-to-the-minute developments, ranging from breaking news and sports scores to reports on specific industries, markets, and technical fields
>
> - weblogs, journals, and other personal sites provide a window on the interests and opinions of their creators
>
> - corporate weblogs, wikis, knowledge banks, community sites, and workgroup journals provide share news and knowledge among co-workers and supply-chain stakeholders
>
> Some of these sites change every week; many change every day; a few change every few minutes. Daypop's Dan Chan calls this the Living Web, the part of the Web that is always changing.

Beyond the now-familiar websites and mailing lists, the living Web is fed by a host of new specific web services and applications, forms of collaborative software such as

- Blogs

- Wikis

- Discussion boards

- P2P filesharing tools like Napster

- Chat tools such as IRC

- Shared workspaces for virtual collaboration

- Commercial and noncommercial web-driven service sites like Meetup and upcoming.org

I use the term "living Web" to also refer to things that aren't really part of the World Wide Web (such as unlogged instant-message chats) or that aren't even on the Internet per se (such as the proliferation of cell phones and other tools for enabling remote presence) and yet are similar in their networks of communication. The living Web is built on standards and protocols that continue to evolve such as

- FOAF (friend-of-a-friend) and tools built on it such as People-Aggregrator

- Dead-easy services such as Yahoo! Groups

- Whimsical attempts to harness the gift economy, such as Lazyweb.org

Besides specific technologies, we can see new guiding technological principles that are enabling these new applications—chiefly the open-source movement—but others as well. In all cases, what is exciting and intriguing are not the technical specifications but rather how it can be possible to have the technology serve the people instead of the other way around.

The glossary itemizes some of the various technologies and technical philosophies discussed in the book, for those who like their lists and references well organized.

It's the People, Stupid

The heart of this book is organized around case studies that examine what methods, technologies, and processes have worked (and which ones have not), and what lessons we can derive from these pioneers and their experiences. The next chapter discusses political organizing and takes a closer look at the 2004 presidential election and the impact of the losing primary campaign of Howard Dean to which I have been alluding throughout this chapter. In the rest of this book, I examine other areas of civic life, from community organizing to business networking to dating, but I return from time to time to this example of this long-shot presidential campaign that nearly shot the moon, because there are still many lessons to be derived from it, whatever the outcome in November 2004.

Sources and Further Reading

Read these web pages for more detail on the ideas in this chapter:

Elizabeth Lane Lawley, "Step Away from the Laptop," *mamamusings*, February 12, 2004:

http://mamamusings.net/archives/2004/02/12/step_away_from_the_laptop.php

Briggs Nesbit's gardening blog, *True Dirt*; and her article in *The New York Times Magazine*, "A Tree Grows in Oakland," May 16, 2004:

http://godetia.com/dirt/

http://www.nytimes.com/2004/05/16/magazine/16LIVES.html

Many-to-Many, an ongoing group weblog discussion of the new model of communication fostered by the Internet; and specifically, Clay Shirky's "Exiting Deanspace" (February 3, 2004):

http://corante.com/many/

http://www.corante.com/many/archives/2004/02/03/exiting_deanspace.php

For why Clay Shirky is seen as an expert on the subject of the living Web, see the interview with him in *Gothamist* (April 9, 2004):

http://www.gothamist.com/interview/archives/2004/04/09/clay_shirky_internet_technologist.php

Mary Hodder, *The Napsterization of Everything*; and specifically, "The Practice and/or The Tool: Journalism and Blogging" (April 16, 2004) on the tools of disintermediation:

http://napsterization.org/

http://napsterization.org/stories/archives/000227.html

Rebecca Blood's laws of blogging, January 2004:

http://www.rebeccablood.net/archive/2004/01.html#06weblogs

Mark Bernstein, "Ten Tips for Writing the Living Web," *A List Apart*:
http://www.alistapart.com/articles/writeliving/

Alexander Galloway and Eugene Thacker, "The Limits of Networking:
A Reply to Lovink and Schneider's 'Notes on the State of Networking'";
a post to the nettime-l mailing list, March 15, 2004, on the organizational
principles that bind human networks:
http://amsterdam.nettime.org/Lists-Archives/nettime-1-0403/
msg00090.html

danah boyd, presentation at the O'Reilly Emerging Technology Conference 2004 on the interaction between human behavior and social-software
technology:
http://conferences.oreillynet.com/presentations/et2004/boyd_danah.txt

Chapter 2   All Politics Is Personal

All politics is local.

—motto of Thomas P. "Tip" O'Neill (1912–1994), Speaker of the U.S. House of Representatives, 1977–1986

In the twentieth century, politics entered the age of mass media, where traditional "retail politics" (whistle-stop tours, baby kissing, and pancake breakfasts) began to be limited to the first few primary and caucus states, before campaigns entered a phase of major media buys driven by steady fundraising from wealthy donors and interests. In this period, some political savants have suggested that the political parties have lost their original connections to their voters and become little more than brands fronting massive fundraising operations.

Tip O'Neill would say that parties have forgotten that, even in a national campaign, voters ultimately make their decisions based on their local environment, issues, pocketbooks, and community.

This is not to say that grassroots efforts and neighborhood canvassing ever went entirely the way of the dodo. Get out the vote (GOTV) efforts have always been important (witness Florida in 2000), and each party has developed shock troops to do most of the work on the ground: walking precincts and phoning voters from phone banks. The Democratic Party has long relied on its union supporters for these kinds of efforts, and the Republican Party has cultivated a network of evangelical churchgoers and nonprofit organizations to achieve a kind of parity on the ground.

The changes now affecting how political campaigns are conducted include a trend toward greater transparency and lowered barriers to entry for folks who want to participate, as well as more control and a greater sense of satisfaction for their efforts. Internet technologies can, according to Mary Hodder of the University of California at Berkeley, collapse the time and space between like-minded people, and individual targeting "can lead to finding people who are the most passionate supporters of a particular cause or candidate." This can ideally provide the core of support online that can translate into a successful campaign "in the real world."

From Insurgents to Frontrunners

Outside of the hierarchies of each party, there have always been insurgent candidates, who railed against entrenched power and whose supporters tended to be bright-eyed and enthusiastic, even when engaged in an ultimately losing effort. At the start of the twentieth century, the populists and later the progressives mounted third-party efforts whose philosophies were eventually co-opted by the major parties. Such incorporation has been the only kind of success really open to third parties since the days of the Civil War, when the disarray in the Democratic Party and withering of the Whigs opened the way for the Republican Party to move from outsider status.

Before mass media, a third-party candidacy was of necessity grassroots—all campaigns were. But "third-party" doesn't equate to "bottom-up" organization. John Anderson's 1980 effort used the same techniques as those of the eventual major-party nominees.

In 1972, George McGovern challenged the back-room kingmakers of the Democratic Party (whom the antiwar movement felt had led the party into a series of disastrous national decisions). The McGovern campaign built a base of independent funding and support through then-innovative use of direct mail, an emerging form of marketing. McGovern's supporters built his war chest from small donations, but nonetheless he was crushed by Nixon.

In 1992, Jerry Brown ran for president a second time and briefly caught fire with "We the People" rhetoric, the then-innovative bandying of an 800 number, and the stated goal of raising his campaign funds in small donations of $100 each as a way of challenging the wealthy donors and interest groups able to donate $1000 at a time or more in "bundled" donations.

In 2000, John McCain ran against party anointee George W. Bush and came close to unhorsing him with an upset victory in New Hampshire. The day after McCain won that primary, more than 40,000 new volunteers joined his campaign and donations poured in, particularly via his 800 number and his website. But the Web was still a fairly new medium at the time, and most businesses were still wrestling with how best to use it for marketing and other purposes. At the time, politicians had little idea of what to do with the Internet, and its subscriber base was still a small percentage of the population.

By 2004, it became obvious that the Internet was poised to become an essential medium of political communication and organizing. We may have reached a tipping point, we may be on the cusp of bigger changes, but it is clearly still just the beginning. A critical mass may or may not yet be reachable through the Web (and other digital technologies such as mobile phones and pagers), but already the Internet has been shown to have the power to extend the reach of an insurgent campaign and incubate the initial connections required to develop a truly effective grassroots political campaign.

In each cycle, the primaries and caucuses seem to be moved earlier and earlier, and the party power structures try to arrange them so that a frontrunner will emerge and have his (or her, but so far always his) candidacy sealed as early as possible so as to best pivot and begin aiming fire at the opposing party's candidate. This means that the 2004 election really got started at the end of 2002, and many of the defining aspects of the primary election took place in 2003. Looking back on that year at the beginning of the voting season, 2003 looked like the year of Howard Dean, in which an obscure small-state governor rode a nimble, Internet-fueled campaign from dark-horse asterisk status to a position of unexpected putative frontrunner, the primaries his to lose. In the end, 2003 *was* the year of Dean, even if 2004 turns out to be the year of Kerry or Bush.

Franklin Delano Roosevelt embraced the new medium of radio for his fireside chats. John F. Kennedy was said to have lost his debate with Nixon for the people listening on radio, but was considered the overwhelming victor among those who had watched the debate on the new television format. But the Internet is a medium unlike television and radio. It reaches a mass audience, but it is interactive. While TV and radio are "one-to-many" formats, the Internet is "many-to-many." Instead of a hub and spoke model, the Internet thrives as a web or cloud of many connections.

Who Was That Brusque Man?

The stated goal of the Howard Dean presidential campaign was to reinvigorate and reinvolve the grassroots of the Democratic Party, and—ideally—of the entire American polity at large in the process of electing a candidate. By giving each volunteer and supporter a stake in the candidacy, a sense of ownership, the dream was to trigger a successful maverick insurgency and topple a powerful sitting president against all the odds.

Although the Internet was only part of the Dean campaign strategy, it clearly played a large part, in several ways:

- Systematically, the Deansters embraced existing Internet tastemakers (influencers), political communities, and services.

- They adopted technical software tools designed for online community building.

- Where necessary, they developed their own custom software solutions to bridge the gaps between what was available in the market and what the campaign required.

And all of these steps were focused on producing the real-world effects necessary to nominate a candidate and, if all goes well, elect a President.

Despite the Internet buzz surrounding Howard Dean's campaign, it was obvious that the candidate himself was no computer geek. One of his top advisors, though, Joe Trippi, had left politics in the mid '90s for the high-tech world of Silicon Valley. He read some of the earliest progressive weblogs—such as MyDD.com, Atrios' Eschaton, and DailyKos—and he sought out advice from some of the more connected people online.

It was these people, such as Markos Moulitsas Zúniga of DailyKos, Jerome Armstrong of MyDD, Matt Gross of DeanNation, and Rick Klau of There Is No Spoon, who advised the campaign to embrace the bloggers who were busy updating the Web every day with their latest commentaries on news, events, and media. From these early consultations also flowed the idea of facilitating face-to-face meetings for local Dean supporters using the Meetup.com web service.

Trippi has spoken about a "concentric circles" approach to political organizing, in which each participant creates their own ripples in the pond, and the whole volunteer community grows out from each circle. The Internet, he realized, might enable a kind of "concentric circles on steroids" approach.

Dean got it too. "Dean himself was on board earlier than Trippi," says Armstrong. "I met with Dean in June of 2002, showed him the webpage I had up, and he talked for about 15 minutes about how to use the Web....[E]ven in 2002, the early staff was reading MyDD and DeanNation."

Trippi also seemed to intuit that there was a large community of potential voters who feel alienated from politics as usual. Trippi believed that an Internet-driven campaign might reach out to those voters and engage them in politics for perhaps the first time in their lives. Nearly half the people in the U.S. who are eligible to vote don't bother to do so. If even a small fraction of those apathetic voters could get excited about a candidate, they might represent the winning margin in a political climate in which each party has poll-tested its views to an almost uncanny degree of parity with the other party. This risk-averse status quo led to the painful deadlock battled out in Florida after the presidential election of 2000.

A metaphor that's often bandied about when discussing the Dean phenomenon is the software-development model known as "open-source." Generally speaking, open-source software can be modified and patched by anyone, and this inherent openness means that a product or application can potentially be improved by any of its users. (Some of the software involved in the technical aspects of the campaign were indeed literally open-source applications, but not all were.) While the metaphor is imprecise when applied to politics, the philosophy of an open process in which anyone can contribute or improve the product was the "juice" that drove the Dean campaign.

In May 2003, Trippi posted an entry to an unofficial weblog supporting the Dean candidacy, entitled "The Perfect Storm," where he wrote, in part:

> They are trying to stop the Perfect Storm.... [T]he storm requires thousands and thousands, perhaps millions of Americans to become actively involved in determining the future course of our country.

Trippi recognized that helping these Americans find each other, organize themselves, and take actions that could help win the election was the crux of the matter:

> It took years to get here, years of millions signing up to their first ISP. Millions making their first Internet transaction. Millions using eBay, or Amazon—and becoming comfortable with using their credit card online.

> The other critical difference is the amazing tools that have emerged.

Trippi heralded the value of blogging, not merely as a direct communication tool for the campaign but as the basis for an ongoing civic conversation that he was signaling the campaign was aware of and interested in participating in.

But no evil-genius campaign manager is going to make a candidate successful unless the candidate himself gets it. A line in Dean's stump speech represented the kind of plain talk that fired up the usually disaffected, in which he refused to offer the sort of easy answers that are common from politicians:

> The biggest lie that people like me tell people like you during the election season is, "If you vote for me, I'll solve all your problems." The truth is that the power to change this country is in your hands, not mine. Abraham Lincoln said that a government of the people, by the people, and for the people shall not perish from this earth. But this president, this president has forgotten ordinary Americans. And you have the power to take this party back and make it stand for something again. You have the power to take this country back.

Don't get me wrong: I'm not suggesting that Dean wasn't a politician. Of course he's a politician. His people do polls, they craft positions, and so on. You don't get to be governor of a state, let alone president, without some powerful political instincts. But it's the unique ability to trust himself and, more importantly, to trust his supporters, that enabled Dean to rely on the kind of decentralized, people-powered grassroots volunteer campaign that propelled him to the brink of the Democratic nomination.

Learning from Webloggers

Trippi was strongly influenced by a pair of young progressive political weblog-gers, Jerome Armstrong and Markos Moulitsas Zúniga ("Kos"), who were at the time the only people writing weblogs covering multiple local political races across the country. (Kos believes this may still be the case.) Armstrong's web-site, MyDD.com—the name stands for "my due diligence"—pioneered the approach. Kos was a regular commentor on MyDD, and when he started his own site, DailyKos.com, Armstrong linked to him. When MyDD's comments became overwhelmed by "huge flamewars," Armstrong shut down the feature and Kos inherited most of his commenter community.

Kos didn't want his own comments to suffer the same fate, so he made a point of deleting right-wing posts: "I was militant about deleting Republicans." One interesting thing about this readership community is its provenance: MyDD inherited the readers from Taegan Goddard's Political Wire, which also no longer supports comments, and many of those readers came from an earlier political website that wasn't a weblog, and in fact many of those readers themselves came from Delphi discussion forums run by Peter Orvetti. Jerome Armstrong says, "Orvetti had what was probably the first political weblog, covering the 2000 elec-tion." His site featured a 150-word daily news update.

Trippi was a regular reader of both weblogs and sought advice from Arm-strong and Kos about how to best engage with bloggers online and convert some of that wired energy into off-line activity. They recommended that the cam-paign have a weblog and that the campaign work directly with Meetup to help volunteers organize themselves locally.

DeanNation was the most important blog in the early stages of the Inter-net campaign. "It was *the* campaign blog from late fall, when Anna (of Annatopia), myself, and Aziz [Poonawalla] began blogging there," says Armstrong. "Joe [Trippi] and Zephyr [Teachout] would blog there, then migrate to BFA [Blog for America]."

Matt Gross is the guy who actually made Trippi do it, Armstrong told me.

> I'd been bugging Trippi nearly daily, to start a blog for the campaign....Matt
> was a regular commenter on MyDD and DailyKos, and I asked him to start
> guest blogging on MyDD.com in early 2003, because he was a big Dean fan

and a good writer. He took to it like a fish in water, and he decided he needed to go to Vermont. He asked me if I knew anyone there and I was like, "Yeah, Trippi! Tell him to start a blog!"

So Matt went to Burlington, walked into Trippi's office, and said, "I blog for MyDD." Trippi replied, "You're hired."

Another blogger who found the Dean campaign early was Rick Klau. In August of 2002, more than two years before the election, Klau read an article about Dean and was impressed by his stands on civil liberties and "a foreign policy driven by alliances not unilateral action." Klau points out that this was before the war became front and center in the campaign: "9/11 was still less than a year old at this point," says Klau. "I saw the Democrats cutting deals, taking a leadership position really in the wilderness."

A lawyer by training, Klau can pinpoint the phone call that motivated him to become involved. He spoke with a friend, a nationally known immigration lawyer, who told him about a client held incommunicado by the government for three weeks, with no acknowledgment that he was being held. He found himself imaging the future, 15 years from now:

> Our kids will be studying this time, and they will come home and ask what we did. I don't want to have to say, "I waited until November 2004 and voted."

Klau remained in loose contact with the campaign, but he launched an independent blog to promote Dean's candidacy. "The blog started getting me contacted by people who would provide me with information or thank me for maintaining the site." Google sent a lot of traffic Klau's way. "When Dean spoke at the winter DNC meeting in February 2003, it was carried on C-SPAN, and my blog saw a tenfold increase in traffic from people googling Dean's name after the speech." This happened again after the California State Democratic Convention in March, where Dean gave one of his most rousing speeches.

"I remember remarking on my tech blog [There Is No Spoon], 'There is google polling going on that I can tell you right now... Howard Dean arrived today. He was nowhere yesterday.'" Eventually people did start monitoring candidate mentions in blogs as a tracking poll. The campaign, says Klau, invested in a lot of expensive but very valuable data along those lines.

When Dean's original campaign manager, Rick Ritter, and his campaign secretary stepped down, Klau posted "a throwaway comment" about the news on his blog. "I hoped this shakeup wasn't a sign of trouble," says Klau, especially after rumors of a fairly strong fundraising quarter. Within three hours, Klau received an email message from Trippi, telling him off the record that the news was not in fact a bad thing for the campaign, that the staff changes were according to plan but "just accelerated because things were going so well."

Klau then helped the campaign set up its weblog using Six Apart's Movable Type software. One of the real strengths of the campaign's weblog, says Klau, is that people could disagree with him and felt it might make a difference." You could suggest a change to Dean's stump speech in the blog comments, and there was a chance your suggestion would be adopted."

First-Mover Advantage

Dean didn't invent the Internet, and he didn't create the conditions that drove flocks of wired "early adopters" to his maverick campaign. He did, however, listen to what the people were saying online (and at his campaign appearances) and tune his message to one that would resonate with this small but influential constituency.

One of the best journalistic analyses of the Dean campaign's use of the Internet was written by Edward Cone for *Baseline Magazine*, called "The Marketing of a President." Cone starts his article with a quick sketch of Zephyr Teachout, the campaign's director of Internet outreach. "I'm obsessed with offline," he quotes her as saying. The real people at the ends of the connections are what matter, so much more than the wiring that ties it all together.

The Dean campaign showed that it was possible to get people out of their houses and involved in activities that required coordination, patience, passion, and cooperation. However, unable to close the deal with enough of the voters of Iowa, the innovations of the campaign also proved to be their own limitations, at least in this transitional election. It already seems clear that future campaigns will ignore online organizational tools at their peril.

Along with embracing the "ends" of the Internet, the campaign realized that it needed to cede power and control to the people who make up its grassroots army. It's impossible to control this kind of network from the top of a pyramid or the hub of a wheel. In fact, it would be counterproductive to do so. A great deal of the energy unleashed by the volunteers emerged precisely because they felt empowered to develop their own tactics, share the most successful "best practices" with each other, and learn by doing. An army of motivated amateurs was out-organizing the best-paid experts in the world.

This is a hard lesson for politicos (and business people) to learn: letting go of control. The old command-and-control structures will not be able to stand against the supple, decentralized networks now made possible by the Internet.

A truism of the technology world, particularly in the Internet age, is that a tremendous advantage accrues to anyone who pioneers a new technology (successfully, of course). While it's possible to imitate, catch up, and outcompete (in fact, Bill Gates' Microsoft has made billions doing just that), the advantages inherent in being the first to succeed in a new way are frequently difficult to overcome.

The MoveOn Example

The Dean campaign was the first campaign (and perhaps the only one) to engage the advice and help offered by MoveOn (more on that presently), the first to embrace the third-party web service called Meetup (more about that coming too), and the first to absorb the concept of weblogs ("blogs") fully into its campaign media strategy.

Joan Blades and Wes Boyd, whose Berkeley Systems software company was best known for the "flying toasters" screensaver, founded MoveOn in 1998 as a response to the ongoing scandal, media coverage, and political response to Bill Clinton's affair with White House intern Monica Lewinsky. While Democratic partisans dismissed the entire phenomenon as a president being persecuted for "lying about sex," and while Republican partisans pushed ahead with an unpopular impeachment process, Blades and Boyd built an organization up from a mailing list in the process of advocating a middle way: the President, they said, should be censured, and then we—the country—should move on.

Fearing that this political distraction was robbing the President of attention that needed to be paid to urgent national priorities, the "Censure and Move On" movement built a large following online. Through a series of subsequent inspired campaigns and movements, MoveOn has continued to build steam as an independent progressive pressure group, sometimes referred to as "the Christian Coalition of the left," while claiming to represent a broad, centrist-minded majority of Americans. A *Salon* profile of MoveOn quoted Columbia University professor Todd Gitlin as saying:

> They get things done. They raise money, they hold straw votes, they're constantly dreaming up practical activities that have a constituency. They've straddled the discourse of mainstream politics and the discourse of outsiders. They seem to be both insiders and outsiders. That appeals to those who are both moralists and hardheaded.

MoveOn volunteered to help various Democrats running for the nomination in 2004, but only Dean's people took them up on the offer. In fact, a MoveOn staffer, Zack Exley, took a several-week sabbatical from his job with MoveOn to help the Dean folks revamp their web site, improving the user experience and making it easier for people to donate money.

Both MoveOn and the Dean campaign exhibited an uncanny ability to make hay from attacks. When Republicans or right-wing pressure groups attacked MoveOn or Dean, with ads or interview campaigns, both entities publicized the attacks and used them as a fundraising source. Both also targeted response ads and raised money from supporters specifically to fund these ads, even soliciting suggestions about how best to respond. In this way, the people donating to MoveOn (and to Dean) felt that it was they who were being attacked, and they felt empowered, as if they themselves were responding to the attacks.

Naturally, for Dean, this dynamic also fueled his image as an outsider whose candidacy was threatening to the "powers that be."

In June 2003, MoveOn scheduled an online Democratic straw poll, which it referred to as "the Internet primary." They deliberately scheduled it well in advance of the official primary season, during what some Washington insiders and the media referred to as the "money primary." They were concerned that people were being left out of this advance vetting process, when the candidates are informally winnowed into electables and unelectables. They scheduled their online vote this way to give people—at least wired people—a voice during this crucial time.

Dean's success in this primary (he got 44% of the vote, not enough for a majority and an endorsement, but ahead of all the other candidates) first put him on my own personal radar screen. I wasn't particularly tuned into MoveOn at the time, and like many, I perceived them as a somewhat far-left group. I therefore expected Dennis Kucinich, the candidate most keeping the faith with traditional liberal constituencies, to easily win that online vote. He did well. Kucinich came in second, but when Dean won, I found myself re-evaluating him and reconsidering my assumption about the people behind MoveOn and who they represented.

In Michelle Goldberg's *Salon* article, Boyd is quoted as saying, "The hardest thing to get across to the political establishment is that this is not just another set of tools you use to manipulate constituencies and tap them for money. This has to be seen as a way to engage constituencies and engage in a two-way conversation."

MoveOn practices what it preaches. It doesn't determine an agenda behind closed doors and then reveal it to the masses. (In fact, there are no closed doors: MoveOn employees work from home and coordinate their efforts via email.) Last year, MoveOn even asked its members to interview each other by phone to determine which issues mattered most to the membership.

Kos feels that MoveOn is hostile to the openness of weblogs. They are still a traditional top-to-bottom organization, he says. "They were this guerrilla Internet organization, rallying people with this email list. Now they've gone all establishment." On the other hand, he couldn't fault their member-driven ad campaign: "*Bush in 30 Seconds* was brilliant," he concedes.

Meetup Ties the Web to the Real World

MoveOn proved to be an inspiration and example to the Dean campaign. But possibly the most effective Internet-driven service embraced by the Dean campaign was Meetup, a startup founded by Scott Heiferman and Peter Kamali. Meetup is based in New York and enables people with common interests to schedule local meetings on a monthly basis, for free. (They get their money from the venues and from members who sign up for advanced features. A "Meetup Plus" membership entitles you to host events and nominate venues.)

Scott Heiferman derived some of the inspiration for Meetup after reading Robert Putnam's book *Bowling Alone,* about the withering of American community and the absence of public spaces. As television watching has replaced more communal activities, Putnam wrote, Americans have become estranged from their neighbors. Heiferman recognized that the Internet was already being used by people to find each other and form groups, and that all that was missing was an offline, face-to-face component to help cement and reinforce those relationships.

While not geared specifically toward politics (fans of TV shows and people who share hobbies make up some of the other active Meetup constituencies), Meetup has fostered the return of politics as a social activity and not, as the MoveOn slogan goes, "a spectator sport."

In an interview for the South by Southwest digital conference, Heiferman said, "The Internet was created to connect people. It's the heart of the thing. eBay, IM, email, craigslist, AOL chat rooms, online personals, LiveJournal...it's all about the people."

Meetup is marketed virally by websites that voluntarily display the Meetup logo. (It's a "Hello my name is"–type sticker, with a series of handwritten variations on the word Meetup.). By January 2004, Heiferman claimed that Meetup was "growing at 2,000 memberships per day, up from 1,000 just one month ago."

Nearly half of the people who attend meetups complete an online poll about the experience the next day, which provides the Meetup.com people with a wealth of feedback and customer data. Venues welcome meetups because they drive more foot traffic. (Many of them are cafés, bars, and bookstores.) The voting process determines which local venues get to host the event, so the participants get to decide where they want to meet.

William Finkel of Meetup originally approached the DeanNation bloggers. Armstrong says,

> I got ahold of Trippi that same week, and pushed the idea until the campaign put the logo up on their website after they saw 200 [people] sign up in one day via MyDD in January 2003.

On a single day in December 2003, more than 177,000 people attended Dean meetups all across the United States. There were only 12 people at the one in Oakland, California, but they knew that many people were working on the same projects and the same purposes right then. In Ed Cone's article, "The Marketing of a President," Zephyr Teachout is quoted as saying, "I can imagine the campaign without the blog, but not without Meetup."

Just as with MoveOn, Dean's campaign was the first to adopt Meetup. Dean meetups happened earlier and were larger than other candidates'. In this case, the campaign itself wasn't even first; it was Dean supporters who began using Meetup, thereby bringing the site to the attention of the formal organization.

The Meetup logo was plastered all over the Dean campaign's official and unofficial websites. It was almost impossible to miss, and was one of the primary movers in converting online energy into face-to-face meetings and real-world activities. At meetups, people discussed the campaign and their political views, sometimes watched videos or DVDs, prioritized local tactics, and performed tasks suggested by the campaign.

The campaign provided meeting organizers with materials, letter-writing kits (more about that later), and forms for volunteer signups.

Not coincidentally, MoveOn has adopted a similar face-to-face community-building approach—for example, promoting house parties last December in which members met to watch a documentary about the Iraq war.

Adopting Internet Technologies

The Dean campaign made ample use of Internet applications geared toward communication and social interaction, most notably at its official weblog, but also in the form of discussion forums and an internal wiki (a kind of website that's very easy for participants to edit, geared toward collaborative knowledge-sharing). The blog, of course, was the sexiest of these.

The campaign's official blog featured new entries posted several times a day and provided followers of the campaign (as well as opponents and the media) with a steady pulse of news, information, hype, and spin. The campaign hired several full-time bloggers, and other paid staff members also posted from time to time. These authentic voices from inside the campaign helped pierce the bubble that so often surrounds a political candidate, giving outsiders at least a glimpse, a kind of cinema verité view into the inner workings of a campaign.

The blog was also used relentlessly to encourage financial donations. Nearly every post contained a link to the Contribute section of the official campaign website, and frequent fundraising mini-goals were flogged mercilessly in the blog.

The blog was even used to recruit volunteers and staff with specific, hard-to-fill skill niches. In Ed Cone's article in Baseline, he quoted Dean blogger Joe Rospars as saying, "The blog is about humanizing the campaign, not just Dean but the staff and supporters."

The Dean blog went through several incarnations, graduating from one application to the next. The first version of the blog was run on Blogger, a free, hosted service of Google. But Blogger doesn't offer a built-in comment feature, so the campaign migrated the weblog to Movable Type, a more robust, flexible blog package made by Six Apart. The popularity of the blog challenged that software as well; most entries generated several hundred comments, a great deal of noise for anyone trying to follow the conversation. The campaign sometimes talked about adopting a more community-oriented blog tool, perhaps one with threaded comments or one that requires people to establish password-protected usernames, but there was a concern that too many barriers to participation would defeat the purpose of an open communication channel.

Many of the commenters were new to blogs, experiencing the media format for the first time in the context of this campaign, and some of the commenters called themselves "bloggers." Traditionally (well, on the Internet, a tradition is something 18 months old), that term applied to people who hosted, maintained, and wrote their own blogs. But the activity of commenting on the blog was so engaging and absorbing for these people that nobody could begrudge them the right of referring to themselves as bloggers. They were "doing" the blog as much as the paid writers making the entries were.

During the many televised debates of the primary season, blog readers with cable posted play-by-play comments to "open threads," narrating the progress of the debate and providing a kind of *Rashomon*-like patchwork view of the proceedings for those who couldn't follow the debate directly.

The blog also contained a "blogroll" or list of related links, linking to official campaign sites, unofficial (independent) sites, and popular political bloggers (more about this later).

One attempt to deal with the sheer volume of feedback arriving via the official website was a section of the Dean site called Forums for America, driven by a popular, free, third-party discussion-board tool called PHPBB. For various reasons, however, these forums were significantly less popular than the blog comment areas, even though they were better suited technically for threaded discussions that carry on a topic through many responses. There was something about the immediacy of the blog or even the feeling that someone "important" within the campaign might monitor the responses (even though the same person could just as easily peruse the forum topics), that seemed to drive most people to make their comments in that more visible medium.

It may just be that the users—some of whom are Internet newbies—found the forum interface too complicated or cumbersome. But eventually any campaign will overcome the user interface (UI) problem and face this scaling problem. One possible solution is the one that was adopted by the Clark campaign, which used an open-source, community-media tool called Scoop to manage collaboratively moderated and filtered comments from signed-in community members. Each member can maintain their own diary (or blog) whose contents, if salient enough, can be promoted to the front page of the official campaign blog.

Another solution might be to convert the blog to the DeanSpace tool that was developed by a group of software developers both inside the official campaign and in the volunteer community. More about that later.

Dean and Clark were not the only candidates with official blogs; eventually most of them hosted a blog (Joe Lieberman's campaign being the notable exception). John Edwards sometimes posted to his campaign blog, and his wife Elizabeth wrote several popular entries, describing the people she had met and the places she had seen campaigning with her husband.

John Kerry's campaign also purchased campaign ads on some of the more influential political weblogs, and other campaigns followed suit.

The effort to draft General Wesley Clark into the campaign was to some extent spearheaded by bloggers who believed that the Democrats needed a candidate with national security credentials sufficient to challenge a sitting commander-in-chief in a time of war. Clark hired Cameron Barrett—whose CamWorld blog is one of the longest running—as his official blogger, and he launched the Scoop-based Clark Community Network late last year. (Clark was at one point the second-most popular candidate in the Meetup network.)

Internally, the Clark campaign used a wiki product made by SocialText to track media coverage and to otherwise coordinate strategy and tactics. Wikis are designed to be edited directly in a web browser, and SocialText markets its products to organizations looking for ways to make their intranets more responsive and interactive and to create more synergy among their users.

Developing Custom Solutions

According to the Dean campaign's director of Internet technology, Jim Moore, the campaign used commercial software products wherever possible, but developed its own custom solutions when unable to find anything that met a particular need in the market.

Zack Rosen, a college student in Illinois, started hack4dean as an effort to develop an open-source, website-management system that could be adopted by anyone wanting to start an independent site to support the Dean campaign. His idea was absorbed by the campaign and rechristened DeanSpace, and he was hired to work as a full-time developer, temporarily dropping out of school and moving to the campaign headquarters in Burlington.

DeanSpace was based on an open-source, content-management system called Drupal, enhanced with custom modules designed to meet specific campaign needs, such as ones that can automatically place blog icons on the site to link to specific fundraising campaigns, house-party announcements, and—of course—the ubiquitous Meetup logo. Other modules enable a local site to download a constantly updated stream of local events used to populate a custom event calendar, thus refreshing the site with updates and announcements of upcoming campaign events, including meetups, other meetings, house parties, campaign appearances, "Victory Days" dedicated to early primary states, and so on.

Late in 2003, Zephyr Teachout put out a call on the Dean blog for people with skills in PHP and MySQL, some of the open-source technologies that underlay Drupal and hence DeanSpace. According to Cone, she got 85 responses immediately, and more than 180 people ended up working on the project. (Including me: I helped the DeanSpace team with some of their documentation needs.)

DeanSpace tied in to other custom tools developed by the campaign and used Really Simple Syndication (RSS), a website content syndication format, as the basic building block of interconnectedness. The dream was to create a truly distributed network of sites that could "bubble up" important ideas and suggestions from the grassroots to the volunteer community at large and, when necessary, to the official campaign.

As the primary season got underway, the campaign rolled out official state websites (Iowa for Dean, New Hampshire for Dean, California for Dean), all of which were built with DeanSpace. Another idea, suggested by a student and embraced by the campaign, was a volunteer site originally called Students for Dean; the campaign renamed it Generation Dean and absorbed it as an official site.

Beyond the blog and the DeanSpace project, probably the most effective internal development effort was the suite of tools now known as Project Commons. (It was briefly named Dean Tools, and the automatic email reminders it generated used that unfortunate appellation for a long time—a reminder that programmers and engineers don't necessarily make the best marketers and branding experts.)

The core features of the Commons were called DeanLink and Get Local. DeanLink was a social software tool something like Friendster, Ryze, or Tribe.com (discussed in depth in Chapter 7, "Doing Business with Strangers" and Chapter 8, "Lonely Hearts' Club Bands"). When signing up for DeanLink, visitors gave their name and address and checked off the activities they were interested in. They could also upload photos of themselves, such as those taken at events.

Members could search for other volunteers in their area (by setting a radius around their postal code) and send them messages, greeting them, planning events with them, or inviting them to participate in ongoing events. Finally, they could designate other participants as "friends" and add them to a buddy list or social network. I joked to one volunteer that after the campaign was over, this would make a great dating tool for progressives.

Get Local was a service that showed events scheduled to take place within some set number of miles. It could be used to plan or sign up for events and, in combination with DeanLink, to send out invitations. Both of these tools were also integrated with DeanSpace, so a DeanSpace site could feature local events and it could show a user the people to whom they were linked.

Software development on the Dean campaign wasn't limited to the official staff. Legions of developers were building sites and spec-ing out applications. Richard Hoefer, a videographer and participant in the DeanLeaders Yahoo! group (formed to enable grassroots volunteers to share their best practices) launched a site called DeanPort because he felt that the official campaign site was too bewildering for undecided voters. DeanPort was carefully designed to attract new supporters and channel them toward the interests and issues that motivate them.

People involved in the GreaterDemocracy.org website built another independent site called the Dean Issues Forum (DIF). There, a series of moderated discussions divided up by topic areas enabled the public to debate what issues Dean should support and marshal arguments in favor of or against various positions.

Another developer created a tool called DesktopDean that automatically subscribed to syndicated RSS feeds containing news, information, and opinions about Dean and the campaign, and delivered these headlines and stories to the user's desktop on a daily basis. Although it was designed for Windows, volunteers immediately came forth offering to port it to the Macintosh platform.

Just a month or so before the Iowa caucuses, the official blog announced the release of an online computer game called The Iowa Game in which users competed to canvass neighborhoods in Iowa and invite Iowans to go to their caucuses and support Dean. The idea came up on a blog. A social network of influential people (including Joi Ito) passed the idea along and found a game-designing software developer; the game came together spontaneously and was offered to the campaign for free. Although it was merely a simple diversion and amusement, The Iowa Game serves to illustrate the ferment of ideas emerging from the techie Dean supporter base.

In fact, the suggestions and ideas came so fast and furious that there was no way the campaign could manage entertaining them all; they vetted the best and decided which projects to encourage. As a result, another independent volunteer organization—Tech4Dean—nominated itself to review technical suggestions, to build a skills database, and to try to direct technical resources where they were most needed. For example, in states trying to organize their precincts, Tech4Dean worked on software projects for generating precinct maps and interactive voter-information forms.

Producing Results: The $100 Revolution

All the website churn in the world amounts to nothing if it doesn't produce results in the real world. The Dean campaign was canny about trying to direct its efforts toward achieving pragmatic goals aimed at winning the nomination. Not least was the importance of fundraising, despite the fact that this turned off some critics (such as the outspoken Dave Winer), who considered the campaign to be treating the Internet as a piggy bank, extracting money that was then spent on media buys and not plowed directly back into the Net.

But, as the saying goes, "Money is the mother's milk of politics." Dean would never have gotten as far as he did if he hadn't been able to demonstrate an ability to generate funds. The fact that this was done mostly with small donations only serves to underscore the grassroots nature of his support, as well as its breadth.

One of the memes promoted by the campaign was "the hundred-dollar revolution." Playing off the Bush campaign's early goal of raising $200 million, Joe Trippi suggested that if two million people each gave $100, this army of donors would be able to match the large-figure donors on the other side.

In the service of this fundraising need, the campaign didn't have to be creative. Tried-and-true marketing tricks apply in cyberspace as in meatspace. The official website publicized its dollar targets and progress using a logo showing a baseball player holding up a baseball bat, with a thermometer-like red zone rising as the dollar target was approached. Commenters on the official blog talked about "hitting the bat" and could set up their own personal bats and compete as fundraisers.

When the campaign was attacked, the official bloggers brought out the bat and asked supporters to donate (they could do so online with a credit card) in response.

When there was good news, such as a major endorsement, the campaign brought out the bat and asked supporters to donate in celebration. At times, the commenters on the blog implored the campaign to put up a new bat for some special occasion, and they talked about the donating process being addictive. Dean's supporters were convinced that if he won, he wouldn't be beholden to the interests that usually direct the large funding amounts to candidates. They felt that if Dean was owned by anybody, it would be by each and every one of them, and this made him an independent candidate.

Sometimes fundraising ideas came directly from the blog's commenters. When Vice President Dick Cheney held a $2,000-per-plate fundraiser, someone on the blog suggested that the campaign post a photograph of Dean eating a sandwich to encourage supporters to match or exceed Cheney's stated goal. Cheney raised a quarter of a million dollars, but Dean raised more than half a million with average donations of just over $50 each!

Because anyone could comment on the Dean blog, it wasn't unusual to see opponents of Dean—whether Republicans planning to vote for Bush or supporters of other Democratic candidates—posting contrary opinions or talking points in the comment area. To some extent, dissenting opinions were tolerated and respected, even engaged, but any relentlessly negative poster who didn't seem to be open to debate was quickly labeled a "troll," a concept that dates back to the earliest days of the Internet.

The Dean blog commenters flipped this around by inventing a disincentive for trolling: a webpage called Trolls4Dean.com. There, regulars to the blog were encouraged to pledge donations in response to specific troll attacks. When trolls realized that each of their negative comments was generating a new donation to the Dean campaign, the fun of stirring the pot diminished heavily, and many of these trolls slunk off, never to be heard from again. The slogan of Trolls4Dean was "Feed the goal, not the troll."

A Virtual War Room Isn't Enough

In the 1992 presidential campaign, the Clinton team was renowned for its "war room," where they planned immediate response to attacks. The conventional wisdom was that Michael Dukakis had not been assiduous enough about defending himself in the 1988 campaign and had let too much time elapse before responding to each new attack. The Clintonites resolved to respond to any incoming attacks within the same 24-hour news cycle, so that the negative information wouldn't have enough time to sink into the consciousness of the casual public without being countered by an opposing view.

In 2003, a self-organized group of campaign supporters calling themselves the Dean Defense Forces organized email campaigns to respond to any perceived inaccuracies in the media, negative press, or attacks from competing campaigns. In so doing, they created a spontaneous, networked war room, with the flexibility to respond to the flurry of negative rumors that can swarm the Internet at a moment's notice.

By itself, an Internet presence would not win a campaign. Not enough Americans are wired, and those who are connected to the Internet don't necessarily use it to get news or to follow politics. Instead, the Internet has to be used as a seed and a starting point for offline interactions, where the real work of a grassroots campaign can take place.

According to one of my sources, over a third of meetup attendees don't hear about the meetings through the Meetup.com site. Instead, they read about it in a local free weekly, see an announcement somewhere, or are invited personally by other attendees. Regardless of how the attendees hear about the meetups, the purpose goes beyond merely showing up at a café and grousing about political trends. The real purpose is to help people meet their neighbors and peers.

For the first six months or so, Dean meetups all featured a segment called The Great American Conversation, in which participants were encouraged to introduce themselves to each other and speak about the issues that mattered to them. This was a deliberate effort to foster community ties and neighborliness. Howard Dean published an op-ed at the Common Dreams website in which he wrote, "I want to restore a sense of community in this country."

Backspin: "They're Not Trying to Stop Me. They're Trying to Stop You."

Just as the Dean campaign used the Internet to build momentum, his opponents embraced the same technologies to try to stop him. Dick Gephardt's supporters, for example, created a site called Waffle-Powered Howard that they used to highlight inconsistencies or flip-flops in Dean's stated positions over the years.

Another group of activists, alarmed at Dean's success and convinced that his antiwar message would doom the Democratic Party to defeat at the polls in 2004, created a Yahoo! group to discuss the best ways to stop him and built a website called Stop Dean Now.

One of the most common responses of the Dean campaign to withering attacks was to rally the troops and suggest that because they owned the campaign—because Dean's campaign was people-powered—the attacks were not so much trying to hurt Dean as trying to stop the movement, trying to stop all of the followers who had invested in the campaign's success. "And this message resonated with the grassroots supporters. In fact, one Dean enthusiast created a parody called *Soylent Dean* of an old movie, but in the new version, the President was shown recoiling and remarking, "My God! His campaign—it's made out of…people!"

This feeling of inclusiveness wasn't limited to Dean's campaign. In an article from *Common Dreams,* Matea Gold reports:

> Faerstein is an evangelizer. Because of her involvement through the blog, she took a six-hour bus ride to New Hampshire a few weeks ago with other Clark supporters to canvass voters. "I feel like I'm really part of this campaign," she said. "When someone says, 'What should they do?' I say, 'What do you mean they?' It's us."

The Blogging of the President 2004

Another key component in the Dean strategy of embracing the existing Internet community, structure, and formats was the adoption of blogging and engagement with existing bloggers. Weblogs can be about anything. The vast majority of them are not particularly political. But an influential minority of blogs is dedicated to politics or even to a specific issue, cause, or candidate. The Dean campaign showed remarkable flexibility and skill in the manner in which it responded to blogging.

As noted earlier in this chapter, Joe Trippi posted to the unofficial Howard Dean blog before the campaign even adopted an official blog. When the campaign did adopt an official blog, some people—including blog visionary, pioneer, and evangelist Dave Winer—criticized the campaign for not blogging properly. It was noted that Dean wasn't writing the blog, and that the blog was sending out self-serving spin instead of objectively citing all possible references pro-Dean and con-Dean and covering the rest of the field.

For Dean's supporters—particularly the ones who read the blog obsessively and the small fraction of those who started responding to the blog in its comments section—none of that mattered. They were happy just to see the voices of real people emerging from within the campaign, and they believed that their commentary could influence the campaign's strategy and tactics. In fact, they witnessed some of their own suggestions and catch phrases (such as "The tea is in the harbor") being adopted by the official campaign, which validated their participation.

Howard Dean also made a guest appearance on the weblog of Stanford professor and Creative Commons co-founder Lawrence Lessig. When some people publicly wondered if his entries were ghostwritten, the campaign's official bloggers joked that if they had been writing the entries for him, they would have been better written. Dean was criticized as well for posting generalities and not taking specific positions on the burning intellectual-property issues important to Lessig's readers and an influential segment of the weblog communities, but he was also applauded for dipping his toes into the medium.

One person commented, "This is unprecedented and fantastic. This is the type of town square dialog that we've been missing." Aldon Hynes (a programmer, researcher, and Internet executive who volunteered for the Dean campaign) noted that candidate Dennis Kucinich, who also had a strong Internet following, appeared on Lessig's blog the next month as a guest poster and took much more specific stands on the issues, interacted better, and was better received by the readers.

Some of the official Dean bloggers started out as unofficial Dean bloggers before getting hired by the campaign. For example, Matt Gross went from the seminal DeanNation independent weblog to become a mainstay of the Blog for America. Others continued working on the independent site, Dean Nation.

Matt Bailey started off with his own Grassroots for Dean weblog. "Back then there were only a few of us blogging on Dean regularly, and it wasn't hard to get to know the other people. I received an invitation from Dean Nation and began blogging with them. The number of us contributing grew and fluctuated since those early days. A number of us went to work for the campaign in Burlington."

Bailey felt that blogging radicalized the fundraising and ownership aspects of campaigning: "The blogs help people to feel as though they 'own' the campaign…. This makes it easier for them to give contributions. This money will allow strength in the traditional arena of campaigning by financing television ads, get out the vote efforts, and the like."

He also pointed out that the official and unofficial blogs played different roles in the campaign's messaging. "The idea of having volunteers use their extra cell phone minutes to do phone-banking is an idea that came from the Internet. The official blogs have a unique access to inside information. Unofficial blogs can cry foul if supporters feel betrayed. I think they all serve a unique purpose, and that's why many readers read more than just one."

Peer-to-Peer Democracy

At one point in 2003, Dean campaign Internet outreach director Zephyr Teachout drove around the country in a barely functioning van to meet the grassroots supporters face-to-face. For a profile of the Internet aspects of the Dean campaign in *Wired* magazine, Gary Wolf accompanied Teachout and another Dean staffer to some small local gatherings. He wrote:

> The day turns into an endless series of encounters with Dean enthusiasts, and what interests me most is to see at meeting after meeting the speech-making function of the candidate distributed among the participants. The speakers are often diffuse and sometimes sentimental; nonetheless, these are hot political speeches, not support group–style confessions or narrowly personal tales. Accustomed as I am to the low style of television and talk radio, to the mumbling of recalled California governor Gray Davis and the swaggering of recently installed governor Arnold Schwarzenegger, I am stunned to hear such high-quality mini-rants in the living rooms and restaurants where random Dean supporters have gathered for mutual encouragement and tactical coordination. These are the Dean blogs come to life.

Perhaps the most significant activity promulgated through the nationwide meetups was letter writing, a pre-Internet technology if there ever was one. In order to capitalize on the individuality and passion of Dean's supporters and repudiate the form letter and poll-tested messaging so often beamed at voters, especially in the early caucus and primary states, the campaign came up with the crazy/brilliant idea of asking supporters to handwrite letters to potential voters in key states. Meetup attendees in California, for example, spent all fall writing letters to Iowa voters, explaining in their own terms why they were supporting Dean and how they hoped the letter's recipient would caucus for him in January. They were encouraged to include personal photographs and to invite the recipients to write back or even call to discuss the candidate.

Marc Hansen, a columnist in the *Des Moines Register,* wrote the following after receiving one such letter:

> Dear Howard Dean backer,
>
> Thanks for your personalized, handwritten, single-spaced, two-page letter. No, it wasn't addressed specifically to me. And at first I wondered what was going on—some guy with perfect penmanship and a California return address writing my wife out of the blue. Whom does she know out there that I don't?
>
> But when I gently ripped the letter out of her hands and read it, my mind was at ease. It was obvious, Pen Pal, you were only after her support in the Iowa caucuses.

He was impressed by the attention to detail but seemed to regard the effort as little more than a novelty. In turn, a commenter on the Blog for America, "Gina in Texas," posted a reply to this column, in which she expressed a crucial element of the nationwide grassroots effort that made an obscure ex-Governor the odds-on favorite at the time, that is, the opportunity for people outside of the early caucus and primary states to express their views:

> We outside Iowa know that y'all have a huge say in who becomes the Democratic nominee, and we just can't help wanting you to have the views of the nation on a topic of national importance.

In addition to attending meetups, campaign volunteers were also encouraged to host, help with, or attend fundraising house parties in which participants learned about Howard Dean. The most advanced bit of technology involved was the speaker phone used to make conference calls. All the house parties in the country (generally scheduled in advance for the same day) called in, and those that had raised the most money were permitted to ask Dean a specific question.

The essence of all of these activities was that they required the volunteers to get up from their computer, leave the house, and meet with other people from their local community. It turned an audience into participants, turned "passivists" into activists. I asked Aldon Hynes what he thought was the "X factor" that distinguished a simple online community from an engaged group of activists, and this was his reply:

> I do not believe that there is such a thing as a purely virtual online social activity. 'Online' is merely one medium for social activity, and social activity does not take place in a vacuum. My social connections that have been established online, and remain predominantly online, still have very real effects on my persona. There is nothing truly virtual about them.

Hynes pointed to Joe Trippi's "Perfect Storm" blog entry. For Trippi's rhetorical questions—about whether the Internet could be used by ordinary people to self-organize and take action offline—Hynes says, "The answer is obviously, yes, they can and have. The question becomes, what is it about an online community that enables, empowers, or even simply just causes people to take their action offline?" The key difference is whether campaigns are willing to step back and let them do so: "This is, I believe, the X factor. The Dean campaign is very enabling of people to do what they want to do. The other campaigns are much more top-down organized."

Clay Johnson worked on DeanLink and went on to co-found Blue States Digital (which now provides I.T. services to Democracy for America). Although he is a huge booster of these new technologies, he also warned about the pitfalls and limitations of digital organizing:

> While it does lower the barrier to entry, it does it for a specific class of people. In the predominantly African-American precincts here in Atlanta, those that control the Georgia democratic primary, online access is around 2–3 percent. I think that with the power of this new process, we've got to figure out ways to lower the barrier to entry for those without Internet access. In South Atlanta, people can't afford air conditioners, much less computers. And these are key, active Democratic voters. Here's the interesting part, though: There is a high level of wireless phone penetration in those areas.

So I think on the "blue" side of things, we've really got to figure out how to provide a level of engagement that can work over a cell phone. That's going to be a tough problem to solve, but to wake people up and get them engaged again, the digital divide's got to be kept in mind constantly.

Incumbency vs. Disruptive Technologies

Not all the unofficial websites pertaining to the campaign were weblogs. There were static websites and seemingly innumerable Yahoo! Groups dedicated to one or another identity group or issue-oriented group supporting Howard Dean and discussing his policies and his candidacy (and the other candidates and their policies). The official website linked to as many of those sites as practical and developed the DeanSpace open-source software to help people set up their own independent sites in ways that were compatible with the rest of the campaign.

When disruptive new technologies come along, they are not always adopted by the established market leaders, because they represent risk and change. So it wasn't surprising that the incumbent Republican administration was slow to adopt the freewheeling blogging ethos of the feistiest Democratic challengers. However, as blogs became an unavoidable story even among political insiders, clearly someone on the Bush team realized that his official site needed a blog, and they unveiled one in the summer of 2003.

The site is sometimes criticized because its entries are unsigned and it is not open to reader comments or trackbacks (automated notifications from other websites that a page elsewhere has linked to the site). Nonetheless, the Bush campaign adopted grassroots tools for motivating its supporters, such as the GeorgeWBush.com Action Center where volunteers are invited to become a Bush team leader and enabled to send encouraging emails to their friends. (The Dean site had an analogous Endorsements feature.)

The Bush site even includes a tool for writing semi-automated letters to the editor and provides checkbox-driven talking points. For example, you can select and include the following paragraph in a letter you're sending to a newspaper:

As a result of President Bush's focused and effective leadership on forest health, his vision has become law. The Healthy Forests Restoration Act

2003 will aid in safeguarding our pristine lands by implementing a more effective and timely process to protect communities, wildlife habitats, and municipal watersheds from catastrophic fires.

This approach has its downside. Letters using the same boilerplate language are sometimes decried as "Astroturf" (meaning fake grassroots) and can easily be discovered using Google. For example, a Google search for the phrase "focused and effective leadership on forest health" yields many results from various letter pages at newspapers across the country, all signed by individuals but all bearing the same boilerplate language.

The Republican Party also has a Team Leaders program in which supporters compete to earn points by responding to various outrages from the left. When MoveOn sponsored its *Bush in 30 Seconds* ad contest, participants were encouraged to create their own ads, which were posted on the MoveOn site, voted on by the membership, and finally judged by a panel of progressive Hollywood types. Several ads crossed the line of good taste by comparing President Bush to Adolph Hitler. The GOP Team Leaders site leapt into action to respond, invoking the memory of millions of Holocaust victims and the few living survivors.

If the official Bush blog is a little on the stuffy side, the same cannot be said for an unofficial effort called Blogs for Bush, which features scathing attacks on Democratic challengers and a long blogroll of weblogs that support Bush. Matt Margolis, the organizer of the Blogs for Bush group site, says:

> I do believe that the true test of the impact of political blogs will happen during this presidential election. Blogs have the potential to perpetuate the buzz of a story that doesn't get media attention or has yet to be picked up by the mainstream media. Blogging has allowed me to continually express my political views as well as defend them. It also pushes me to be constantly aware of what's happening and write about it so I can keep my content up-to-date.

Margolis is more skeptical about the potential for Internet campaigning as a way of getting votes: "It is too early to tell at this point. Clearly, a successful Internet campaign did not translate into votes for Howard Dean. At this point, the Internet has been useful in organizing a candidate's base—but I have yet to see any evidence of influence with independent voters.... The Internet will certainly always have a role to play in politics, but I don't see it as the dominant force in politics for quite some time. A bad candidate (like Howard Dean) can have great organization with the Internet, but in the end, it takes a good candidate to make it all come together."

The Whole World Is Watching

Even for nonpartisans, there is a role to play in leveraging the online community. Long before there were blogs supporting (or opposing) a single candidate, there were independent political weblogs. The best of these have become tastemakers that are influencing the professional pundits, and to some extent routing around traditional media.

Frank Rich wrote an op-ed piece in *The New York Times* called "Napster Runs for President in '04," in which he suggested that the mainstream media did not "get" the Dean campaign:

> In that sense, the candidate is a perfect fit for his chosen medium. Though his campaign's Internet dependence was initially dictated by necessity when he had little organization and no money, it still serves his no-frills personality even when he's the fund-raising champ. Dr. Dean runs the least personal of campaigns; his wife avoids the stump. That's a strategy befitting an online, not an on-TV, personality. Dr. Dean's irascible polemical tone is made for the Web, too. Jonah Peretti, a new media specialist at Eyebeam, an arts organization in New York, observes that boldness is to the Internet what F.D.R.'s voice was to radio and J.F.K.'s image to television: "A moderate message is not the kind of thing that friends want to e-mail to each other and say, 'You gotta take a look at this!'"

Rich pointed out that a general election between Dean and Bush would have been "utterly asymmetrical," in that the political structure around Bush is entirely a top-down hierarchy that matches perfectly with the CEO style of its leader. Bush's campaign is "accustomed to broadcasting to voters from on high rather than drawing most of its grass-roots power from what bubbles up from insurgents below."

The claim that the political class is tone-deaf—that they don't "get" the Net, they disbelieve the power of the many, and they can't imagine that the process might be racing ahead of them was echoed in a blog entry by journalism professor Jay Rosen. A commenter to Rosen's piece (Fontaine Maverick) suggested that the candidate's identity still matters:

> What hasn't been said (very well, in my opinion) is that the brilliant and timely use of the Internet to connect and empower supporters and raise money would not have been so successful without a very attractive candidate.
>
> I, for example, fell into the Dean camp when I saw him call Bush on the carpet on Russert's show in early March—(LOVED IT!), and then got an invite/flyer to a Dean event handed to me at a peace march down Congress Avenue in Austin on the eve of the war. It was only then that I logged on.

Political weblogs of the left (Daily Kos, Eschaton, Talking Points Memo, Blogging of the President, Pandago, and Oliver Willis, to name a few) and of the right (InstaPundit, Daniel Drezner, the Volokh Conspiracy, and Roger L. Stone, to name a few more), are emerging as filters and recommenders for emerging political thought. It's in the dialogues and sequences of comments and replies, like Fontaine Maverick's, that we're seeing a new form of public political discourse emerge.

Beyond the partisans of the left and right, there are also nonpartisan blogs and website projects, dedicated to exposing political information to the light of day. Some examples of these include Open Source Politics, Taegan Goddard's Political Wire, and Open Secrets, which tracks and publicized information about money in politics.

Watching the Whole World

Meanwhile, the rest of the world is catching up with the U.S. in terms of connectivity. The Internet population in Asia is growing by leaps and bounds. They used fax machines to coordinate the Tiananmen Square protests in China and mobile phones to protest the seizure of the parliament in Russia in the coup that brought down the Soviet Union. More recent political change in the world has been accompanied by weblog, mobile, and text-messaging coordination.

The "Velvet Revolution" that peacefully forced Eduard Schevardnadze out of office in the former Soviet republic of Georgia relied heavily on uncensorable mobile phones, Internet, and text-messaging techniques for planning and organization.

The protests in Spain over the way that the incumbent government was handling the al-Qaida train bombing investigation just before the election were likewise organized by mobile phone, despite government restrictions against demonstrations so late before elections. (The incumbents were defeated.)

Jeff Jarvis of BuzzMachine frequently points out that it's the webloggers in Iran and China who are going to press for change as those nations continue to grapple with connectivity to the rest of the world.

The Internet is also bringing geopolitical information into the homes of anyone interested enough to Google around for country names. Respected publications such as EurasiaNet publish news stories every day sourced in the countries they cover. EurasiaNet, whose geographical mandate includes Afghanistan and Iraq, doesn't have to make a profit. It operates under the auspices of George Soros's Open Society Institute, filling an information void in these countries.

Justin Burke, the editor of EurasiaNet, reported that democratic reformers in Iran are indeed using modern technology to evade ham-fisted attempts by the conservative authorities to control debates. "We're trying to shed light on what's going on in Afghanistan, Central Asia, and the Caucasus—real countries where radical Islam has taken root and where the war of ideas will be won or lost.... Turkey is the secular model for Islam. Turkey is the antidote to the Taliban and al-Qaida. They want to join the EU. Even the religious party [there] is moderate." The stringers for EurasiaNet are a mixed bag of Americans (native English writers) and people who live there. "Increasingly, we have to be concerned about protecting their identities."

Meanwhile, the situation in Iraq in the summer of 2004 looks almost infinitely complex, all the more so since the revelations of prisoner abuse in the notorious Abu Ghraib prison complex. When digital photos showing sexual humiliation of Arab prisoners by American military and contract personnel circulated on the Web, the Administration's policy of democratizing the Middle East starting with Iraq was dealt a serious setback.

At this point, the ubiquity of digital recording and communication devices (such as digital phones)—even in the theaters of war—has begun disrupting the military's ability to shape media coverage of its activities. Even with the formal mass media thoroughly embedded in military units, the urge to document and discuss one's own experiences is turning our soldiers into reporters and bloggers. The prison itself had an Internet café for the soldiers.

Ironically, a story circulated online a week or so after the Abu Ghraib story broke, reporting that Secretary of Defense Donald Rumsfeld had responded to the scandal by banning the use of digital cameras in the field. The source of the story proved to be a humorous website, but the story was accepted at face value on much of the Web.

Internet analyst Clay Shirky tells us that Abu Ghraib is part of learning to live in a "fully disclosed culture":

> I remember hearing about the security efforts being put into place around delivery of Ken Starr's Whitewater (Lewinsky) report as it was delivered, and thought "Why are they bothering? It will be in the Web in 48 hours." I was wrong, of course—it was on the Web the next day. Now I hear that military officials are debating whether to release other photos with evidence of American torture of Iraqis, and I wonder again why they are bothering. If the images exist, they will be released. It's a fantasy to assume that they can re-assert control of the spread of images by fiat. ... At a guess, filtered versus unfiltered information, in many settings and particularly around control of audio and visuals as opposed to words, is going to precipitate the same sort of conflict [as the Protestant Reformation]. (The music industry is a canary in that particular coal mine.)

Let 1,000 Flowers Bloom

Shirky also points out that the successes of the Dean campaign and Meetup at getting people to show up at events isn't the bottom line in politics: "Prior to Meetup, getting 300 people to turn out would have meant a huge and latent population of Dean supporters, but because Meetup makes it easier to gather the faithful, it confused us into thinking that we were seeing an increase in Dean support, rather than a decrease in the hassle of organizing groups."

Still, the Dean experience jumpstarted a thousand initiatives and inspired hundreds of thousands of people to increase their involvement in political organizing. In the wake of Dean's primary defeat, the campaign and its associated grassroots organizations underwent a period of re-evaluation and retrenchment. Many participants feared the fragmentation that would inevitably ensue, whereas others viewed it as the ultimate market of ideas, a quasi-Darwinian open source-ish competition among movements and groups, web applications, and memes.

Rick Klau gave a presentation to a graduate school class on political strategy, attempting to extract the lessons of the Dean campaign, and then turned it into an entry at his There Is No Spoon weblog. In Klau's view, there were four primary lessons:

- Give up control.

- Let the fringes have input.

- Be transparent—the decision-making process should be visible.

- Changes in course should also be visible.

When you encourage supporters to do things on their own, to engage their own creativity, the moment that they have an active outlet for their energy, says Klau, is the moment they are committed. "Give them room to play and some control, and encourage them to be creative," he says.

On the other hand, Klau thinks that what worked for Dean may not make as much sense in local races:

> I had a conversation with a guy trying to start up a Democratic organization in this town. I told him, "The last thing you need is a website. Face-to-face meetings, phone, email, yes, but you don't need a website.

Kos explains the failure of the Dean campaign in simple terms: "Dean failed because of the candidate, the air game, and the ground game. Also, the Internet portion of the campaign became really complacent. The tech effort got caught up in inward-looking stuff—a Friendster clone [DeanLink] that enabled Dean people to talk to Dean people, or an aggregrated RSS feed from Dean-friendly blogs. Instead of the Internet group reaching out and getting new supporters, it insulated itself."

Kos says this insularity of the campaign manifested itself in the caucuses in Iowa, where the wind really went out of Dean's sails: "Edwards and Kerry people were really aggressive about going after Gephardt people. Dean people stood around talking to each other. This is really symbolic of that 'we're Dean people,' attitude, part of the cult-ishness. For me, it was never about Dean. I'm a Trippi loyalist."

Klau is frustrated by some of the facile explanation bandied about in the first wave of postmortems after the Dean campaign visibly went off track. "It was never about the technology," says Klau. "A lot of what Dean did worked because he was who he was, not because of the technology but because of who he was.

"It wasn't all geeks looking to talk to each other. 600,000 people handed out fliers, went to meetups, put on bumper stickers, marched in parades." Klau says that Dean lost because he mismanaged the campaign, especially in the final two months, failing to mediate between his two competing strategy factions (his closest advisors from Vermont vs. Trippi and company). "It was Dean's job to fix that," he says.

From Klau's point of view, the Dean campaign wasn't brought low by its innovative tactics but, if anything, failed because in the end it didn't dare to be transparent enough. Trippi has spoken of how, in the end, he felt that the blog conversation was too public and that the campaign couldn't ask for help or admit that there were serious problems without tipping off their opponents to their vulnerabilities.

"I had a long chat with Joe about this," says Klau. "Everyone accepts that there is a lot of blame to go around."

An Open Civic Space

Zack Rosen and Neil Drumm took the core of their DeanSpace project and with the help of some venture capital aimed more at social progress than at reaping a profit, launched CivicSpace Labs to continue the open-source development started during the Dean campaign, with the aim of providing organizing tools to any grassroots campaign.

Rosen describes the package he wants to build as a "groupware tool set" and says he hopes, according to journalist Dan Gillmor of the *San Jose Mercury News*, "to establish a permanent foundation that can spearhead social software development projects for nonprofit organizations." Rosen also put together a website that aggregates RSS webfeeds from a large number of progressive weblogs and websites called Progressive Pipes.

In my own corner of the grassroots Dean campaign, we discovered that our core organizers still shared a common purpose, perhaps more widely than we had expected. (Dean activists were always more pragmatic than they were given credit for.) As Californians, we had discovered that there was a role for us in the political landscape beyond the traditional one of "giant ATM" funding early-state campaigns over which we have never had any direct influence.

My local grassroots organization changed its name to East Bay for Democracy and joined with other Northern California groups in an umbrella organization called DFA-NorCal that coordinates with the Southern California group and with the national Democracy for America entity. There is still a center, but it has even less control over the fringes than it did during the primary campaign.

Local activists have started groups such as Party for America to continue the phenomenon of neighbors meeting and discovering their shared concerns and Citizens Vote, a "voter registration drive pyramid scheme."

Zephyr Teachout, Dean's Internet outreach coordinator, is now playing a similar role in the new Soros-funded ACT (America Coming Together) 527, formed to provide soft-money–issue campaigning to the anti-Bush campaign effort.

Clay Johnson insists:

> The blogs of this campaign, including Blog for America, along with the online organizing software, really served as a dramatic disruptive technology to the political process because they drastically lowered the barrier to entry to the active political process. It used to be hard to get involved with

a political campaign. You had to figure out where an office was of a campaign, you had to then drive to that office, and sit there and lick envelopes until somebody told you to go canvassing or make phone calls. The secret to the Dean campaign's success, I believe, was lowering the barrier to entry. Blogs like Blog for America and the Kerry blog now keep you informed of what's going on in the campaign and take a little bit of the mask off the process of campaigning.

Johnson says he thinks the influence of the Dean campaign won't show its full effects in this campaign cycle, but it will definitely pay off in the next. "While we did not win, we created a broad systemic change. In the next cycle, I don't think that you will see a single candidate running without a blog." He thinks this is more than simply a matter for the Democratic Party but something good for Americans across the ideological spectrum. Johnson is hopeful that the apathy he sees surrounding politics today will yield to what he refers to as "this disruptive technology," as campaigns learn to give people something to do beyond voting.

The challenge will be the same challenge the Dean campaign faced—figuring out how to create a two-way channel of communications between headquarters and the activists. That's the nut that didn't really get cracked enough at the Dean campaign, and really, I think it is the current holy grail of online activism: A campaign that can engage its supporters with things to do, listen to them and provide resources to them, and maintain a level of control and stability.

Aldon Hynes posted an interesting essay at the Greater Democracy site in which wrote that this is not a Republican/Democratic conflict. Rather, it's a conflict between the goal of an informed, involved populace and the current reality of a powerful elite:

The person raising the issue went on to say: "Peer to Peer facilitates communications between individuals, but then again, how can we control or monitor each individual actions to make sure that they are beneficial or disrupting?"

Again, the less we attempt to control and monitor each individual's actions, and the easier we make it for people to connect with one another and talk about what is going on and the issues that matter to them, the more possibility for the truth to be discovered.

This post generated a heated discussion about the risks of giving up control and power. It seems clear, though, that you can't generate enthusiasm among a networked community without opening up your processes to participation and debate.

Mary Hodder notes that being freer consists of both lowered transaction costs and less control over behavior. "Under the old model, you had to pay people, or at least pay for paper and stamps and mailing materials, to get the word out. The transaction costs here go very close to zero—and that is key."

Kos feels that there is the potential to re-engage with voters and transcend the political campaign culture of message discipline, which is designed to exclude wavering voters. "They only want their supporters voting," says Kos. Each party has a base of about 30 to 35 percent of the voters, with the rest in the middle, "the swing vote." Campaigns "don't want them voting," says Kos, "because they aren't predictable." Instead the tactic is to run negative advertising and get the uncommitted voters to hate both candidates. "Drive up your opponent's negatives, drive away the mushy middle, and then turn out your partisans."

Kos feels the impetus for changing this will come from open-source politics, which will give voters a role, allowing them to participate directly in politics:

Reading comments on a message board on a campaign blog, that could be it, that could be enough: "My candidate is talking directly to me, not being filtered at a press conference."

Kos points to Brad Carson, running for Congress in Oklahoma, as an example of a candidate with a great blog and a great netroots effort, and he sees the influence of bloggers on politics growing: "In the next contested election cycle, there's going to be a blogosphere primary."

Meanwhile, more people each day realize that they can have a voice on the living Web and most importantly, they can connect with other people who share their dearest concerns. Of course, the people who take advantage of the greater ease of connecting in real space and communicate with each other will represent the most motivated segment of the populace, and are not particularly representative of the masses as a whole. In these cellular groupings, highly involved participants can discuss and even rant to each other and have a greater influence on the debate, just as the people who attend political conventions are less representative of the whole but are more engaged.

The general public, points out Hodder, can now choose to watch the political debate by surfing around to the relevant sites or blogs. This may then spur on more debate or may act as a call to action for the person doing the research. In the past, at best you got this kind of insight filtered through the occasional "inside baseball" news article written by some reporter who covered that beat, but that felt distant, not accessible. The Internet helps make these activities transparent, helps us discover different forms of participation, and makes it easy for us to connect with each other.

Sources and Further Reading

Read these web pages for more detail on the ideas in this chapter. (Some of the candidate-specific sites are now defunct, however.) Many sites can be found through Yahoo! Groups > Government & Politics > By Country or Region > Countries > United States > Politics > Federal Politics > Presidential Elections > 2004.

> There's a ton of research available on Tip O'Neill; here's just one place to find his words:
> http://www.bc.edu/bc_org/rvp/pubaf/chronicle/v7/n12/archives.html

> Howard Dean sites:
> http://deanforamerica.com
> http://blogforamerica.com
> http://deanspace.org
> http://deanport.com

http://deanissuesforum.com

http://tech4dean.org

"Stop Dean" sites:

http://wafflepoweredhoward.com

http://www.stopdeannow.com

Wesley Clark sites:

http://theclarksphere.com

http://www.ex-deaniacsforclark.com

http://www.clark04.com/techcorps

irc://irc.forclark.com

http://www.clark04.com/chat

The post-campaign Dean organization, Democracy for America:

http://democracyforamerica.com

George W. Bush sites; and the "Astroturf" healthy-forest page:

http://www.georgewbush.com/GetActive/Default.aspx

http://blogsforbush.com

http://www.georgewbush.com/GetActive/WriteNewspapers.aspx?aid=102

GOP Team Leader site; and the MoveOn "Hitler" ad page:

http://www.gopteamleader.com

http://www.gopteamleader.com/myissues/view_issue.asp?id=1358

Non-candidate political blogs and sites:

http://www.ospolitics.org

http://bopnews.com

http://politicalwire.com

http://opensecrets.org

http://civilities.net

http://www.dkosopedia.com

http://civicspacelabs.org

Learning the Lessons of Nixon blog:
http://www.cadence90.com/blogs/nixon.html

Aldon Hynes, "Open Source Peer to Peer Democracy," *Greater Democracy,*
December 19, 2003:
http://www.greaterdemocracy.org/mt/archives/000016.html

Joe Trippi, "The Perfect Storm," *Howard Dean 2004,* May 11, 2003:
http://dean2004.blogspot.com/2003_05_11_dean2004_archive.html

Edward Cone, "The Marketing of a President," *Baseline,* November
17, 2003:
http://www.baselinemag.com/article2/0,3959,1386982,00.asp

Ed Cone blog entry on North Carolina politics, December 31, 2003:
http://radio.weblogs.com/0107946/2003/12/31.html

Michelle Goldberg, "MoveOn moves up," *Salon*, December 1, 2003:
http://www.salon.com/news/feature/2003/12/01/moveon

Scott Heiferman interview for the South by Southwest interactive
conference:
http://www.sxsw.com/interactive/tech_report/recent_interviews/scott_
heiferman

Aldon Hynes' paper to the Association of Internet Researchers:
http://ahynes1.homeip.net:8000/dean/aoirpaper1.htm

Gary Wolf, "How the Internet Invented Howard Dean," *Wired*,
January 2004:
http://www.wired.com/wired/archive/12.01/dean.html

Comment on Dean's appearance on Lawrence Lessig's blog, July 12, 2003:
http://lessig.org/cgi-bin/mt/mt-comments.cgi?entry_id=1348

Dennis Kucinich's appearance as a guest poster on Lessig's blog (scroll down to entries of August 11–17, 2003):
http://www.lessig.org/blog/archives/2003_08.shtml

Peter Orvetti's website:
http://www.orvetti.com

Early history of MyDD.com, DFA, and blogging:
http://bopnews.com/archives/000/33.html

Howard Dean, "Bush: It's Not Just His Doctrine That's Wrong," *Common Dreams* op-ed, April 17, 2003:
http://www.commondreams.org/views03/0417-07.htm

Marc Hansen, "Advice to Dean team: Thaw him out," *Des Moines Register* op-ed, January 6, 2004:
http://desmoinesregister.com/opinion/stories/c5917686/23180457.html

Jay Rosen, "Politically Significant Cluelessness," *PressThink,* December 22, 2003:
http://journalism.nyu.edu/pubzone/weblogs/pressthink/2003/12/22/rich_clue.html

Frank Rich, "Napster Runs for President in '04," *The New York Times* op-ed page, December 21, 2003:
http://www.nytimes.com/2003/12/21/arts/21RICH.html?ei=5007&en=035abc452122c4ec&ex=1387342800&pagewanted=print

Matea Gold, "Where Political Influence Is Only a Keyboard Away: More Than Ever, the Internet Gives People a Connection—and a Voice—in Campaigns," *Common Dreams,* December 21, 2003:
http://www.commondreams.org/headlines03/1221-03.htm

Stirling Newberry post at the Draft Clark site (site is now defunct and page is inaccessible):
http://www.draftclark.com/archives/004484.shtml

Stirling Newberry, "Nothing but Net," *The Blogging of the President*, December 27, 2003:
http://www.bopnews.com/archives/000108.html

Robert Greenwald documentary, *Uncovered: The Whole Truth About the Iraq War*:
http://www.truthuncovered.com/home.cfm

Clay Shirky, "Moblogging from the front and the new Reformation," *Many-2-Many*, May 11, 2004:
http://www.corante.com/many/archives/2004/05/11/moblogging_from _the_front_and_the_new_reformation.php

Matt Stoller, "A Beginning of the Dean/Clark Campaigns," *The Blogging of the President*, January 11, 2004:
http://www.bopnews.com/archives/000133.html

Markos Moulitsas Zúniga, "KY6: Chandler Wins!," *DailyKos*, February 17, 2004, on how a blog-supported Democrat won an off-season congressional seat:
http://www.dailykos.com/story/2004/2/17/233027/847

Brian Dear, "Dean-Counters," *BrianStorms*, February 22, 2004, on how Dean's site revealed trends in membership:
http://www.brianstorms.com/archives/000277.html

Rick Klau, "Dean: Technology, campaign strategy and what went wrong," *There Is No Spoon*, April 13, 2004:
http://www.rklau.com/tins/archives/2004/04/13/dean_technology_ campaign_strategy_and_what_went_wrong.php

Chapter 3   Getting Off the Couch

While some of the leaders have become highly visible, what is perhaps most interesting about this global movement is that it is not really directed by visible leaders, but, as we will see, by the collective, emergent action of its millions of participants.

—JIM MOORE, "The Second Superpower Rears Its Beautiful Head"

In the 2004 presidential campaign, we saw that a period of anxiety or heightened political urgency, at least on the national level, can motivate people to take actions—from going to meetings to knocking on doors to phoning or writing undecided voters. All of these activities can be coordinated and spurred on through technological aids. But it's not just elections and political campaigns that motivate people to hit the streets. In 2002 and 2003, worldwide antiwar demonstrations were planned and coordinated on the Internet. Other issues, such as environmental regulation, social services, and even medical research, can also motivate people to take action.

The urge to get involved, to help people, or to make a difference in some way can be a strong enough motivation to move someone away from their computer screen and out onto the street. This is true whether the goal is to raise money to help combat a deadly disease, or to head to a Red Cross center to donate blood to help those at risk from disasters and other emergencies. In each case, the key elements are

- An issue or cause that is powerful enough to motivate a person to find out how to participate.

- Some kind of facilitating tool that can help people identify the activity or location or event that they wish to participate in.

- A way of enabling a person to make the commitment to actually go and perform the task that needs doing.

What Motivates People

I was chatting on an IRC channel named #joiito one day when Howard Rheingold, author of *The Virtual Community* and *Smart Mobs,* showed up. I private-messaged him a brief request for an interview. He asked for email, and I mailed him from my Well address, implicitly inviting him to ask around the Well as to my bona fides. We set a time for a phone interview, during which I took notes in Microsoft Word.

I asked Rheingold about the sort of things that motivate people to take collective action. The first element he identified is the need for a shared interest to provide the initial motivation for people to find each other online. He says,

> The great advantage of Meetup, the way the Dean campaign is using it, is that it uses the power of the virtual world—the Internet—to connect people who don't know each other but share an interest, and combines it with the ability to accomplish things in the face-to-face world. That's an important step, but in terms of political action, just getting together and meeting only has a certain amount of power. If your objective is to get your candidate elected, you need to use that meeting to leverage that meeting to accomplish the sorts of the things a campaign needs to accomplish: going to Iowa, ringing doorbells, and so on. There's another step of commitment that's required.

In Rheingold's view, the Meetup process was sufficient to bring the most dedicated volunteers through three crucial stages of involvement:

- Using the virtual world to connect with like-minded people.

- Meeting in the face-to-face world.

- Taking the steps to perform the collective action.

"In the online world, you can talk about anything and everything," he observes, "but talk only goes so far." Rheingold acknowledges that in some circumstances, a virtual community of people sharing a strong interest is sufficient unto itself. He describes a medical support group in which the participants can't leave their homes. In that circumstance, the virtual community inherently enriches their lives, without requiring that the participants meet in person to bring about a benefit. Likewise, many virtual communities consist of people living in different parts of the world, geographically separated in a way that, for the most part, prevents face-to-face meeting.

"That has its value," says Rheingold. "But if you have an online communication and you have a need to move that towards community, then it requires getting together face-to-face and doing things that people in communities do—going out to dinner, seeing movies, doing activities, babysitting each other's children.

"Not to discount the value of meeting people online, there are limits of what you can know about someone" through that medium. In *Smart Mobs*, Rheingold recounts much of the early history of the Well, a virtual community whose participants (many of whom lived in the San Francisco Bay Area) started getting together face-to-face, "dating, having parties, starting businesses."

What gets people over the threshold to use virtual technological tools to meet other people is a compelling interest: a sick child; a rare breed of dog and no other owners in your neighborhood; a '52 Chevy that you're trying to fix without knowing where to get the parts; a problem configuring a computer network that isn't explained in the manual. "Any need you can't meet yourself," says Rheingold, can provide "a sufficient motivation to get over the barrier of using an unfamiliar medium."

When introducing a new person to the potential of the Internet, Rheingold doesn't start by explaining the technology to them. He asks them what their interests are. "Oh, I'm a butterfly collector." "OK, let's see what's happening online with butterfly collectors." Then he shows them newsgroups, listservs, and weblogs dealing with that subject. This is what motivates people to participate.

"They're not interested in the medium," says Rheingold. "They're interested in what they're interested in. When starting a virtual community, the sine qua non is a virtual interest that's strong enough to draw people together."

The intensity of the need is "a powerful determinant of whether you're going to climb over that barrier." It's easy for people who have already surmounted the barriers themselves to forget, and quickly, how forbidding the technological hurdles may have been at first. Many people understand email, but few really know how and when to use mailing lists, chat rooms, and weblogs. "These things are esoteric," says Rheingold, "so why learn them? You have to have a reason that's personal to you."

What People Need

Deciding who will be the next leader of the free world is—for some people—a very powerful motivation. Trying to prevent war and bloodshed, regardless of the political merits of the specific case, is a powerful motivation for others. The strongest motivations are the perennial drives: survival, comfort, and well-being. The best-known analysis of these drives is Abraham Maslow's hierarchy of needs. In *Motivation and Personality* (1954), Maslow posited a sort of pyramid in which fundamental, base needs must be met before subsequent needs can even enter into the picture. In his scheme, he elaborates on five levels of needs: physiological, safety, belongingness/love, esteem, and self-actualization.

> **Physiological needs** are biological needs that include food, water, oxygen, and the chemical, temperature, and other homeostatic balances required for the maintenance of life. When these needs are threatened, survival is at stake and it isn't possible to worry about higher needs.

> **Safety needs** include the need for security, protection, freedom from fear, structure, laws, and so on.

> **Love, affection, and "belongingness" needs** emerge when physical well-being and safety are relatively assured. "The love needs involve giving and receiving affection. When they are unsatisfied, a person will feel keenly the absence of friends, mate, or children.... He or she may even forget that once, when hunger was foremost, love seemed unreal, unnecessary, and unimportant. Now the pangs of loneliness, ostracism, rejection, friendlessness, and rootlessness are preeminent."

Esteem needs include "the desire for strength, achievement, adequacy, mastery and competence, confidence in the face of the world, and independence and freedom" and "the desire for reputation or prestige, status, fame and glory, dominance, recognition, attention, importance, dignity, or appreciation."

Lastly, **self-actualization needs** come into play when all of the more fundamental levels are satisfied: "Even if all these needs are satisfied, we may still often (if not always) expect that a new discontent and restlessness will soon develop, unless the individual is doing what he or she, individually, is fitted for. Musicians must make music, artists must paint, poets must write if they are to be ultimately at peace with themselves. What humans can be, they must be. They must be true to their own nature. This need we may call self-actualization."

The Internet isn't yet so entwined with human life that it has much to do with physiological well-being, but this is on the very near horizon. For instance, some heart monitors now broadcast their data, so that wearers no longer have to download the information by telephone. Doctors not only receive the data sooner, but they can access it from anywhere there's a web browser. Surely matters of medical health—both mental and physical—can provide sufficient motivation for people to find help and commonalities with others online. (Chapter 5 looks at online support groups.).

The Internet's relation to safety and security needs is primarily as an information source or as a source of advice and help as in, say, the example of a person seeking support from within an abusive relationship. And because financial well-being is a fundamental aspect of security and safety—especially in our capitalistic societies—for many of us, the Internet even has a (minor) role in our safety needs through our employment.

Once people have their more fundamental needs met, the Internet and other virtual community tools provide a wealth of avenues for exploring the higher levels of motivation:

- People seek intimacy, love, and "belongingness" through trying to meet lovers and friends online.

- People work on establishing their reputations or their status through participating in discussion groups of their peers or by maintaining weblogs that promote their expertise or inventiveness or brilliance.

- More and more people use the Internet as a tool of artistic expression or self-actualization.

The needs that drive and motivate people are ancient and perennial. What's new are the virtual realms that provide additional venues for the exploration of these needs.

Critical Mass

Politics is, in some ways, more urgent and deadline-driven than even commerce, the usual agent of mass organized activity in the 20th century. In the same sense that medical advances come from the stress and trauma of battlefield emergencies, lessons for organized action throughout society can be drawn from the exigencies of political races. For these campaigns, the crisis-driven inventiveness of (often unpaid) dot-com-like teams enable them to engineer multiuser applications in the blink of an eye.

The fact that some people respond to a strong motivation to participate in politics is fairly easy to understand. But motivation may not be enough to get them to participate, or participate in a specific way.

The Internet itself has been around in one form or another since the 1970s; the World Wide Web first appeared in the early 1990s and began to emerge as a mass phenomenon in 1995 or 1996. Yet the Internet wasn't a significant *political* medium until the last couple of years. For example, talk radio was credited as the most influential medium in the 1994 midterm elections, and political weblogs only gained traction in late 2001 in response to the terrorist attacks of September 11. It's clear that the 2004 presidential campaign is intertwined with the Internet in an unprecedented way—why?

What was needed was an additional element: a critical mass of people using the Internet to find information, to share their own ideas, and to meet and communicate with other people, both to commiserate and strategize with those who share their views and to debate with—or vilify—those who oppose them.

In the last few years, the number of people with regular Internet access at home or at work has continued to expand. Along with that, the sort of Internet literacy required to track down information and discover online communities has also grown.

According to a report by the Pew Research Center for the People and the Press, in the winter of 2003–2004, more than 40 million people had used the Internet to research or participate in the current presidential campaign: looking up news and information, exchanging emails, joining discussion groups, signing petitions. Also, 18 percent of Internet users had sent or received email messages from campaigns, political organizations, or acquaintances.

Rheingold points out that in the run-up to the first Gulf War in 1990, "you didn't see worldwide antiwar demonstrations." While this might partly be because there was less opposition to that war, it's also clear that there wasn't the same kind of virtual infrastructure for planning, publicizing, and coordinating mass demonstrations at the time. "Far, far, far fewer people knew how to use…a listserv or even email forwarding," says Rheingold.

For that matter, the first Gulf War played out before the advent of the World Wide Web protocols in 1991, which hid enough of the underlying technicalities to render the Internet a sufficiently transparent interface to enable nonmilitary, nonacademic, nonprogrammer types such as business people and artists and activists to start contributing to the daily dialogue. In the '90s it was still mostly nerds, but somewhat less geeky nerds started to have their voices heard as well.

Now, the pressure is on to make it all work for people who aren't nerds and who don't like dealing with condescension. (The Apple Store "genius bars" seem to address this, offering free customized tutorials, but the "genius" branding is surely offputting. I guess it's the flipside of promoting products for "dummies.").

Only recently has the Web emerged as a medium for personal political expression, but a threshold number of people is required before the engagement becomes effective. With a critical mass of participants, says Rheingold, "a magnetic or gravitational force starts to draw in people who are marginal."

He cites the example of The Well, an Internet community founded by the progenitors of the Whole Earth Catalog in the San Francisco Bay Area in the early 1980s. Media people, technologists, and progressive problem-solvers met and influenced many of the early developments of the Web, including *Wired Magazine*'s influential HotWired site, Salon.com, and other online communities. "The Well worked partly because they started with a pretty large group of people. Several hundred people were given accounts to start it: Whole Earth people, Stewart Brand's friends, hackers, and journalists."

Achieving a critical mass of people has always been important to online community, because it creates what people familiar with gardening sometimes liken to composting. A compost heap is a place where you put your cut weeds and discarded vegetable peels and other wholesome trash and allow it to all break down and intermingle through natural processes (detritovores, mostly, but this ain't a biology text). In time, it becomes rich nourishing soil for future growth. Sometimes you even get "volunteers": seeds that love the compost so much they grow without much nurturing at all.

In some ways, the only way to manage a living website is to think of it as a perpetually ongoing project, much like a garden. You need people to water it when you are on vacation. There is a degree of self-selection. Things that thrive get more attention or spread. Some things wither, and some require special treatment to take root, such as favorable light or water or air.

No website can scale if the content is to be created entirely by the website's owner. If your community grows to be 100 times as large, will you multiply your "editorial staff" (if you have one) by 100 people? No, you won't. So where do the economies of scale come from? They come from cultivating a readership community that feels empowered and comfortable enough to contribute its own content to the commonweal. You have to facilitate it, encourage it, weed it, use the proper tools, accept setbacks, take it on as a life project. Or someone does. Not necessarily you.

The Second Superpower

In February 2003, a front-page *New York Times* article by Patrick Tyler about demonstrations against the impending war in Iraq led off with this line:

> The fracturing of the Western alliance over Iraq and the huge antiwar demonstrations around the world this weekend are reminders that there may still be two superpowers on the planet: the United States and world public opinion.

This two-superpower analysis was immediately adopted by many organizations and leaders in the peace movement. In the following weeks, announcements from the Hague Appeal for Peace, Greenpeace, and even U.N. Secretary-General Kofi Annan all echoed the idea that the peace movement constituted a potential balancing power to what had been considered the "sole remaining superpower" (or what the French have taken to calling a "hyperpower")—the United States.

The day of the *Times* article, a weblog called Industrie Toulouse linked to it and made first use of the phrase "a second superpower." The following month, Jim Moore, a fellow at the Berkman Center for Internet & Society at Harvard Law School, wrote a blog essay that recast the second superpower idea—placing it in the narrower context of online engagement, as opposed to worldwide direct action by citizens opposed to U.S. policy regardless of the position of their own governments:

> There is an emerging second superpower, but it is not a nation. Instead, it is a new form of international player, constituted by the "will of the people" in a global social movement. The beautiful but deeply agitated face of this second superpower is the worldwide peace campaign, but the body of the movement is made up of millions of people concerned with a broad agenda that includes social development, environmentalism, health, and human rights.

Moore's article got a lot of attention, but it should be noted that he redirected the discussion from "world public opinion" to "world online opinion." Moore claimed that "cyberspace-enabled interconnection among the members" of this global movement—web connections, Moveon.org, Slashdot, text messaging, and more—were principally responsible for the scope and success of the global antiwar protest coordination community.

Moore, who went on to play a role in the Dean campaign's Internet outreach effort, also took a narrower, provincial view of the antiwar movement. Although he briefly noted the international nature of the peace movement, his concrete examples of results were drawn from U.S. political campaigns and populations.

That said, we can definitely see that (as Moore puts it), "the Internet and other interactive media…provide a means for instantaneous personal dialogue and communication across the globe." On one level, the formless second superpower is self-organizing, arising from the intertwingling of cybercommunication, spontaneously forming a sort of undirected, anthill-like neural network. But it's also possible to rally these communities deliberately or to motivate intentional action, as opposed to simply waiting for a community to invent itself, emerge, arise, and start taking action.

Moore continues,

> The collective power of texting, blogging, instant messaging, and email across millions of actors cannot be overestimated. Like a mind constituted of millions of inter-networked neurons, the social movement is capable of astonishingly rapid and sometimes subtle community consciousness and action. …
>
> Thus the new superpower demonstrates a new form of "emergent democracy" that differs from the participative democracy of the US government. Where political participation in the United States is exercised mainly through rare exercises of voting, participation in the second superpower movement occurs continuously through participation in a variety of web-enabled initiatives. And where deliberation in the first superpower is done primarily by a few elected or appointed officials, deliberation in the second superpower is done by each individual—making sense of events, communicating with others, and deciding whether and how to join in community actions. Finally, where participation in democracy in the first superpower feels remote to most citizens, the emergent democracy of the second superpower is alive with touching and being touched by each other, as the community works to create wisdom and to take action.

It seems that there are some tried-and-true organizing techniques that can be used to facilitate online-coordinated actions. While you can't necessarily lead a virtual community around by the nose, you can cultivate, host, or otherwise foster a community of like-minded people who have demonstrated their motivation to participate through their engagement and self-selection, and then inform them and provide them with activities and suggestions about how to translate their interest or concern into positive action in the physical world.

Think Globally, Act Locally

Global causes will always demand attention, and some issues (such as climate change and the preservation of species and habitats) inherently transcend national borders and regional governments. However, there is a strain of thought that suggests that the most natural way to further good governance in your communities and larger constituencies is through meeting in your neighborhoods and discovering whether you share any unmet needs that you can collectively request be resolved.

Most people don't consider themselves activists, but it's fairly easy to find ways to meet with your neighbors and learn what each other's values and priorities are. It's sometimes easier to plan and take actions in one's own community than it is to coordinate worldwide rallies, and I believe in making things as easy as possible, especially when starting and learning.

Fortunately, the organizing techniques that are available to people using the Internet to gather together like-minded others scale pretty well. You can use many of the same methods to restore a local wetland or oppose a local tax increase as you would to mount a campaign of much wider scope.

Online Methods for Real-World Organizers

Partnership for Parks is a public-private partnership in New York City that helps manage and maintain city parks from Central Park on down. I spoke with Christine O'Connell, technical assistance manager at Partnership for Parks (but "advocacy coordinator" during the campaign we're looking at here), an experienced Internet outreach coordinator with a good grasp of Internet organizing strategies and what works and why.

She points out, for example, that the tried-and-true, somewhat unglamorous technology of email and electronic mailing lists are the workhorses of Internet organizing. (Such tools are known as list servers or colloquially as "listservs," although technically Listserv is the brand name of a particular mailing list software package. Others include majordomo, mailman, and PHPmail.) As MoveOn has shown, simply getting an email alert out to a large receptive audience or forwarded virally from one person to the next can do wonders for raising awareness and encouraging people to respond to a news item or perform an activity.

The tried-and-true methods for automating what the geeks call "the back-end" of the activism business generally come down to a database of contact information for use by the people in your organization. This can scale up to include people who've signed up for your activities and can incorporate escalating levels of involvement.

In the most basic sense, a mailing list can function as a simple database of email contact information, but a full-fledged database can also be used to maintain information such as physical addresses, demographic information, or contact preferences. A database can be maintained in anything from simple spreadsheet formats to inexpensive office software or more robust database management tools.

Beyond email and contact information, the Web itself is an inexpensive communication tool. With weblogs and simple syndication technologies (such as Really Simple Syndication [RSS]), it's also possible to use a web page as a cheap, effective form of "push" marketing, in which updates are regularly streamed to the site and to subscribers to your newsfeed. (Acronyms such as RSS and other geeky names and abbreviations are all explained in the glossary at the back of this book.)

The nonprofit, NGO (nongovernmental organization), and digital divide communities, especially online, are starting to discover each other's weblogs and projects and are trying to find ways to work together as a loose network. This section contains some suggestions I've floated that have generally met with positive responses. (Nobody seems to suggest that nonprofits, for example, should be less transparent or less accountable than they are now.)

As a community of likeminded organizations, nonprofits (for example) could be adopting RSS and weblog technology in order to promote their causes and to better interact and interrelate with each other. Many of these suggestions would apply equally well to any kind of advocacy group, or even to any kind of organization at all. These include the following:

Make it easy to contribute thoughts and ideas. Create the most minimal possible barriers to entry; make a real attempt to learn what works in bringing people to speak up and what doesn't. Have a willingness to admit imperfection and a commitment to improving that which can be improved. This way, you will empower as many people as you can who are affiliated with your organization in any way to start or contribute to weblogs if they want to.

Organize all your publishing (content) across multiple media channels. This includes syndicate and reprint news, analysis, announcements, and alerts. The RSS-based syndication network has recently become the primary way for people to publish microcontent and communicate on the Web. Websites should have an RSS feed and should include site updates, alerts, and any other news in that feed. Email-based alerts should be duplicated as RSS feeds. When possible, RSS feeds should be registered centrally or at local community switching stations, and organized by topic or interest so that people can find your resource. By networking with other organizations, you can encourage them to publish headlines (and links back) from your feed on their websites, and enliven your own website with headlines from other RSS feeds.

Use weblogs internally and externally. A weblog at a public-facing site can be used for alerts, news updates, clipping services, human-interest stories, to promote a personal voice for the entity, and to communicate by, with, and about volunteers. Weblogs can also be used internally as knowledge logs or project logs for employees, volunteers, directors, and even board members.

Watch what's happening around you. Assign one employee, intern, or volunteer to start using an aggregator (newsfeed reader) in-house to track many related feeds, both news-filtered and from weblogs and nonprofit sources. Use trackback, commenting on other blogs, and reposting of each other's key stories as a way to strengthen your network and motivate larger groups when issues require attention. Repost content from incoming RSS feeds when it amplifies your own message or provides needed context.

Listen to your users. Never dismiss a request for help from a user as a sign of their unevolved ignorance. Respond as if it were a bug report and fix the bug. Make your application (or user experience, or whatever trendy metaphor you use to describe your interactive web presence these days) work the way people are expecting it to; don't spend time trying to teach them to think like your engineers.

(As a user, talk back to the interface. If something makes no sense, type "This makes no sense" in the box and press OK or whatever. Someone will see it, and maybe they'll take a clue.)

O'Connell has studied a lot of the available resources, both online and in the environmental community, and she boiled down the collected wisdom into a few fundamental tips for people who are adopting technical strategies for the first time. Some of these may sound obvious, but trust me—these are hard-won "learnings" (as the consultants call them), usually paid for in expensive projects that failed to pass the "user acceptance" test called the real world:

Know your technology budget and specific technological capabilities and limitations. Keep things simple. Understand the total cost of ownership of any new technology—this includes not just the cost of the software, but also the costs of upkeep and maintenance.

Don't expect, allow, or force technology to replace personal contact. If you rely completely on technology and substitute it for face-to-face interaction, it may act as a deterrent for your campaign. Use the right medium at the right time.

The TechSoup website also has a great deal of helpful advice on "Writing Effective Email Alerts." Some of it is reasonably valuable folk wisdom based on experience, such as "Get to the point right away; tell a timely, compelling story; use everyday language; personalize the message; stress the urgency; keep it brief; give readers a sense that their actions can have a real effect ('can make a difference')."

Other suggestions are good to bear in mind for any important email message—"Ask for one clear action" and "Follow up!"—and some are simply good email formatting: "Limit paragraphs to 1–3 short sentences, include blank lines (vertical spacing) between paragraphs, and clearly mark the message's beginning and end."

Finally, TechSoup recommends good "viral" marketing: "Encourage recipients to forward the alert widely." Be sure to include the basics, probably in the form of a brief signature: who you are, how to contact you, your web address (including http://, which most mail programs still require before they notice the link and make it clickable), the current date.

O'Connell adds some email tips of her own:

> Use a catchy subject line. Don't hide your alert in a newsletter. And protect privacy: When sending emails from an email account (instead of from a list server), use the Bcc field, which stands for "blind carbon copy." This field hides the individual email addresses so they are not displayed to everyone who gets the email. In addition, recipients of the email cannot reply back to the entire list.

Bringing It Home

In Maslow's hierarchy of needs, survival issues come first. For some people, environmental activism motivates them on that same fundamental level. For them, the very survival of our ecosystem and of the human species—and even more specifically of one's own self and one's children—might be at stake. Thus, anyone trying to persuade people to take direct action in support of an environmental cause has the advantage of—at least among a target sector of the population—a highly motivated set of individuals.

O'Connell told me about her experience working with the Green Corps leadership project on the Heritage Forests Campaign, also known as the Roadless Forests Initiative. It was a national campaign, but it was heavily localized, with an organized effort to influence local politicians all the way up to President Clinton.

Clinton was considering a rule for the National Parks Service that would prevent roads from being built in national forests. The campaign undertook what felt like a huge initiative to solicit as many supporting public comments as quickly as possible. The tactics were successful. Response was tremendous and Clinton put their policy in place.

I asked O'Connell how they generated so much public comment. "At first it was email," she said. "We also used postcards, as a way of dealing with the problem with any Internet organizing campaign: Her sense was that you should rely entirely on the Internet to disseminate your message, and that some of the more successful efforts she's seen have involved providing simple Internet technology (such as email and forms) to help supporters create and send "snail mail" appeals, blending the various media in the way that plays each to their advantage—the Internet and email for gathering support cheaply and rapidly and the U.S. Postal Service for generating physically bulky, impossible-to-ignore appeals.

When trying to influence politicians, remember that they respond to the level of effort required when assessing the weight of the public comment they get. If they perceive that something was too easy to generate (such as with the push of a button), they tend to discount the volume of those comments.

"We had a massive postcarding campaign involving college campuses, many environmental groups," says O'Connell. "We used pre-printed postcards with room for custom comments."

One important tip, says O'Connell, is to not have the postcards sent directly to the ultimate recipient but to have them sent to your own organization, so that you can deliver them en masse and generate news coverage for the volume of your delivery. "For the Heritage Campaign, we delivered 10,000 postcards on the steps of Congress. We staged a mock delivery of 500,000 public comments to the president."

This brought to my mind the climactic scene in the movie *Miracle on 34th Street*, when the letters to Santa are triumphantly delivered to the judge's bench in a huge pile of bulging mail sacks. The overwhelming bulk of those sacks of mail swayed the opinion of the fictional judge who was torn between the literal truth and the sensitivities of children.

The physical representation of so many opinions can soften even the stony heart of a professional politician, or more likely, bring home the idea in a concrete way of how many voters are motivated to take action or express an opinion to effect or prevent change. Opinions may remain abstract but, like dollars from campaign contributors, bags of postcards and letters and thousands of email messages represent concrete evidence in favor of an action or change.

The campaign publicized Forest Service hearings around the country in an effort to increase attendance and public comment. Such hearings were legally required, but they would not necessarily have been heavily publicized or attended. (Regardless of regulations, no bureaucracy goes out of its way to solicit public input.)

Beyond promoting the regional hearings online and to their announcement mailing list, the campaign provided transportation for people who wanted to attend these hearings. "Again, we worked with college campuses, which can provide a lot of energy for a national campaign," recalled O'Connell. "We flooded the public hearings."

They also assigned organizers to work in key states and to communicate with key elected officials. While the ultimate decision was going to be up to the Clinton administration, the campaigners knew that other government officials would influence the decision. O'Connell traveled to Colorado, for example, rather than relying solely on remote communication. She worked directly with mayors and City Council members to communicate the roadless forest policy message.

Urban Activism

Partnership for Parks is a joint program of the City of New York Parks & Recreation department and the City Parks Foundation. It's a public-private partnership formed to support and help maintain the parks in New York City.

The Parks 2001 campaign was an effort by Partnership for Parks to encourage all of the candidates running in that year's mayoral election to commit to raising the city's parks budget to a full 1percent of total expenditures. Christine O'Connell worked on that campaign and says it had a "huge technical component." The campaign didn't just target mayoral candidates but also all politicians running for election or re-election from the City Council level up in New York City.

The campaign was a joint effort by a number of organizations, and its technical aspect had both successful and unsuccessful elements. "The grand idea was to build a 'greenlist,'" says O'Connell—a database combining the membership and notifications lists of many environmental organizations in a single repository. Some of the groups were willing to contribute their data, but others weren't. "They'd say, 'Just send me the action alert and I'll send it out to my people,'" says O'Connell. "In some ways, it got more complicated than it needed to be. We got the database designed, and member groups needed a code to access the database via the website. We tracked people who used the site to send action alerts or faxes, and captured their information for the future to continue building our database and our network."

One problem she ran into was trying to merge a number of incompatible databases, all with differing fields and record structures. You can generally output a flat (nonrelational) database as a simple comma- or tab-delimited text file, but if the fields are inconsistent or even if their names differ, then merging the information requires a fair amount of data "massage".

Parks 2001 found that with smaller scale groups—those with as few as 10 participants—it was easier to just band them together and ask people to sign up for an email list. In the end, O'Connell found that setting up new mailing lists was more effective than some of the more ambitious database-driven web concepts.

For some of the participating groups, there were also privacy issues. If they had promised their memberships that their information would not be shared outside of the group, then the members would need some way to manually opt in to the new aggregated system (or they could be encouraged to sign up for an action-alert mailing list instead). For other groups, this wasn't an issue, and members were willing to be included in the new system.

"We found that for sending action alerts, emails provided the best way to reach as many people as possible," says O'Connell.

The website set up for the campaign was one of the success stories. "People interested in the campaign could be directed to one online site and send their faxes or emails of support from there." The success lay in capturing information about and tracking the people who used the site. This meant that the organization could identify people who were expressing support for the campaign and also keep track of the raw numbers of people using the automated facilities to send messages of support.

"The larger idea of a single combined list turned out not to be necessary," says O'Connell. "One of the most effective organizing tools was the ability to send action alerts and faxes online. The website enabled people to make public comments and send faxes to public officials. It also included phone numbers."

Because the campaign involved working with a number of different organizations of various sizes, O'Connell found that the information had to be tailored to each group. The campaign worked at the local level, with many groups that had been formed to support a particular neighborhood park. In these, "a lot of people didn't have email or Internet access at all, or if they did, they didn't necessarily understand listservs or how to use them."

O'Connell had to do a lot of local hands-on organizing and couldn't necessarily depend on using the Internet as the campaign's sole organizing tool. "We still had to use old-fashioned techniques. Still, the mailing list was helpful for getting action alerts out. "We had 950 people on that" at the height of the campaign.

After the campaign was over, O'Connell evaluated what had worked. "We realized we had to bring it down to the local level, so we set up a listserv for each borough to support coalitions that united all the park groups in each borough."

In doing outreach with smaller groups, O'Connell learned she had to train organizers to start asking for and keeping track of email addresses, not simply postal addresses. "Once you have [an email communication channel], people will start using it, and then you will grow." For example, O'Connell worked with Fred Kress, the president of the Queens Coalition for Parks, to develop a simple, easy database model for storing their information electronically using a free hosted database service and setting up a mailing list on the TreeBranch Network.

"This works really well," says O'Connell. "It's not like there's a problem every day, but if one group has a question, they can send it to everyone and have a discussion on it. There was a long process of getting people comfortable with using a listserv." Some of this involved getting people used to online netiquette, such as keeping one-on-one communication offline. "Most of the park population wasn't used to using email, so the etiquette was tricky for them at first. Most are retired people who never used a computer at work. Of course the younger population takes to it more easily."

In the end, Partnership for Parks did not use the database-backed site to manage the mailing lists. "It was unnecessarily complicated. We used the free topica.com service and set things up so people couldn't respond to the entire group. Instead, replies go to a moderator." They used the list for broadcasting on a one-to-many model—more like a newsletter or an action-alert system, not as a way of hosting a discussion community.

The campaign also involved getting people to attend public meetings, such as a parks mayoral forum. "It was the highest attended mayoral forum the city had. We did that on the Internet. We did outreach as well. We brought volunteers into phone banks to call the memberships of larger groups with a stake in the process, such as New York Roadrunners, and put announcements and invitations in their newsletters."

Unfortunately, the Parks 2001 campaign culminated on Election Day— September 11, 2001. The terrorist attacks that day disrupted the election and reordered the priorities of the city for some time to come.

Some community groups that had participated in the Parks 2001 campaign understandably wanted to focus on healing instead of park advocacy. The attacks also brought about a major budget crisis, so all of the candidates (including Mayor Bloomberg) who had signed the pledge to increase the parks budget to 1 percent of the city's budget and had taken strong stances in support of parks, recreation, and green space, had to acknowledge the changes to their funding priorities. Partnership for Parks didn't press the cause after September 11. However, about three-quarters of the City Council members had also signed the pledge, and they have since been very vocal about pushing for increases in the parks budget, going so far as to create a parks committee to look over park issues in the city.

"I wouldn't say the campaign was unsuccessful," says O'Connell. "We were able to raise awareness of parks as an important resource to a city's health and economy." The parks-related budget cuts have been less severe than other cuts, she points out. "I think the most important thing that came out of the campaign was the growth of five strong borough park and green space coalitions and the linking of community park groups throughout the city."

Saving the Bay

The Save San Francisco Bay Association is a nonprofit in Oakland, California (disclosure: my significant other works on restoration projects there). They recently revamped their website and introduced a new feature called BaySavers Action Alerts. It's managed on the backend by some custom software installed by CTSG Consultants in San Francisco, whose practice is focused on nonprofit customers and their unique outreach needs (as compared with profit-oriented business customer relationship management practices discussed in Chapter 7).

The list of Bay Savers members grew out of a campaign against the expansion of San Francisco International Airport, which was a 501c(4) organization run by a man named Jim Stevens, who had the list of signatories (including ZIP codes) and gave it to Save the Bay. Save the Bay's policy director told me, "He was that for the coalition. We asked for the list. They gave us the list." One key learning from all of this: You have to get ZIP code. That's a required field."

Identifying Stakeholders

One invaluable organizing technique for a campaign is to make community asset maps. This involves brainstorming who has a stake in the issue that you're trying to address or fix. This might include churches, businesses, schools, community organizations, clubs, and so on. Then you pitch the campaign to each organization and find out what they might be willing to do to support you. Some will offer to do whatever you want. Some might be willing to do just one thing, like make phone calls to members but not send them mailings, or to include information in an organization's newsletter. Some groups will invite you to come and make a presentation to their membership. Others will hand over their mailing list to you and tell you to "use it for whatever."

A related technique for targeting campaigns, developed by public interest research groups (PIRGs) such as US PIRG, is called *power mapping*. This can be done on paper, but it can be more effective when done electronically with a wiki or other associative note-taking software that makes it easy to build connections and make relationships (such as Eastgate's Tinderbox software).

In the example of the Heritage Forest campaign, O'Connell said they started with a target: the President or the head of the U.S. Forest Service. Then they asked, who influences the decision-maker? Each of the influencers are noted or written on the map surrounding the key target. For each of the influencers, you again ask yourself who influences that person's decisions. You repeat this process five or six times to build as rich a map as possible and to identify as many targets as possible to maximize the impact of your campaign. The power map helps you determine who or what route you want to use to influence the decision-makers.

Then for each individual or organization—no matter how far they are from the ultimate result—you need to find a way to make your issue relevant to them.

In the case of the Parks 2001 campaign, O'Connell learned that the most important issues for voters were education, health care, and youth or seniors. For each of these issues or interest groups, she had to find a way to make the parks relevant.

"Education was easy. Parks are a healthy place for students to go after school, and a number of school programs use the parks and recreation centers. Also, having a place for students to go between 5 and 7 P.M. lowers crime levels."

To make the parks campaign relevant to people's health-care concerns, the planners emphasized the fact that the parks help reduce asthma rates and offer avenues for healthy recreation. They also noted that parks lower temperatures, which decreases summer cooling costs in nearby neighborhoods, and that they enhance property values. So for each stakeholder or constituency group, the importance of parks had to be pitched in a different context to bring it home.

They also asked themselves, who has the most influence? Random people who visit parks are important, but they don't represent an organized constituency group. Organizations such as teachers' unions and runners' clubs, however, have greater influence and impact, as well as the biggest databases and largest mailing lists.

Finally, O'Connell recommends, "When doing an electronic campaign, have a mix of real-world actions people can do. People like to see what they're doing. And whenever you send out an action alert, be sure to send a follow-up alert after the action to let people know what effect they had."

Millions of Moms

How can a successful campaign, or even a losing campaign that helps a community emerge, recognize itself and begin gravitating toward the most effective organizing principles?

Joan Blades, one of the co-founders of MoveOn, has been working hard lately facilitating the online efforts of other groups. The AFL-CIO has 2.2 million members, says Blades. The Natural Resources Defense Council has 600,000 members. Planned Parenthood has 400,000 members. True Majority has 450,000 members. "I'm working with 100 organizations with a million members."

"We are reinvigorating the democracy. Now we have people that haven't been engaged, being engaged in huge numbers, which is exactly what our democracy needs. We amplify each other's voices when we come together and people love it. So many people have felt cut out of the conversation."

I asked Blades for some advice for nonprofits beyond listening to their members to determine priorities. She had some practical suggestions: "It's important to figure out what's actionable. For example, for years, people cared a great deal about the health system, but there was nothing to support or oppose—no leadership to give support to. We engaged on [the] Medicare [reform bill] because it was a significant opportunity."

There are different paths to activism success. Another example—and possibly a counterexample—of an organization trying to maintain the impact and momentum it established at its founding is the Million Mom March. A 1999 incident in Southern California, in which a gun was used in a daycare center, resulted in an aerial photo of a daisy chain of kids being evacuated. Donna Dees-Thomases, a politically connected New Jersey publicist, saw this on the news and "flipped out, 5,000 percent" according to a coworker.

She started organizing a reaction by emailing people, and she quickly realized that she'd be unable to do it *all* over email. She asked her family for advice, and they told her she needed professional help. Dees-Thomases had momentum, and she had the nerve to scale things up. Her idea, the Million Mom March, became a coalition of five entities, each with a separate identity and agenda. Besides Dees-Thomases representing the MMM, participating were Handgun Control, the Coalition Against Gun Violence, Ask, and The Bell Campaign.

Each had different constituencies, different ideas of what to do. The specific effort was beginning to expect 50,000 to 100,000 people (the "Million" name was just a reference to prior political marches). They needed a consultant, and put out a call for proposals.

Jasculca/Terman and Associates, a Chicago-based public affairs firm, got the job. Felicia Borrego opened the firm's Washington office in part to deal with the work of promoting and managing the march. The march's lobbying goal was, in shorthand, gun licensing and registration or just "L&R."

Mailing lists and signup lists were managed with databases in FileMaker Pro at the firm's Chicago office. Tech problems were handled ad hoc in the back-office IT department. At times, Jasculca/Terman worked directly with the makers of FileMaker Pro to develop custom database design.

Then Rosie O'Donnell signed on, and a lot of hard news and free media ensued, with Donna Dees-Thomases becoming a presenter on Sunday morning shows. "We used to try to temper her 'mom' language…," says Borrego. They wanted her to cut back on mentions of carpools and laundry, "but she kept saying no, and people really responded."

When Jasculca/Terman got the gig, Borrego told me, "Then our lives changed." However, the change wasn't about the money the firm was being paid, but about the rush of public participation. At times, as many as fifteen people were in the D.C. office, and on the day of the march there turned out to be 1,500 workers, subcontractors, and volunteers.

A million people registered to show up. Not all could show up, but online momentum was demonstrated, and people were on record saying, "Yes, I support licensing and registration."

They used a cross-media strategy, Internet and mass media. The coalition ended up granting 1,500 first-level press credentials for the day of the march; this included network affiliate coverage. There were also many second-level credentials, weeklies, and documentaries.

Borrego believes that 750,000 people marched that day, based on a traditional method of counting heads in a block from overhead photos and estimating the rest. Around 69,000 more people attended local marches in their home states. Another 500,000 people sent Mother's Day cards in 2000, highlighting the campaign.

Who Gets the Data?

One lesson to learn from the Million Mom March is that traditional media techniques can be combined with new direct-connection tools. Another, however, is that even the best tools can't eliminate the human factor.

The March combined living-web and old-school publicity methods. According to Borrego, the "sign up to show up" feature of the website was a significant contributor to the bigger numbers of participants overall. This was "organizing the easy way," she says. You can do it in the middle of the day; there were tools for chartering buses, custom features for churches, information kits.

"Moving bodies, I think, was huge," says Borrego. The March made a partnership with the D.C. Metro subway, which ran two extra trains, offering great PR for public transportation all through the march. Celebrity names helped too, "whether they showed up or not," says Borrego, "but email and the Web probably helped tip it over the edge."

The founder of Monster.com, Andrew McKelvey, paid for full-page ads in the Washington papers and for giant screens and speakers at the March.

However, on Mother's Day 2004, a follow-up March was held that received no media attention. Says Borrego, "I only knew because I'm on the listserv." What happened?

Gun control has a lot of support, but it hasn't had sustained success. It was even a backlash issue against Al Gore in 2000, probably losing him West Virginia, New Hampshire, and possibly his home state of Tennessee.

The gun control movement has also spent time fragmenting and reorganizing. McKelvey founded Americans for Gun Safety, which puts its focus on gun safety, not L&R. The Million Mom March organization merged with Handgun Control Inc. (to form the Brady Center to Prevent Gun Violence) and has never recovered its initial mass support.

In the last few days before the first Million Mom March, it became clear that a struggle for power would follow the great success. One big question emerged: Who gets the database? The fight over this marked the end of the March as a coherent movement.

They couldn't get it together at the national level. It appears to me that they killed the golden goose, caring about ownership instead of reasonable ways to cross-promote together.

This is a cautionary tale for campaigns trying to sustain momentum—such as, for example, Howard Dean's Democracy for America. Organizers can undo all their living-web, critical-mass improvements if they return to old-fashioned, top-down structures, behaviors, and problems and lose sight of the mission.

To Your Health

There is no charitable action more physical than giving from one's own body. The American Red Cross depends on people donating their blood in order to maintain blood banks so that they can respond in emergencies and save lives. It might not be an obvious candidate for online technology, but the Red Cross's GiveLife website provides a way for motivated people to sign up and schedule an appointment before showing up at a blood bank to actually donate blood.

For signed-up members, the Red Cross site also sends reminders when a blood drive is scheduled and recruits donors to participate in other activities related to their mission, such as disaster-preparedness training.

Other causes are equally as compelling and motivating for participants as environmental and neighborhood development efforts. The Avon Foundation and Susan G. Komen Foundation organize walks (Avon Walk for Breast Cancer and Race for the Cure, respectively) in major cities to raise money for breast cancer research, and they offer websites for signing up, participating in, learning about, or donating to the campaigns:

- Participating walkers are given resources for keeping a diary (or blog) to discuss their reasons for joining the walk, and they can run an email list to keep their sponsors informed about their plans and their progress.

- Visitors to the site can sign up to support a walker or her crew member or can use the site to send information about the project to others. There is also a resource for donating directly, prominently linked from the site's main page.

These campaigns illustrate how to get people together to take part in a physical activity, but using Internet technology to publicize, recruit, raise awareness, and keep people informed about the cause they're supporting.

The Avon website runs mainly on the software from a customer relationship management (CRM) firm that caters to the nonprofit sector called Convio. Convio's suite of software applications manage content and activist alerts, fundraising, and other behaviors. In a sense, Convio is pioneering a new flavor of enterprise software, activist relationship management (ARM).

The Avon Walk uses Convio's TeamRaiser software, which offers functionality for online volunteer fundraising that is applicable to various scales of organizations and events, from the national multi-walk efforts to a single fundraiser such as Why Me, a nonprofit that provides emotional and financial support for children with cancer.

"If you participate via the Why Me website," says Whitney Otstott of Convio, "you can create your own personal site with the TeamRaiser software, explain why you're walking, announcing how much money you've raised, and so on."

TeamRaiser is also the software that drove the personal fundraising bats on the Dean for America website, as well as the Dean Team Leader functionality.

The gun-control activists with the Brady campaign and the Million Mom March used different elements of the Convio software suite to focus more on advocacy and less on fundraising. "They are constantly sending out alerts," says Otstott, with the email marketing tool, "about bills that are coming up for a vote, such as the assault weapons ban set to expire in September." They help their participants write letters to their congressional representatives.

"If you sign up for the email newsletters," says Otstott, "Your information is captured on the backend in a database, which then tracks which email alerts you forward on to other people, every time you donate, and other information." This marketing tool can be regionalized, prepopulated with your local representatives and other information useful for you."

Convio CEO Gene Austin gave me the big picture: "From our perspective, the thing we hear over and over again from the nonprofits we work with are two fundamental problems:

- 'My support base is not growing.'

- 'I would like to further motivate my support base.'"

The goal is usually to get the support base more actively involved in the specific cause—as a volunteer, issue advocate, or fundraiser. "If you step back and look at the demographic change that's going on, you can understand why the Web is growing," says Austin. A Pew study shows that Web use is growing among those 55 and over; the Web has been adopted by the nonprofit community in greater numbers than during the dotcom boom, and there's the constant influx into the nonprofit sector of recent college grads for whom Internet literacy is a given. They are, says Austin, "more willing to form relationship with whatever entity, using electronic media."

Austin says nonprofits are using the Web for outreach in numbers that are growing exponentially. "In the year 2002, we had half the customers we had in 2003. The base in 2002 raised 3 million dollars. Twice as many people in 2003 raised 40 million dollars.

"One of the things about our network, we can sit back and look at every dollar our customers are raising, how much email is sent, how fast the databases are growing. We have an operations-center view of the combined operations of Convio customers."

In some ways, marketing is marketing, whether the financial incentive structure in the nonprofit sector obeys different rules than in the private sector. In a sense, the product of a nonprofit is the business of motivation and recruitment of supporters.

"Classic CRM in a commercial space is all about managing a customer," says Austin. "We have a partnership mentality versus a vendor/customer relationship.

"You can build customizable appeals. For example, if they gave $100 last year, you can ask for $125 this year. That happens dynamically. They can pre-populate the details of the appeal based on the issues you've expressed interest in through opt-in checklists."

The fundraising events known as "a-thons" involve motivating people already within a cause's support base to go out and recruit new supporters. "The Web has turned out to be really good for that because what it allows you to do is go out and build a page or create an email that is easily forwarded to all the people you care about."

Frequently, 60 to 70 percent of the donors to a nonprofit do not give again the following year. An enterprise with an analogous rate of repeat business would be asking itself where the customers were going. ARM software enables a nonprofit to build profiles of its contributors and members—who they are and what they want—but it also raises privacy issues. Who owns the data and is it right for the nonprofit to mine the data? "We're still unraveling the data mining, which is key," says Austin.

"When I go back, if I've given money, many of them personalize my welcome: 'Hi Gene, thanks for supporting us last month.' In the future, we'll see more and more customized appeals and maybe be able to drive even more segmented campaigns to get overall support up."

Any system that generates bulk email these days has to worry about losing their messages to spam filters. I asked Austin how Convio's customers deal with that problem. Austin said, "We train customers on best practices, make sure our domain names are whitelisted. We have an ongoing dialogue with AOL, Earthlink, and the other big service providers. We get feedback on any issues they see and our messages always come with an opt-out." Perhaps because their customers, if you will, are more likely to be activists or people who are concerned about privacy and other rights, most nonprofits seem to err on the side of avoiding spam and giving the end user as much control as possible over their privacy.

I asked Austin about the RSS syndication format that some are touting as a purely opt-in oriented replacement for bulk email that avoids the spam filter problems, but Convio hasn't looked into it yet.

"CRM is all about having one single version of the truth," says Convio founder Vinay Bhagat, contrasting it with the services that nonprofits require: "If I get your newsletter but am not a donor yet, the development department needs to know I exist and am not just a cold prospect, whether I have been to events, an activist, or not. It seems obvious, but to most groups, it wasn't."

A lot of people with for-profit experience are moving into the nonprofit sector and noticing some of the inefficiencies there. Meanwhile, nonprofits are starting to look for better ways to reach out to volunteers. Howard Dean's campaign was a wakeup call for a lot of these organizations.

Says Bhagat, "Philanthropy is sales and marketing. That may sound crass, but it really is. It's the charity connecting with you, pushing you through a series of steps. If they ask for money, you're responsive; if they ask you to advocate, you're responsive. If all you've done is taken an online survey or read a blog thread, that's one thing, but if you go to an event or act as an activist, the chances of becoming a donor are higher."

Direct marketing, peer-to-peer marketing: engaging someone in the cause. It's powerful to leverage someone they all know, bringing them into the fold.

Every time an organization sends out an alert, roughly 10 percent of those who respond by taking the requested action on the alert are new, having received a message forwarded from current activists. This grows the organization's list of supporters and gets these new people into the entry level of participation. After that, the software can push them through a program of communications, polls (to gather their priorities and opinions), and interactions. They will be asked to take another action, and eventually, if they keep climbing the escalator, they will be asked to contribute a donation. The email forwarding tools work as viral marketing when they come from trusted friends. The tools enable people to reach out to their friends and encourage them to take action on issues they care about.

"We are leveraging human dynamic relationships," says Bhagat. "At our core, all of us trust a message from a friend or family member more than any brand or any marketer."

To Nonprofit or Not to Nonprofit

In comparing rich data-collection ARM systems (such as those supported by Convio) with the less-structured environment of craigslist, I asked Craig Newmark if his site gathers any data on its users. "craigslist doesn't have much hidden information," says Newmark. The site doesn't do data mining on its users and doesn't track them with cookies.

"We do read everything in our feedback forum," although they usually don't reply to each comment, instead acting on suggestions or waiting for consensus to emerge.

"As far as we can tell," says Newmark, "we are much more responsive than anyone we've ever heard of, much more so than the law requires. We hold ourselves more accountable than any entity that we know about."

I asked Newmark why other businesses seem to find it so hard to be responsive to their customer's needs. "In the American corporate culture…customer service is not a priority. It gets a lot of lip service people don't follow." Nearly half of craigslist's staff is customer-service representatives, "and I am one of them," he says.

None of craigslist's competitors seem to be able to copy its success. "People have copied the site, but they haven't copied the obvious good will, the attention to customer service, the commitment to keeping the sites running fast. We have had outages. We screw up. We get better.

"They copy the look and feel, intending to make a lot of money, and some resort to some serious spamming, try to steal addresses from our site. It's outright spam. Some scrape ads from sites, including ours."

Newmark once described craigslist as a for-profit business that runs something like a nonprofit, perhaps not unlike Newman's Own, which donates profits to charity but does not use the nonprofit tax status. I'm interested in Newmark's thoughts about the concept of "sustainable" businesses rather than endlessly growing profit-maximizing businesses: "We decided on what felt right and did it. I don't have any need to make lots of money. I'm not making a value judgment. I just want to live comfortably and then change the world a little."

Newmark definitely wants to make a difference. "I'm still learning at the right time and place to help the country. Our tipping point hasn't come. No one has figured out how to get beyond a few million people. I hope MoveOn or DFA will figure it out. When they do, I'll be there."

"Give Me What MoveOn's Got"

People in the web development world tell me everyone wants "what Dean had" or "what MoveOn's doing." MoveOn, along with some of the other organizations it has inspired and helped, has popularized a model of moving the masses that had eluded the market thus far. The crucible of political opportunities forged a synthesis that it turns out a lot of us have been working on for a while.

MoveOn's origins, of course, go back to the Clinton impeachment, but its momentum has carried it to new missions since then. MoveOn has demonstrated an ability to motivate people largely by listening to them and communicating useful information to them. As I said earlier, it is now helping other organizations learn from its experience.

Joan Blades points to the Dean campaign as another example. She calls it "a transition point in politics" and points out that grassroots support does not necessarily transfer to any candidate. "Democracy is hollow without grassroots," says Blades. "Paid staff took over from volunteers. We got stuck with sound bites instead of policy. One wonderful transformation is making possible a deeper level of two-way dialogue with constituents."

I asked her what the organization was "about," deep down. "Listen," she said.

> We listen to what our members are telling us. We have to go to the place where our members are most passionate. We've created systems for listening that help us out.

> Dean did it with Meetup. It's still very experimental.... People want it, crave it. We amplify each other's voices when we come together...and people love it. So many people have felt cut out of the conversation. The MoveOn members, many of whom were not active, found it tremendously satisfying. It's exactly what they wanted to be doing.

How have we drifted so far from civil comity? "Political conversation in the last couple of years have become so partisan and not civil," said Blades. People worry about having political conversations at work, but "a community can work out an understanding together." And this understanding can reach across policy and even partisan lines:

> We are often asked: aren't you just preaching to the choir? The Bush in Thirty Seconds contest...they were all wonderful, they were great but that ad that won, the clear winner, was "Child's Pay," created by a man who comes from a very conservative family, a man with some very conservative views, concerned about a serious problem...about the deficit. That's talking across party lines. That's why the members wanted to show it during the Super Bowl. That's not preaching to the choir. It's getting into a real conversation about these long-term issues.

Sources and Further Reading

Read these web pages and books for more detail on the ideas in this chapter:

> danah boyd, "Processing Trippi," *apophenia*, February 9, 2004: http://www.zephoria.org/thoughts/archives/2004/02/09/processing_ trippi.html

Howard Rheingold, *Smart Mobs* (Perseus Publishing, 2002):
http://www.smartmobs.com

Howard Rheingold, *The Virtual Community: Homesteading on the Electronic Frontier, Revised Edition* (MIT Press, 2000)

Jim Moore, "The Second Superpower Rears Its Beautiful Head," March 31, 2003:
http://cyber.law.harvard.edu/people/jmoore/secondsuperpower.html

TechSoup tips on effective email marketing:
http://www.techsoup.org/howto/articlepage.cfm?articleid=307&topicid=5

My essay on syndication and web technology for nonprofits:
http://radiofreeblogistan.com/2003/10/03/weblog_strategies_for_nonprofits.html

Eathan Mertz, "Power Mapping: How to Identify and Contact the Key Individuals Who Will Help You Achieve Your Goal":
http://www.frugalmarketing.com/dtb/powermapping.shtml

Research sponsored by the Pew Charitable Trusts has recently provided excellent, detailed statistics on web use, political communication, and people's perceptions of the media.

The Pew Research Center for the People and the Press, and its report on the Internet in the presidential campaign:
http://people-press.org/reports/
http://people-press.org/reports/display.php3?ReportID=200

The Pew Internet & American Life Project, and its report on older Americans and the Internet:
http://www.pewinternet.org
http://www.pewinternet.org/reports/toc.asp?Report=117

I mentioned quite a few nonprofit organizations and activist efforts in this chapter; here are their websites:

Habitat for Humanity:
http://www.habitat.org

Green Corps, a leadership training program and field school for environmental organizing:
http://www.greencorps.org

The Heritage Forests Campaign, also known as the Roadless Forests Initiative:
http://www.ourforests.org

New York City's Partnership for Parks, the Parks 2001 campaign, and the TreeBranch Network:
http://www.itsmypark.org
http://www.nycparkscampaign.org
http://www.treebranch.com

CyberFeminism:
http://projects.ups.edu/honors_thesis/lhandy/

American Red Cross's GiveLife blood-donation site:
http://www.givelife.org

Full Circles' Online Community Toolkit:
http://www.fullcirc.com/community/communitymanual.htm

The Million Mom March:
http://www.millionmommarch.org

Jasculca/Terman and Associates public relations firm:
http://www.jtpr.com

Avon Walk for Breast Cancer:
http://www.avonwalk.org/site/PageServer

The Susan G. Komen Breast Cancer Foundation:
http://www.komen.org

Easter Seals, providing services to children and adults with disabilities and other special needs and support to their families:
http://www.easterseals.com

Why Me, a nonprofit charitable organization that provides essential emotional and financial support for children with cancer:
http://www.whyme.com

American Society for the Prevention of Cruelty to Animals (ASPCA):
http://www.aspca.org

For deeper exploration into Abraham Maslow's hierarchy of needs, you might read Maslow's *Motivation and Personality* (1954; third edition, Addison-Wesley, 1987) or his *Toward a Psychology of Being* (1968; third edition, John Wiley, 1998), but other analyses can also be revealing. For example, in *Driven: How Human Nature Shapes Our Choices* (Jossey-Bass, 2002), Harvard authors Paul Lawrence and Nitin Nohria offer four categories of human motivations: our drives to acquire, to bond, to learn, and to defend. Like most recent studies on motivation, *Driven* concentrates on behavior in the workplace, but the authors also understand and use examples from other types of organizations.

Chapter 4   Meet the Neighbors

I knew that Vesta Copestakes, the editor/publisher of the *Forestville Gazette,* wanted to put the paper's stories online. But she didn't have the budget or the technical people.... So we teamed up. I see it as an intelligent blending of the 19th-century community weekly with the instant-coverage capabilities (and extended discussions) of modern blogging/conferencing.

—ROGER KARRAKER of 95436.com

One of the ways that the Internet as a tool for connecting people is changing our lives is that it has reduced the importance of geographical proximity for personal relationships. It's not that it has eliminated physical closeness as an important factor. As David Weinberger noted in my interview with him, when virtual and physical relationships are harmonized—with the best available tools used for each situation—the richest kind of social web can thrive. Just as telephones altered the idea of conversation, enabling a form of live talking between people in different locations, the Web is now similarly broadening the concepts of immediacy, presence, and intimacy, forcing us to re-examine how these concepts are related to each other.

For a while, the old metaphors helped us get a grip on the new paradigms. It must have made sense to someone that telephone operators yell, "Ahoy ahoy" into the phone when picking it up, perhaps because it was the way ships hailed each other at sea. But eventually people figured out that only some of the conventions of face-to-face conversation make sense in telephonic communication, and that other, new conventions needed to be invented to provide important social cues—such as announcing who you are after the initial greeting when the recipient of a call picks up.

The exciting part is that over the course of the next generation, as we invent and socialize new norms of behavior that enable us all to make intelligent use of our communications and information devices, we're going to discover that

- Intimacy is possible at a distance.

- Two or more people can negotiate together and schedule blocks of time in which they provide each other with their undivided attention, and thus are fully present, even if communicating through the intermediation of a satellite orbiting the planet.

- The importance of proximity, neighborliness, and local community will not be in any way diminished by our suddenly globe-sprawling collection of friends, correspondents, colleagues, mentors, protégés, and lovers.

In the living web, patterns of community and communication repeat themselves on larger and smaller scales, building up from smaller cellular groups with ties to larger groups and bridging nodes. The fundamental building block of society will continue to be the individual, but any pair of people and their relationship can be a building block of the living web society. What follows from the bonds that individuals form with each other are bonds of respect, dignity, and trust. If I can negotiate the boundaries between my needs and yours and we can work together toward our shared goals, then we can also widen the circle and interact with other, larger groups. At the edge of every group is at least one person who has at least one trusted relationship with at least one person in some other group (no group is an island), and so the building block of the bond between two people continues to be important at every scale.

Geography will never cease to be important. We will always share a huge number of common concerns with the people who live closest to us—in our communities. In some way, the United States has been for a century or more too big to allow intimacy as one community. It's a continental-sized country governed like a commercial empire and to a large extent, a society that has lost the local community scale of things as the smaller communities have dwindled and the large cities became dominant (and for many, impersonal and scary).

We're beginning to see the possibility of re-engagement on the local community and local neighborhood level. This quite possibly heralds a revolutionary reinvigoration of civic life in, but by no means should be limited to, the United States. It waits only for the tools to become adequately distributed for these new social networks to be widely adopted.

A Sense of Place

Roger Karraker hosts a community website for the town of Forestville, California using Six Apart's TypePad and other technologies. Called www.95436.com, the site is a community-centered news organ and online calendar with weblog and group discussion facilities. It's a community site in the truest sense; it asks people not just to take in information, but also to participate in sharing information, commenting, interacting, meeting each other, and conversing, and it provides them with the tools necessary to do so.

Karraker says of his site, "I believe you can trace the genesis of this system to an off-hand remark made by Stewart Brand, a legendary guy, perhaps 20 years ago." Brand is well-known for his social-technical vision, especially for several key innovations:

- In 1968, Brand published the first *Whole Earth Catalog*, "a revolutionary publication touting access to tools (books, ideas, etc.) in a format similar to how L.L. Bean sold clothes and shoes."

- In 1969, Brand was an assistant to Dr. Doug Engelbart in demonstrating early forms of now-familiar technology, including the Web, the mouse, hyperlinks, and a modern human-computer interface. "This was the first time when anyone got a glimmer that computing could be different from a corporate behemoth," says Karraker.

- In 1985, Brand helped found The Well, the first public online community.

As Karraker puts it,

> In the midst of all this techno derring-do, Brand surprised us all one day
> by saying that if he had his life to live over, he would want to be the edi-
> tor/publisher of a village weekly. He thought that would be the most pro-
> ductive role possible.

> That got me to thinking, because I'd written for community papers for many
> years. In my case, I would *not* want to be the publisher of a weekly print
> paper because the economics of small newspaper publishing is horrible.

Based on his Well experience, Karraker experimented with various types
of online discussion systems. He began systems for students at Santa Rosa Junior
College and helped found The River, a Well alternative, in 1995. By 2003, he saw
that blogging software could be tweaked to provide essentially a very-low-cost
"community newspaper," and some version of cheap conferencing or forum software could provide the dynamic exchange that communities need.

Vesta Copestakes, publisher of the *Forestville Gazette,* weighed in as well:

> There are so many clubs, associations, councils, committees, etc. that not
> only meet on a regular basis, but that also meet for specific purposes, and
> sometimes with not enough lead time to let the media know about them.
> The immediacy of this weblog allows them to post those meetings.

When you start thinking about the kinds of clubs and organizations that
people join and attend locally, the logistics involved in pulling together people for
regular meetings or activities, some of the more universal issues of community
organizing come into focus: These include meeting attendance, planning, scheduling, as well as the challenges of self-organized management in which people
need to take on responsibilities (such as "I will drive the children to the game," "I
will pick them up at the train at 5 P.M.," etc.) or to ensure that others do.

Bearing in mind that the technological fixes we're using these days are still
evolving, the critical threshold benefit of the blog-plus-webfeed model is that
it combines the following:

- The flexibility of the blog tool for publishing (personal expression, in
  public, with nearly the ease of email)

- The linking power of the Web itself

- The convenience of webfeeds (usually RSS) as a medium for distributing messages on an opt-in basis

Berkeley graduate student and Technorati advisor Mary Hodder commented to me on why this system may work better than phone trees and other ways of coordinating activities. In part, the reason may be ownership: the quality of information is higher because someone specific takes responsibility for a blog. But another reason is "the very *fact that it's in writing*—that last bit being crucial because our education system trains us to take writing more seriously than other, more ephemeral means of communicating." Yet blogs are still perceived as casual and easy, so the process of getting the message out to people is not like getting, say, a law review article published.

Again, a critical mass of participants is needed so that within the larger group of readers, you can find higher involvement people spending more time, working harder, taking on leadership roles, or applying their energy or talents to the furtherance of your group's well-being.

The Dean Commons event calendar has a facility for offering or requesting a ride to an event, to encourage people to carpool whenever possible. This information (where to sign up to offer or request a ride) is even available via a syndicated RSS feed so that any local website can offer one-click access to the rideshare tool for events within a certain radius of the site's ZIP code.

Another example is RideMatch at RideshareOnline.com in Washington State's Puget Sound area, which offers confidentiality, daily updates, and more than "1,000 vanpools for commuting to work or school." The website is supplemented by a toll-free hotline number and an email contact address.

In the park-related activities discussed in the preceding chapter, the major constituencies are people with recreational needs such as athletic leagues, water sports, and even dog walkers.

Park restorations and reclamation of public space rely on people to organize themselves, to plan and schedule events, and to demand that their recreational needs be met.

Portland Communique

Near the end of 2002, Christopher Frankonis, who is known on the Web as The One True b!X, launched a site called Portland Communique. "While I'd made an earlier attempt or two to publish a Portland Communique site, it never really came together until I finally secured the locality-based domain name that it uses: communique.portland.or.us. I wanted the site's URL to clearly 'brand' it as being from Portland."

Having lived in Portland for more than four years, b!X felt he needed an excuse that would force him to learn more about the city. "*Force myself* meaning, I was making a commitment to myself to write about the city every day, which meant I needed to do far more (and far more consistent) reading about Portland than I had been doing previously."

As is typical for weblog-type publications, b!X's early coverage consisted primarily of entries commenting on the local news, but he soon began to add original reporting from community meetings. He covered controversies over urban design such as "the burial of our City's open reservoirs and the ill-conceived plan to put a seasonal ice rink in Pioneer Courthouse Square." Reflecting on the issue of the public's role in the city's governance led b!X to begin attending meetings of the city's task force for discussing new standards and modes of public involvement.

> Those early stabs at original reporting on those types of issues in essence became my sideways entrance into Portland politics, which over the site's first year of existence became an ever-increasing portion of Communique's content, and gradually moved me to more direct attendance at City Council meetings and other events around town.

Communique is a classic cottage-industry publication, running out of b!X's apartment on an OpenBSD box, powered by Six Apart's Movable Type and served up over a DSL line. Thus far, b!X does all the writing and other work as well, although, as he says, "in recent months (after reading an anthology of writings from a women's suffrage newspaper published in Portland in the 1800s), I tend to use the editorial 'we' when posting items to the site."

The publication also serves as a kind of community hub for its readers. "I adore my readers," writes b!X. "They are extraordinarily good to me.... They are an integral part of the 'commentary' component of Communique—as exemplified fairly well by one day during the local same-sex marriage controversy when I was out of the house for 12 hours straight and came back to find 50+ reader comments busily discussing the issue while I was gone."

In addition, over the site's first year, more and more reporters for the traditional media in Portland have made Communique part of their reading routine, as have an increasing number of people in local government (both elected officials and staff). Although it stops short of full two-way or many-to-many communication between officials, paid media, b!X, and the readers, the site points to a future model of civic involvement that will become more commonplace and will depend less on one dedicated seeker with computer skills.

Habitat for Humanity

Carpooling and reducing the use of fossil fuels is one way to help save the world. Another is to address the chronic housing shortages endemic to our urban areas. The nonprofit that former President Jimmy Carter made famous, Habitat for Humanity (HFH), builds houses but also fosters home ownership by arranging at-cost no-interest mortgage loans for first-time homebuyers.

Grounded in local communities, the organization's central habitat.org website helps people find the local affiliates in their area. The site offers the ability to make a secure online donation, and it solicits donated materials, volunteers, and sponsors.

> Habitat for Humanity International is a nonprofit, nondenominational Christian housing organization.... Since 1976, Habitat has built more than 50,000 houses with families throughout the United States and another 100,000-plus houses in communities around the world. Now at work in 92 countries, we are building a house every 26 minutes. By 2005, Habitat houses will be sheltering 1 million people.

Homeowners and volunteers build the houses. The site has a Get Involved page where people can sign up to volunteer to help build a house, contribute supplies, donate funds, or make other forms of donations. This requires some of the back-end logistics involved in e-commerce but without the same form of transactions accompanying the exchange of goods in the nonprofit sphere. Because of tax issues, there are still transactions involved, but they are not shaped the same as a simple credit card charge over the Net.

People who don't want to build houses can work on committees, do office work, work at a warehouse or a resale store, or do the fundraising and leadership equivalents of sales and executive roles in the for-profit business world.

The organization offers a team-building program, so that groups can participate in the home-building activities and network with other service organizations such as AmeriCorps.

But the international site is not the only face of the organization. Habitat for Humanity International is the umbrella organization. It has regional divisions, but the local entities are organized as affiliates and not as chapters; each is a separate nonprofit corporation for funding purposes with its own name and board of directors.

The International group maintains a set of principles and goals, such as these goals:

- Each local group is to build homes.

- Work toward home ownership and not rental.

- Charge no interest on mortgages.

- Involve the benefiting family in the building of the home.

- Employ volunteer labor for the rest of the work.

Each local affiliate signs a "covenant agreement" with the International, which allows them the use of the Habitat for Humanity name as an official affiliate. Local groups are governed by their grassroots, recruit their own volunteers, select their own partner families, and—for the most part—raise their own funds. Local groups generally "tithe" 10 percent of their funding to the International group to support home building in other countries.

In return for agreeing to the covenant, the local affiliates get the public relations benefit and goodwill of being associated with the international Habitat effort. But they have flexibility. "We can pick a specific country to direct our funding to—for example, South Africa," says Krysta Morgenthaler, who works in the local affiliate near me (Oakland, California), maintaining its separate website and email newsletter. Morgenthaler also works with corporate development (fundraising), volunteer outreach, and coordination with partner relationships such as with AmeriCorps.

The local website features volunteers, providing them some much-needed props for giving of their time and skill (not unlike an employee-of-the-month award), and there's an email newsletter distributed via a Yahoo! group. The website offers information about current and future projects and those completed by other volunteers, explains the mission of the organizations and history of the local affiliate (whose budget for 2003 was more than $3 million), and offers a signup form for new volunteers.

Volunteers can specify a construction site they'd like to work on, their availability, and their experience with construction or the building trades (general contractor, carpenter, electrician, plumber, landscaper, and sheetrock and roofing specialists), although construction experience is not required to volunteer.

How these federated-type macro-organizations work is just as interesting as how the local organizations work directly with real people in their neighborhoods, so I asked Morgenthaler about the lines of communication among the various groups. The regional centers help foster communication from the affiliates to the umbrella group, and a site called PartnerNet is used to share best practices up and down the line and enable lateral/horizontal communication among local affiliates.

PartnerNet is what we in the web development business call a "member extranet": a collaborative resource organized into topical sections where members can post messages to bulletin boards and share links to various resources in a dynamic environment. Morgenthaler got a little sheepish when I asked her more about this because, she said, she finds the site burdensome and goes on it only when she is looking for something specific. "I should probably use it more."

I don't like it when users blame themselves for not adopting a tool that is recommended to them, so I suggested that perhaps the site itself wasn't as useful for her as it should be.

Each HFH affiliate files an annual survey report with International detailing how many homes they built and how many volunteers they used. The regional centers also sponsor annual conferences for idea-sharing and workshops. One recent workshop was on the subject of "greenbuilding," meaning construction using as much environmental sensitivity as possible—alternative materials, recycling construction waste, maximizing passive solar energy, and installing photovoltaic cells, for example.

Habitat's western regional center publishes an affiliate newsletter, which used to come out on paper but is now primarily in email form. But International's regular "affiliate update" still goes out on hard copy.

A "You Are Here" Toolkit

The Dean campaign used a radius of x miles around a ZIP code to tell you who lives near you and what events are scheduled nearby. In one form or another, many other initiatives are adopting similar tools.

Joshua Schachter's GeoURL.org site established a standard header format for coding geographical location in terms of longitude, latitude, and other metadata (such as the name of your location). This format can be facilitated by incorporating it into templates driven by other programs and databases when publishing information online. The more that people use this format, the easier it is for others to build tools that support geolocalization (as opposed to another recent phenomenon: cool-looking but otherwise fairly useless maps of the globe showing where people have blogged recently).

In principle, geolocalization enables people to aggregate content from multiple sites within the same community, as long as those sites offer webfeeds or some other form of subscribable update. Maps of community organizations will be useful for the groups themselves as a way of learning about their neighbors and networking possibilities, as well as to researchers, reporters, and even marketers. A localized view of community organizations might also be a useful resource to review when considering moving to a new location.

Years ago, I remember someone suggesting that a community website would be useful in a large apartment complex, gated community, or housing project. The site could host the community's shared calendar, serve as a place to work out disputes, or plan events. This hasn't been made to work in a dramatic way yet; most seem to think that an old-fashioned corkboard is just as good for this kind of thing.

There's still a digital divide, and it's still just a small fraction of the people in most neighborhoods who use their Internet access to organize their time and relationships. However, as the tools for remote communication and spontaneous (or scheduled) partial presence become more and more ubiquitous, it's inevitable that small neighborhood groups will avail themselves of these tools to

- Solve conflicts

- Build consensus

- Plan block parties

- Determine their political and civic needs as a small community and communicate those to the next level of power, whether that be some kind of regional ad-hoc group, a city council, a mayor, or a board of supervisors

As always, the people involved in any potential (or latent) community group still need to have shared goals, if only an inchoate desire for community based on location. Otherwise, no widget or gadget is going to bring anyone closer together or help anyone understand each other's needs and priorities. A homeowners' association, for example, can be a well-defined geographic space that includes people with similar lifestyles and a shared financial interest. But if they have no interest in communicating with each other—no wish to participate in governing their association, let alone being close-knit in other ways—no amount of tech tool-ness will make them share.

It wouldn't be hard to build a site for a physical community using a free community weblog tool such as Drupal or Scoop. I found a discussion of ways to do this using ColdFusion tools, and someone pointed to a free (if generic) "community web portal" product offered by Ultra Apps, which is described as "an online community management system for a Club, Association,

Corporation, Nonprofit or any other company or organization." The portal tool offers

- An event calendar

- Some categorization (taxonomy)

- Multilevel, user management, transaction services via PayPal

- Moderated forums

That's plenty of services to tap into when there's a critical mass of interested people able to use it.

Andy Baio, a web developer and blogger (his popular weblog is called Waxy.org) created a free service called Upcoming.org that any individual or group can use to log upcoming events or appearances. People can see or subscribe to each other's lists, and upcoming events can be subscribed to as a syndicated feed and mirrored or summarized on a website with ease.

Educating Locally

To facilitate homeschoolers, who need the resources and curricular discipline of the local public school system but choose to enact the physical face-to-face component of teaching within the family in their homes, the city of Akron, Ohio, offers an online school (K–12) called the Akron Digital Academy.

Its programs are carefully synchronized with the public school's agendas, and its teachers are certified professionals with the same credentials required for teachers in the public schools. This enables students who decide to return to the conventional school format to do so at any time without a disconnect. The school system provides the necessary online equipment required for participating in the academy's classes.

Even homeschoolers benefit from interacting with other students in educational circumstances, and Akron Digital Academy students are encouraged to attend field trips and participate in after-school activities with other students.

A writer I know, Jon Shemitz, offers homeschooling advice on his personal website and considers it important enough that he includes the URL in his standard email signature. His site is offered as a public good, with no commercial motive. It includes links to useful books, frequently asked questions, links to mailing lists and support groups, and other types of useful information for anyone considering teaching their children at home.

Serious Tools for Playing Around

Almost every kids' sports league in California has its field schedules, referee assignments, and tournament data on a website. Numerous companies offer specialized website construction services and forum or community software technology for sports teams, with brand names like eTeamz, League Pro, and HotStat.

While sports may seem like a trivial matter of fun and games, the fact is that sports and park recreation are traditional community interactions that frequently transcend the demographic divisions that can separate neighbors. While some consider sports to be purely a matter of hobby and recreation, for many parents and educators, athletics are the arena in which children learn fitness, teamwork, commitment, and fair play. Anyone who has organized a league or planned a runners' or cyclists' event knows that a lot of work is involved—coordinating schedules; delegating responsibilities; and keeping track of standings, tournaments, and who is playing against whom next weekend.

The tasks involved in getting a league together include

- Registering players and collecting registration fees

- Recruiting businesses as sponsors

- Raising funds from individuals (such as through fundraising events and candy sales)

- Recruiting, training, and scheduling coaches and referees

- Reserving fields and scheduling the actual games

If only because of the automation of standings, statistics, and scheduling, these digitally mediated sports leagues offer some logistical advantages over the traditional phone, photocopy, and fax methods. (It's odd to a lot of people to see "fax" as an old-fashioned, "traditional" technology.) In addition, the encapsulating of the various organizational functions of sports leagues into a series of web-enabled applications make it easier for a beginner to launch a team or league without much help from an experienced coach or organizer. In a sense, the collective wisdom of how best to do such things can now be made available in an interactive form instead of simply lodging in the heads of each neighborhood's wise elders.

Services like eTeamz facilitate the building of a customer's own custom website, even with its own URL (they walk you through the domain registration process for a small markup), they help with fundraising, and their basic site formats include message boards, a tournament scheduler, practice/drills/instruction information, photos, and merchandise.

The rallying cry is "No HTML necessary" as the critical mass of participants rolls beyond that small core of early adopters who needed to memorize ciphers to get into the club.

LeaguePro targets people who've used free hosting services and are itching for more specialized services such as team pages, complete schedule management, a rain-out tool, standings, and tournament setup. LeaguePro also brags about its customer service in its user testimonials, understanding that people want this stuff to "just work."

Team sports aren't just about kids, either. When my editor and I were researching local recreational community facilitation, one of his co-workers told him about a group in the San Francisco area who play kickball. Yes, kickball, and yes, these are grownups. They organize their team meetings and administration online, through the World Adult Kickball Association (WAKA). They claim to be "huge" in San Francisco, Boston, Chicago, and New York, although participation is clearly not on a par with summer softball leagues or other forms of adult recreation. Less common sports such as kickball can benefit from the Internet's ability to connect people around specific interests by making it easy to find each other and gather together.

WAKA provides a clickable map of the U.S. and other countries for finding the league nearest you. WAKA is pitched not just as athletics but as a "co-ed social experience." The league finds a bar to sponsor its parties (with discounted food and drinks), including an awards ceremony at the end of the season. The Missouri Gateway division's page even recruits for its board of directors, for people more interested in running organizations than in participating in the sport.

Localized Social Networking

While I was writing this book, an engineer at Google released an alpha version of a new social networking tool called Orkut. It began with an invitation-only introduction to the network of the site's inventor. Its mix of interface advantages and functional disadvantages will be discussed in more detail in Chapter 7. I don't particularly endorse Orkut, but its beta-test period began just as I was polishing this subject, and the opportunity to experience the growing pains of a social network site from within was too good to pass up.

Orkut offers users the ability to create communities by defining a group and then introducing the group to the Orkut public or by invitation only. People's profiles in Orkut show which communities they are a part of. When I was invited to sign up, I looked for local communities, as I always do whenever I find a new information resource or collaborative site. I look for my interests (in music, in books, etc.). I also look for the place I live and sometimes other places where I have lived or that I love for other reasons. It seems natural to me that among the thousands of users of Orkut, some should be in Oakland or the Bay Area, and among them might be some people I already know or would like to get to know. Our geographical commonality, combined with some implicit commonalities (that we could get invited into the beta test for a Google social network, if nothing else), lead me to think that searching by location still makes sense, even in a supposedly post-geographical Internet-mediated "non-meat-space" world.

I found several Orkut communities related to where I live, such as "Oakland," "East Bay," and "Oaktown" (a nickname for Oakland), the latter founded by a Rev. Smokey T. Burnout, Esq. I looked at all the groups and briefly joined all of them but found that none of them had much content (yet). It also annoyed me that I might have to choose. I wanted to have the ability to instantly consolidate the information into groups that made sense to me, not necessarily ones that made sense to other people.

Such frustration isn't new. Back in 2001, Oakland mayor Jerry Brown hosted a technology summit in Oakland in hopes of encouraging more investment in high-tech businesses in the city during the ebbing period of the dotcom boom/bust cycle. The handouts included a CD-ROM directory of participating businesses, and there was a website for the conference. The East Bay is, and was even then, crowded with wired people and shouldn't be too hard to organize.

Of course they set up a website. You can still see it at http://www.techoakland.com/about.htm—a page that hasn't been updated in four years. As we've learned, static web pages are a pain to update. Even if the steps involved aren't onerous, they become so after repetition. Had they built the page as a wiki—or even simply included or linked to a wiki—the nascent community members would have been able to enter information as they found it and connected with each other, yielding the possibility of sustaining the site as an information resource to its users. Maybe next time.

Meanwhile, from the ground up, a collective called Nonchalance.org has created a brand ("Oaklandish") and a website that goes with it to teach people about the deeper, lesser known history of Oakland, to support local arts organizations and activities, and to sell stickers with the Oaklandish logo.

All Politics Is Local

One of the driving influences of the Dean campaign was Robert Putnam's book *Bowling Alone,* about how Americans have become disconnected, with fewer public and common spaces and fewer group activities getting them out of their homes, away from their TVs, and even out of their cars.

At the end of 2003, the Dean campaign raised so much money and was polling so well that the ensuing media hype created an expectations bubble—both within and without the campaign—that was not met by the results in the crucial first two states, Iowa and New Hampshire.

The Dean campaign's Internet-driven approach to organizing these states involved letter-writing campaigns from across the country and thousands of volunteers paying their own way, to travel long distances to help with canvassing or any other jobs that needed doing. In spite of this, the poor quality of the Dean campaign's television advertising, the negative (some would call it "comparative") dogfight between Gephardt and Dean, the media gauntlet from January of this year (for weeks, there was at least one negative story about Dean daily), combined with the lack of institutional know-how and follow-through in the actual community-level precinct work, led to the disappointing third-place finish for the campaign.

Looking back, it was apparent that Iowans didn't necessarily welcome political advice from out-of-staters who take off a week and volunteer for a campaign.

Why didn't the Dean campaign set up community-level organizations in Iowa and foster the Great American Conversation right there in the state where the campaign focused so much time and energy? Perhaps the Internet-focused fervor wasn't reaching the 80 percent of not-highly-wired people.

Still, the Dean campaign in my local community changed its talking points but not its ground-level strategy: raise money, recruit volunteers, walk the precincts, organize phone banks, leverage endorsements, and sponsor a voter registration drive. All of these things take place within one's immediate community.

So what did the Dean campaign accomplish, if it didn't elect a nominee in its party's primary? Their use of Meetup and blogs (both their own and those of people already established with trustworthy online reputations) galvanized people and channeled their passion into a belief that change is possible.

For the most active volunteers, losing the primaries was a blow to the system that was eventually processed along the lines of "Of course, what made us think we could change the system in one single presidential election cycle?" With that, many of the grassroots volunteers girded their loins, as it were, and re-entered the fray for the long haul.

Even in the thick of the fight, there were disconnects between the self-organized grassroots and the people at the hub of the official campaign who found themselves riding a tiger that they didn't know how to direct. In the wake of the primaries, with no candidate or single focus, the grassroots groups took some time to reorganize. Most groups realized that even while working together on national goals (the presidency, Congress, the national party), the real meat of the matter was going to take place locally, in each state, in each congressional district, over nearby state boundary lines, and so on.

The primary results stripped away the illusion that 50 dedicated supporters in a congressional district would automatically translate into 2,000—let alone 20,000—votes. But when all was said and done, in meeting hall after meeting hall across the United States, groups of 25 to 50 people stared at each other and realized that they represented in each locale a potent force for grassroots community activity and political change.

Somebody Call 311

I went to see Howard Dean's announcement of Democracy for America (aka DFA 2.0), the successor organization to his presidential campaign Dean for America, at a hotel in downtown San Francisco in March 2004. In many ways, it reminded me of a Grateful Dead show in the late '80s. Many people came early to get the best positions. The time spent waiting for the headliner to come on (late) felt festive and raucous.

As it got crowded and stuffy, I began to feel claustrophobic, especially when they started leading the crowd in protest songs. I stepped into the hallway and watched passersby being drawn by the noise emanating from the ballroom. I got an idea of what the rallies must have been like in the heat of the campaign: excitement generated by the crowd and energy for the rock star Dean whose downfall was screaming into a unidirectional microphone.

When Dean came onstage, the audience roared along with all of his hooks, including the tagline about how even tiny Costa Rica "has health care for all its citizens." He summed up in preacher style a list of goals and ambitions of the primary campaign. He ended each line with "…and we did!" to the accompaniment of great cheers from the crowd.

You could feel the fervor of the room from across the hall, and I was reminded of Phil Wolff's comments to me just days before about "the dark side of the mob."

Craig Newmark came out of the room into the hallway. He spotted me and told me he was going to address the San Francisco Democratic Club and would I like to tag along as a journalist. Of course I said yes.

The Democratic Club has been around since 1980; it claims to be centrist, interested in analysis of politics and good-government reforms. Newmark was invited to address the group specifically to discuss his involvement with new San Francisco mayor Gavin Newsom's transition team and in particular, his involvement with the 311 initiative to provide one-stop city government customer service to constituents.

Newmark is a great believer in customer service as an overlooked key to business process re-engineering, a discipline that is much talked about but rarely practiced. He recommends providing customer service representatives and other "line workers" (workers who interact directly with customers and other people across the boundaries of an organization) with the support they need to do their jobs well and with pride.

In particular, he supports empowering line workers to report on what they see that needs fixing or what customers are reporting to them (complaints, requests, or suggestions) and to suggest improvements in the processes used to fulfill the organization's mission.

By increasing transparency in an organization so that it's clear who is responsible for what, and by demanding accountability so that people are called upon to fix what they see going wrong, Newmark believes that the people actually doing the work in an organization can work on healing its dysfunctions and enabling the system as a whole to learn from its experiences.

At the Democratic Club, Newmark quoted Adlai Stevenson, "Sources of information are the springs from which democracy drinks." He described 311 as a "non-sadistic phone system" or at least "much less sadistic."

But some of the club members who work in the civil service—and have their own notions about who isn't doing a good job—and other members don't agree with the ethos of transparency and accountability that Craig is advocating. True to his ideas, Newmark asked for contact information from the naysayers, so he can learn better what they know about what is working and what isn't.

He ended with a quote attributed to Victor Hugo: "There is nothing so powerful as an idea whose time has come."

Now, local improvement doesn't necessarily have to happen locally. Freecycle is a network of local mailing lists dedicated to recycling property by giving it away to others for free instead of trashing it. People can post items to their local list that they wish to give away as well as items they are hoping to find. No money can exchange hands. My local list is rather low traffic, averaging only about one post per day. Nonetheless, Freecycle stands as example of how even very small neighborhoods can apply the power of the global living web to solve their problems.

Not every big system will reach out to the little. Newmark loves the idea of local neighbors—perhaps even tenants in the same apartment building—having a shared website and discussion area in which to safely meet each other and hash out their ideas for the neighborhood they share. "Probably in the future," he says, he can imagine offering a version of craigslist.org that has been customized for that degree of locality. In the meantime, though, that type of site never quite makes it to the top of craigslist's priorities.

Moving into Communities of Interest

People like to meet with their friends and other people with whom they share interests or experiences. Through the Internet, it's become much easier to find people who share your concerns or priorities, without regard to location. You can cast a wide net and communicate and build relationships with people across the U.S. and around the world. When the time comes to look for places to go or things to do in your own local world, the community you spend the most time in, that same critical mass/economy of scale benefit of the Internet may not be available to you. If there are no other parrot fanciers in town, the Internet isn't going to help you organize a local chapter.

But if the interest group you are looking to join or form or support or meet with has sufficient people involved or available at the local level, then national and international groups can help you pinpoint these nearby meeting places and help support fledgling or otherwise less-than-visible groups. Chapter 5 carries us into those groups and places.

One example of a community that has had to learn how to support itself and its loved ones is veterans, some of whom may understandably wish to find and associate with people who share their experiences or have reckoned with some of the same problems. I'll look at veterans groups as well as other kinds of support groups in the next chapter.

Sources and Further Reading

Read these web pages and books for more detail on the people and ideas described in this chapter:

Roger Karraker, "About 95436.com: the interview begins:"
http://karraker.typepad.com/95436/2004/01/about_95436com.html

TechTV bio about Stewart Brand:
http://www.techtv.com/screensavers/showtell/story/0,24330,3614694,00.html

Habitat for Humanity, International and San Francisco East Bay regional sites:
http://habitat.org/

http://www.eastbayhabitat.org/home.shtml

The One True b!X's Portland Communique:
http://communique.portland.or.us/

Akron (Ohio) Digital Academy:
http://akronschools.com/site/digitalacademy/digitalacademy.html

Ultra Apps community web portal tool:
http://ultraapps.com/freecommunitywebportal.html

World Adult Kickball Association (WAKA):
http://www.worldkickball.com/

Jon Shemitz's homeschooling resource site:
http://www.midnightbeach.com/hs

Robert Putnam, *Bowling Alone: The Collapse and Revival of American Community* (Simon & Schuster, 2000)

Robert Putnam, Lewis Feldstein, and Don Cohen, *Better Together: Restoring the American Community* (Simon & Schuster, 2003)

There are far more soccer, softball, and other sports leagues—and companies providing services to them—than I could ever point you to in a single book. Here is a tiny sampling:

http://www.vividdream.net/ccsl/

http://www.neighborhoodsonline.net/

http://inlandsoccer.net/youth_soccer.htm

http://www.littleleague.org/

http://www.eteamz.com/

http://www.leaguepro.com/

http://www.hotstat.com/

Chapter 5   Visible Means of Support

> Everyone gets all excited because the Dean campaign had an
> interactive communication scheme online. [...] Somehow, I
> get the impression that the digital interactive environment
> allowed those with the same views to talk to others with the
> same views. This is *great* for support groups, but dreadful for
> changing the system.
>
> —DANAH BOYD, "processing trippi," *apophenia*

When we experience major changes in life or situations that involve loss, mourning, or crisis, some of us instinctively reach out to the people in our immediate or extended family or in our social clan. This medium-sized social unit can pull together to support a member who needs help from the entire group. Increasingly, the people we turn to when we need this sort of help are not necessarily blood relations or people who live within our environs.

Clearly, some types of online communities perform a function or service equivalent to and often directly modeled on that of traditional group therapy or counseling *support groups*. This is a good thing; however, there is an assumption that support groups are great for "talking things through," but not so good for "getting things done." Is this true? I submit that this is a false dichotomy, as "talking things through" may alone help people heal or recover from injury or deal with grief or depression.

Internet-mediated forms of communication leave out much of a person's affect, removing many of the cues that structure but also inhibit social interaction in traditional face-to-face contexts. Generally, this paucity of social cues in online interaction is taken as a drawback, something that makes the experience alien and difficult to navigate. Ironically, the impoverished social environment online (as compared to the much richer face-to-face experience) can function like a social lubricant for people who otherwise feel overwhelmed by social signals that discourage them from speaking up, reaching out, or asking for help.

Beyond that, online communication forms provide a supplement to whatever type of support, friendship, family, or collegiality we can find in our immediate environs. If a family member is struggling with a rare medical condition, it may be easier to find a support group online than to find enough people sharing your experience and concerns in your locale to meet with face-to-face. The online world is all about "search;" in the real world, searching, and finding, can be trickier.

Internet groups are helping people handle the challenges and the struggles that can enter anyone's life, whether through sharing a profound or difficult experience, grappling with a medical condition in your family, dealing with loss or grief, even marking major milestones.

Mutual Support from Shared Experiences

The number probably mounts every day, but one day when I checked, there were 3,748 Yahoo! Groups listed under "Support" in the Health & Wellness category. The Support category offers more than 16,000 ad hoc communities, systems, and professionals. Nearly 3,000 of these are in its main listing, such as Life Coaches (for those who provide support), Soft Shoulder Advice (an ezine promoting "peace, harmony and love"), and Love Is the Killer App (a community for readers of a book by that title), just to mention a few. But beyond the master list of groups that deal with support is an extensive set of major subcategories, including

- Abortion Recovery (47 groups)

- Abuse Survivors (601 groups)

- Addiction and Recovery (1,907 groups)

- Care Giving (267 groups)

- Domestic Violence (195 groups)

- Hospice (23 groups)

- Illnesses (10,639 groups)

- Mourning and Loss (1,594 groups)

- Procedures and Therapies (276 groups)

- Rape (143 groups)

- Suicide (201 groups)

- Weight Issues (3,684 groups)

- Infertility (456 groups)

- Teens (219 groups)

A Yahoo! group can be defined in many ways—by physical characteristics, by shared experience, by knowledge interest, in fact by any means anyone has devised to categorize people. Yahoo! Groups includes Hurting-Hearts, limited specifically to Christian women, greypower for those over 50, and Handicap-able for those with physical challenges.

Even assuming that some of these populations overlap, clearly thousands of web users feel they benefit from communicating with others who have shared some aspect of their experiences. And this goes beyond merely reading messages on a monitor and typing replies.

As an example of the power *in the real world* of what we commonly consider the virtual Web, consider shut-ins. If people cannot leave home, the Internet can be the connecting tool for shut-ins to find enrichment in their lives by offering a channel of communication with other real people—no matter how attenuated. These connections are more robust than the telephone and certainly preferable to complete solitude, but does it matter if the physical aspect of the experience is minimal or impaired? Is an experience complete and rich enough merely through exercising the sphere (in this case, the virtual sphere) that is available?

That's not to say that remote emotional and communication connections are the only ones available for shut-ins; physical contact can be web-driven, as when a visitation service is set up online. For instance, one service centers around a collaborative process of designing and making lap quilts which are then delivered to convalescing people, providing a convenient opportunity for a visit to the shut-in. Beyond the tangible gift of the quilt is the less tangible but just as important gift of human contact.

The Unique Experiences of Veterans

I recently saw a pickup truck with several POW/MIA stickers and related messages plastered to its back bumper and rear cab window. One of them read, "Do Draft Dodgers Have Reunions? If So, What Do They Talk About?" It occurred to me that for many veterans, the shared experience of service in defense of the nation, whether during active wartime or not, represents a qualifying status—a brotherhood of sorts—that underlies any other relationship in the context of meeting together *as* veterans.

Over the course of a lifetime, a former soldier, sailor, airman, or Marine will likely spend many more years out of the service than in. But any veterans' reunions will hark back to that defining time in the veteran's life, providing the grist for conversation and friendships that can persist and even form outside of the original military context.

The military is an early adopter of many of the technological advances that will eventually be considered vital parts of ordinary life. Active-duty military personnel work with some of the most advanced sensory, deductive, and artificially intelligent equipment on the planet. Yet networks of veterans use the Internet in much the same way that most civilians do, and they face the same digital-divide issues: less fortunate, less wealthy, and homeless vets must rely on minimal or nonexistent public communications resources to become connected to the wired network of vets.

Beyond the economic issues that make Internet access and other technological tools more readily available to some people than to others (often referred to as the "digital divide"), there is also the matter of simply knowing whom to turn to for advice or to get started online. And getting online often requires having a network of people who want to communicate with you and can help you along during your first few months or years online; many veterans don't meet such prerequisites.

Veterans have Yahoo! Groups, web message boards associated with ICQ chat channels, chat rooms, pager ("buddy") networks, and more. Veterans groups require members to be "military active, a veteran, or a veteran family member," and they educate users in ways of recognizing phony veterans. They're still forced to explain to prospective participants how to use the arbitrary communications tools they've inherited from their immediate online environment: "You are eligible to join if you have ICQ & Yahoo! pager installed and at least one posted on your webpage…. Don't have an online pager? Free (yes, they are free) Download & install now…."

Active-duty veterans and their friends and family members are also using the Internet to organize and communicate with each other. In addition to the increasingly prevalent "ship-to-shore" type email access and cell phone communication, Soldiers Radio lets visitors record a message on an 800 number, which can be played back by soldiers with web access. Soldiers Radio includes other webcast shows geared toward the active-duty audience, with newscasts, chat features, and communiqués from Army brass:

> Keep in touch with your Army, and stay on the same sheet of music as your Army buddies wherever you're stationed. Soldiers Radio has the day planned with music, Army news, features and interviews, plus live Pentagon and Department of Defense press briefings, live remote broadcasts from special events, and Army football broadcasts.

The communication channel for soldiers on active duty uses the Internet and is tremendously more sophisticated—both in terms of its underlying architecture and its presentation—than the ad hoc networks of veterans. But it is only mildly interactive, with the few people who can send messages in the brief time allowed for that. It owes more to traditional broadcast models than to anything having to do with the living Web. Give me a soldier's weblog—even if it has to pass muster with the censors—over a professionally produced radio show any day.

Getting Beyond the Stigma of Asking for Help

Because death, loss, and other forms of suffering are inevitable, people have always needed to find ways to share feelings in a safe environment as part of moving through the difficult stages involved. This need exists whether the person has lost a loved one, their health, a part of their past, or their innocence—it exists even in circumstances that can seem trivial to external observers. For some people, what works best is face-to-face group therapy or other encounters with people willing to talk and listen and sympathize. Some may not respond to the intensity of such an environment; others may want to do so but may not be able to find a suitable group nearby. Still others are physically unable to join such groups.

Social network tools, from email on up, can supplement a traditional support group or can be used to create the virtual equivalent, with minimal or no physical face-to-face contact. But online tools used for support purposes must be used carefully. For example, in a group set up to help people through depression, anxiety, panic attacks, and suicidal feelings, the introductory message includes this warning:

> Do NOT EVER stop taking Paxil or any SSRI without medical supervision. This group sometimes discusses sensitive issues, including self-harm and abuse of all kinds. Please be aware that adult language may, at times, be used.

Also, in a virtual group, it can be hard to trust strangers who reveal little about themselves. For example, many rape survivor groups have to police their memberships to prevent people with prurient interests in the subject matter from interfering in the therapeutic goals of such groups.

As with any mailing list or similar online community, one can always read the archives of a group passively and try to get a feel for the tenor of conversation and the personalities of the most highly interactive people involved, taking as long as you like before speaking up or revealing intimate details about yourself. Even then, bear in mind that almost nothing on the Internet (outside of what's on your own computer, and sometimes not even then) can be expected to be wholly and completely secure and private. There are simply too many ways for possible eavesdropping. The future will likely hold more of the kind of awkward revelations that were experienced by some early Usenet participants when Google resurrected a large chunk of the Usenet archive in its Google Groups feature (after acquiring DejaNews). Suddenly you might find the youthful indiscretions of a boss or co-worker—or your own!—on full display.

I asked Craig Newmark of craigslist.org whether there is a new category of information somewhere between public and private; he thinks not. There is still just public or private, but the line between the two has become increasingly nuanced. Further, the line has shifted dramatically, with what was traditionally kept private (or at least opaque or hard to find) opening up into the transparency of the public sphere. People instinctively worry about losing a grip on their own privacy; it's sensible to pay attention to who can know what about you and who is the gatekeeper for this or that tidbit.

There are some demonstrable benefits to sharing some personal information with the Web. However, even a general trend toward greater openness does not imply an endpoint with zero privacy. Instead, you are required to carefully examine most thoughts, utterances, and scraps of information you have shared and decide quickly whether to discard or save them—and, if you save them, whether to make them visible to someone, anyone, or any group.

Doc Searls has said in conversation with Mary Hodder that the scariest thing about going online with personal information is the fear of what we will do to each other (as opposed to the fear of what the government or some other large impersonal entity will do).

Those concerned with their reputation—including anyone working in a job where discretion requires that some personal facts be kept out of the public sphere—should always think carefully before revealing information about themselves, even in theoretically private or secure environments. This is especially necessary when the issue or cause is in any way controversial, such as politics, war, drugs, sex, and other interesting topics.

Having said all that, clearly large numbers of people get enough of a benefit from participating in online support groups that they accept whatever loss of privacy may be involved. (At Yahoo!, there are 342 mourning and loss groups, running the gamut from funerals for lost family members to lost pets, and 360 abuse survivors' groups, dealing primarily with child abuse and incest survivors.)

The entire spectrum of addiction-model recovery programs can be explored online—matched up with every possible addiction. Such programs and addictions, clinically recognized or not, might include

- Twelve-step programs

- Rational recovery (such as AA but without the higher power)

- Moderation programs (in opposition to the abstinence called for by the anonymous and rational approaches)

- Drugs

- Gambling

- Sex

- Overuse of the Internet

Once again checking Yahoo!, the first group-oriented social-network system most people encounter, I recently found 607 addiction and recovery groups.

More and more behavioral peccadilloes are being medicalized and viewed as illnesses, frequently—as with drug and alcohol addiction—with a suspected genetic component. The realm of medicine itself—in Western scientific terms and increasingly in terms of holistic, Eastern, and otherwise experimental therapies—is becoming available online. One can join groups for:

- People with obsessive-compulsive disorder

- Family members of people with cardio-pulmonary obstructive disorder

- Homeopathy groups

- People lobbying for more congressional aid to research into cures for this or that part of the body

- People considering or recovering from plastic surgery, eye surgery, and organ transplants

- People trying to recover from or continuing to experience other eating disorders. (Overeaters Anonymous, for example, has a website that makes it easy for you to find a meeting near you.)

A Tale of Two Mail Lists

Christopher Filkins is the writer behind one of the most popular sites run on Salon's servers: Chronotope. And some of Chronotope's "Googlejuice"—the search-engine results sending traffic there—comes from Filkins' other website, safersex.org, a perennial high-relevancy, non-pandering result for the popular search term "sex."

My weblog, Radio Free Blogistan (RFB), focuses on the developments of the web as a living written medium—through blogs, wikis, personal publishing, and other forms of microcontent distribution. I publish this blog-about-blogging through Salon's weblog server, where I met Filkins and eventually invited him to join the contributing staff of RFB. Filkins has been working on solving content-management problems for even longer than I have, so we enjoy comparing notes and discussing our earliest experiences online. Filkins—who is also known online as filchyboy—told me about two support groups that he participated in at separate times in his life.

On the first occasion, Filkins was married to a woman who had begun showing signs of mental illness. He found a mailing list called Madness-L (run on a majordomo server of an East Coast university) and subscribed to it, using just his first name. (As a counterexample to the privacy problems I noted earlier, this list seems to have disappeared. When I asked Filkins about his memories of the list, he told me he could find "no traces of the mailing list's archives on the Web anymore.")

The recipients of Madness-L included people with mental illness, family members of people with mental illness, doctors, nurses, and other health-care professionals. Filkins noted that it was rare at the time for people with these different perspectives on mental health, its treatment, and the health-care system to have any particular way to meet and exchange views.

Some online groups schedule lunches or picnics if enough participants live near enough to each other, but Madness-L never did so. It "would have been extremely unlikely, as many of them were shut-ins and the professionals involved likely would have avoided such a thing."

As disorienting and alienating as it must have been to watch a loved one go mad—Filkins' wife eventually became a violent risk to him and to their daughter—Filkins was able to find some degree of comfort from being able to communicate his experiences with people who might understand what he was going through, whether they could offer useful advice, empathize, or help Filkins try to understand the experience—as unpleasant as it was for him—from the perspective of his ailing wife.

Indirectly, this experience led to his second online group experience. Filkins is bisexual; after his wife (in his words) "flipped out," he went through a homeless period. Once he got back on his feet,

> I started seeing a therapist. My wife had outed me to her family as "a dirty faggot." I had never been closeted before and had not had much experience with this particular [form of] hate, so I broached the subject of my sexuality with my therapist. This led to a discussion of the role of Madness-L in my ordeal with my wife. My therapist suggested that I find a similar online support group which dealt with issues related to bisexuality and marriage. I did some research and found BMMA [Bisexual Married Men of America].

Filkins got a lot less out of this group, because it centered more on issues of coming out to one's wife or loved ones. "Most of the discussions didn't seem to have much bearing on me or my issues," he says, "but it was nice to know that there were others not unlike myself." Ironically Filkins ended up stepping in to save the group soon after he joined it. The list's manager was leaving the University of Michigan, where it was hosted. "I volunteered to host it, as I had the technical chops and the resources to do so. This was in 1997. I still host it to this day." Although Filkins lives in Southern California, the server is a Lyris setup run out of North Carolina.

The group has had several thousand members over the years and currently has about 500. It has also produced several subgroups, particularly one known as HOW (Husbands Out to Their Wives).

According to Filkins, members of the BMMA list meet in person all over the country on a regular basis. "We have had too many deaths, marriages, children born, etc., to count." Lately, Filkins has been evaluating Flickr, a chat-and-media-sharing social network system (described more fully in Chapter 8, "Lonely Hearts' Club Bands"), as a possible tool for BMMA members to meet online in real time and to share photographs.

From Shared Needs to Concerted Action

In the aftermath of the Dean campaign, some commentators suggested that the meetups and other community-building tools that were used had functioned more as an outlet for group therapy than as an effective get-out-the-vote operation. (Note the quote from danah boyd at the start of this chapter.)

However, there's no reason why these two ways of engaging in group activities can't be complementary as well as alternatives to each other. People who form communities around shared experiences or around health or medical issues may find that their needs aren't being met by providers or the government and that can be addressed only if a sufficient number of affected people speak together with one voice. People who meet to share experiences and support each other online may also share ideas about where active participation in civic life or communicating as a group with the government is called for.

When people are researching a medical condition online, they can compare symptoms, learn about experimental treatments, help each other find qualified help with caregiving, and so on. If in doing so, people learn more about how their state provides care for the needy or what expenses can be reimbursed, then they are a step closer to having some control over these systems.

The mission of the Osteogenesis Imperfecta Foundation is to find and connect people with this particular birth defect, and to provide mutual support and education to them and to the parents of children with OI. The Internet has transformed this organization. They have a budget of just over a million dollars—small for a charitable foundation—but Convio's software toolkit (described in

Chapter 3, "Getting Off the Couch") has allowed them to reach nearly all the people scattered throughout the United States afflicted with this rare ailment. Beyond just information and fundraising, the foundation's events, online forums, and conferences help people feel connected.

The model of organizing people around special events can help rally less-involved people who might not become part of a regularly meeting group but who want to show support on a yearly or seasonal basis. The Susan G. Komen Breast Cancer Foundation supplements affiliated local walks with virtual fundraising events. If someone is walking for Avon or diabetes, running a marathon, riding a bike, and so on, they can raise money on behalf of the campaign. All of the information about donations and participants can be managed easily online.

The Internet enables us to create support groups out of thin air, as we find people who have shared our life experiences or have common issues or affinities. The living Web is not about the technology of webfeeds, notification methods, or hardware protocols. It's the *people*. If my Yahoo! group has an RSS feed, great, but the interesting part is you and me.

Sources and Further Reading

Read these web pages and books for more detail on the ideas in this chapter:

danah boyd, "processing trippi," *apophenia,* February 9, 2004:
http://www.zephoria.org/thoughts/archives/2004/02/09/processing_
trippi.html

Yahoo! Groups, Health & Wellness, Support category:
http://health.dir.groups.yahoo.com/dir/Health___Wellness/Support

Yahoo! Groups, Hurting-Hearts support group:
http://groups.yahoo.com/group/Hurting-Hearts

Yahoo! Groups, depression-anxiety support group:
http://health.groups.yahoo.com/group/depression-anxiety

Soldiers Radio and Television:
http://www.soldiersradio.com

Overeaters Anonymous:
http://www.overeatersanonymous.org

Christopher Filkins' blog *Chronotope*:
http://chronotope.com

Bisexual Married Men of America (BMMA):
http://www.safersex.org/bmma

Osteogenesis Imperfecta Foundation:
http://www.oif.org

The Susan G. Komen Breast Cancer Foundation:
http://www.komen.org

Chapter 6 CultureJamming the Hollywood Megalith

> But fanfic turns writing into a communal art, as folk culture has always done. Writing and reading become collaborative. We share the characters and work together to make them interesting and funny and sexy. Write a short story about your crazy uncle and post it on the Web, and no one will read it. Write a short story about Dr. Who, and hundreds of folks will flock to your site. Fanfic writers meet at conventions ("cons"). Thanks to the Internet, writers communicate constantly on e-mail listservs. They invite e-mail responses and crave feedback.
>
> —DAVID PLOTZ, "Luke Skywalker Is Gay?
> Fan Fiction Is America's Literature Of
> Obsession."

Every medium of communication is potentially an expressive medium, equally applicable to accounting recordkeeping, distress calls, and poetry. Every new communication medium ends up being used to make art (and pornography, but that's another book). There were probably people who used semaphore to make poetry or who figured out how to make their oscilloscopes draw pictures like a child's Spirograph. The nontechnophobic strand of artists has been experimenting with electronics and perception and representation and remote presence and interactivity for decades.

On the living Web, artists can collaborate more freely than ever before. Performers and their audiences can contribute to an online comity. The image of the auteur as the artist, the genius, mastermind, the solo masterpiece—these are all under assault from increasing transparency. That transparency reveals all the people who are helping Sir Christopher Wren build the cathedral, all the little transactions of time and energy, some voluntarily, some under the duress of "needing to eat" that creates advertisements for Scotch or digital passion plays.

Perhaps more interesting, however, is the way affordable web-suitable digital cameras and camera phones have entered the hands of "almost everyone" (a subjective observation from my privileged perch in the upper-left corner of the U.S., I understand). More broadly, the tools of expressiveness, the free press, the microphone, the right to help frame the narrative, the range of allowable ideas about what people might use their free right to assemble to do together.

Art and performance and event and activity can blur together. Because the Internet is, among other things, a means of communication and an expressive medium, it was inevitable that artists would see the potential of the Internet as a creative tool, for knitting together geographically disparate collectives, for planning and scheduling performances, events, and happenings, and as an art form in itself.

PLATO was an educational computer network created in 1960 that thrived in the 1970s and 1980s. It was developed to deliver interactive multimedia instructional programs, but it rapidly evolved into one of the first online communities. PLATO anticipated other similar online community systems and features—CompuServe/AOL, the Internet, and the World Wide Web—by as much as 20 years.

I asked Brian Dear, who is writing a history of the PLATO online system, about art in that early online context. He told me,

> PLATO's core mission was to deliver high-quality educational courseware through the terminal to the student. That courseware tended to be heavily illustrated. Colleges of medicine, physics, chemistry, etc., all used PLATO to teach tens of thousands of students over the years, as well as corporations to train airline pilots, nuclear power engineers, soldiers, etc.
>
> [But we also wound up with] drawings, illustrations, poetry, interactive animations, complete feature-length interactive stories, blog-like self-publishing,

extended humor pieces. Art departments of various universities taught fine arts lessons on the system and did art exhibits using PLATO. Musicians built synthesizers and weird sound gadgets and hooked 'em up to PLATO to do musical pieces, which were sometimes performed live in front of audiences. There were even music sequencer apps written on PLATO so you could create your own music. (I remember sequencing a version of The Who's "Baba O'Riley.")

PLATO was an incredibly rich medium for creative expression of all sorts; people figured that out quickly, and it became one of the major factors that drew people from so many different backgrounds (not just hackers, not just techies) to the system.

There was a lot of face-to-face communication within the PLATO community, at least at the major sites like the University of Illinois. But as PLATO installations began to appear all over the country and then the world, a user increasingly knew most other users only by their online presence.

I asked Dear why it took so long for the innovations first seen in PLATO to reach the Internet and later the Web. Besides the very high price of hardware (PLATO IV terminals cost about $5000) and the even higher cost of telecommunications at the time, he said, "The micro revolution distracted a lot of people for a long time, to focus on stuff going on inside the desktop machine rather than (to me anyway) the more interesting stuff going on inside the network of connected machines. PLATO made me focus on the network right from the beginning. It seems to have taken a long time for a critical mass of people to discover the network was the place to be."

The instinct toward community creativity was there. But with its focus on productivity, the PC in a sense delayed or obscured the importance of human factors and interpersonal communications as the binding glue of organizations.

Jamming in Real Time

One of the first online artist network collectives I encountered back in 1994 that's still going strong today is SITO. (At the time it was called OTIS—"operative term is stimulate"—but then the Otis School of Art in Los Angeles made them change the name, so they simply reversed the order of letters without worrying about making it stand for anything.)

SITO offers hosting space for digital artists, and serves, among other things, as a directory of such artists. A major interest of the SITO participants is online collaboration. A whole section of the SITO website called Synergy is dedicated to various online collaboration vehicles such as HyGrid, a never-ending set of tiles created by numerous artists, all of which fit together to create a larger synthetic artwork. HyGrid is an example of asynchronous collaboration—you download the surrounding squares from the grid and then create your own image so that it integrates with them smoothly on all four sides. But SITO also hosts a number of synchronized (real-time) collaborative "jams" such as the weekly (since 1994) Friday night Panic collaboration facilitated via IRC. In a Panic jam, someone uploads an image, someone else grabs it and alters it, another person changes it further, and so on. A Panic jam is not unlike a musical jam session in which riffs and changes are traded and improvised upon around a room in real-time.

In fact, as the technologies of digital music and online bandwidth have converged, the potential for real-time (or asynchronous) musical collaboration has become much more accessible for musicians, even without access to professional-quality recording studios and equipment.

Some people have put together websites to host artists or have built websites to showcase their own work or found ways to collaborate or work with partners in creating Internet artwork. Others began the process of developing more involved online collaborations such as

- The invitation-only Hell.com website created collaboratively by some of the most well-respected web artists and designers of the '90s.

- birdhouse.org, a site built by Scot Hacker to showcase the writing and art and music of his network of artist friends scattered across the country and around the world.

Some sites flourished briefly and then went dry such as Art on the Net, with its coveted domain name, art.net, which has been sadly dormant since 2002. Likewise, my own webzine—Enterzone—was conceived in 1994 as an online salon, but it never developed the kind of rich interactivity that the web medium is best suited for; it petered out in 1998, subsequently mutating into a series of disjointed weblogs and other collaborative writing spaces.

One lesson that emerges from these various projects is that the more an endeavor is dependent on the energy and enthusiasm of a single person, the more vulnerable it is to running out of steam. Those that harness the power of many have a much greater shot at becoming self-sustaining in the long run.

The old Panic jams and other real-time collaborations pioneered by SITO were precursors of the universe of interactive art creation now taking place over the living Web. These often take place on bulletin boards for graphic artists, where they swap and critique art, most commonly with Adobe Photoshop images, Macromedia Flash animations, or 3D stills or animations from Alias Maya or discreet's 3ds max.

In a lot of cases, the art is collaborative or competitive. The biggest genre for this is something called Photoshop Tennis (PT). To "play" PT, some parameters are agreed on first such as file format, time limits, or even artistic theme. One person creates a Photoshop file and then sends it to a second person. That player alters it—whether minimally by touch-up or extensively, even perhaps throwing out the entire image and starting over—and then returns the file. This back-and-forth can go on haphazardly or for a prearranged number of rounds; the end result is more than just a single image but an artistic sequence.

Just as no two artists are identical, no two art matches are the same either. The participants can range along the spectrum from collaboration—agreeing on a common theme, subject, motif, or purpose—to competition, with each trying to outdo the other in a demonstration of digital-art "chops."

Although Photoshop Tennis developed and evolved spontaneously in several places, it was at Coudal Partners, a Chicago design house, where PT was finally formalized in a significant way. (As my editor and blog-collaborator Pete Gaughan points out, "Coudal also has one of the best freakin' blogs on the planet, right on their home page, but nobody knows about them outside the graphic design community.")

The collaborative art trend eventually led to a book (full disclosure: also produced by my publisher) called *Photoshop: Secrets of the Pros*, which teaches

Photoshop techniques through the medium of Photoshop Tennis matches by 20 designers and artists.

Jamming in Unreal Time

Just as visual artists are now able to collaborate (or compete) in real-time or near real-time by kicking art works back and forth across the Net, musicians can also collaborate more easily in asynchronous ways. They can layer new tracks or remix old ones while working with remote musicians to evolve their shared compositions.

I spoke with musician Yaniv Soha about the methods he's been using lately to compose music with remote collaborators over the Net. As is often the case with online work, the killer app is still email. Soha told me,

> At the outset, one of us songwriters will generate an idea independently. It could be a set of chord changes or a partially written song, but it's almost always something incomplete or rough around the edges. That idea is then translated into a scratch version of the song (a rough draft, essentially), which is then delivered to the collaborator by way of email.

At this point, the second person offers input and suggestions. For example, a recent song had a spot that his partner wasn't too thrilled with.

Soha explained, "The song started to drag at that point, he seemed to say, and he thought I should consider scrapping that section. I did, and what resulted, I think, was a song that was much tighter and less meandering."

After the initial demo and the first round of feedback, whichever participant initiated the recording produces a more polished, definitive recording of the basic tracks and then sends them to the long-distance collaborator, who may add new instrumentation, harmonies, rhythm, effects, and so on. This draft of the song is then sent back via email to the originator for a final mix of the various tracks.

Soha elaborated,

> The collaborator might suggest bringing a certain section more to the forefront of the song or cutting out a certain element. In the end, I think we assemble something that's satisfying in a way that individual writing often isn't.

It's important for me to recognize that my collaborator's opinion of one of my performances is always way more objective than my own (and vice versa), so there's a certain amount of letting go that we both depend on to get through it.

The common thread in all these network-mediated forms of creativity is that they favor the social context of multiple people working together and sharing ideas over the traditional image of the artist as a lone genius who incubates his ideas and then delivers his bounty onto a waiting, grateful world. If you demythologize and deromanticize the creative process, you'll find that people can accomplish much more by working together—even on unfinished or half-baked ideas—rather than hiding them until they're "perfect" for fear of criticism or the kind of withering unhelpful gaze that all artists fear will render their creations stillborn.

This is not to say that individual artists will stop feeling motivated to create their own solo works of art, although the artist's image has often been one that tends to overlook the contributions of partners, helpers, assistants, studios, ateliers, and so on. No one is going to force artists onto collectivization art farms, but a great many people who might not consider themselves professional artists or musicians—and who might not be willing the shoulder the entire burden of an aesthetic movement—can now find more community-based ways to express their humanity and their ideas in concert with others.

Internet killed the artist-star—and when I say artist, don't leave out tele-visual art, advertising (that truly original American art form), all forms of popular entertainment, all forms of orchestrated, in-concert show, performances that break the fourth wall and require that the participant be a player (how gamelike, how interactive, how webby, how kewl).

A lot more "let's put on a show / my father has a barn" samizdat self-publishing and self-expression is happening online. And it's not all for creativity's sake only: American soldiers, as we are learning, have been documenting their doings in Iraq with cell phones and digital cameras and blogs.

Friends of mine filmed a fake infomercial (as opposed to a "real" infomercial) in super-VHS in the early '90s. Today, the same group plus a few more amazingly talented people are making radio theater playlets as three-minute, two-megabyte MP3s for download from a reconditioned PC running Linux web server…and this will suffice until or unless they get famous, in which they ought to be able to afford hosting or…what was the business model again?

A great Kurt Vonnegut story made the point that at one time each family, clan, or tribe had storytellers, singers, people who told jokes, and so on. To be creative in public, someone didn't have to be a member of the Olympic-level talent distributed widely by jukeboxes, radio, or eventually, TV.

It's My Happening…

At the same time I was starting Enterzone, I saw another writer building a site called Literary Kicks, which started as a kind of free-form encyclopedia of Beat writers composed of a series of interlinked essays. Its creator, Levi Asher, recognized the need for a creative website to foster and grow a participating community of contributors. He attached a discussion-board feature to the original hyperlinked set of articles and cultivated LitKicks.com as a creative community site. Founded in 1994, LitKicks thrives to this day.

Asher understands an important thing about online community and did another thing right: Every year or so, he plans a large public "happening" and invites people who've contributed to or inspired the LitKicks community to come and perform. These readings have taken place all over the country, and a small group of his contributors went on a college tour last year. These real-world happenings—in which writers and art lovers come together to perform, celebrate, and enjoy their work—mirror the motley patchwork world of online creativity: a college professor, a punk musician, and an undiscovered poetic genius may take turns reading on stage, backed by a rock band, a jazz combo, or David Amram, who accompanied Jack Kerouac's "go! go! go!" Beat performances half a century ago.

After tending this community for more than a decade, Asher told me,

> I've learned that online communities are unique in the sense that they don't follow patterns or templates established by any other medium in the world—if you drew a biological chart of human interaction, online community would have to be its own tree.

As a participant in communities, I've learned that a magical sort of thing happens the moment you post to a public area. At that point, your relationship suddenly shifts from disengaged to engaged, and you may find yourself obsessively interested in whether anybody responded to you. Your interest in this may be completely out of proportion to everything else in your life. For a short time, you will put aside all your other work and responsibilities in order to compulsively check for responses.

As an operator of online communities, I'm sorry to say that I've learned that a few people can be really dumb, selfish, and bossy. We [the LitKicks staff] expect people to treat us like human beings, and we're disappointed when they don't. I should mention that 99% of our members are great, but the other 1% can be really annoying. I've also learned that members of online communities can be very emotional, very intense, and very needy—more so than people would be in face-to-face interaction.

I also asked Asher how he found ways to balance online-mediated community with face-to-face interaction. "I always prefer face to face. I've found that people are usually more likable in person."

When it comes to getting people into the same room at the same time, the Internet is much more than a tool for creating mind-bending, computer-automated, or touch-screen-animated visual extravaganzas: it also provides scheduling and calendars, announcements and promotions, getting listed and selling tickets. Just as art always involves a degree of inspiration and a much greater degree of perspiration, creativity, and hard-won craft, so it is with the deft use of Internet technologies to reinforce the communicative threads that bind together a like-minded community. Developing community to bring consensus and organization to promote an event enlarges the crowd of people who can find the time to show up in person or learn about what's been happening behind their computer screens. These are the tools to make art live within and beyond the Internet.

Someone has to coordinate and synchronize. Someone has to get all the people in their Santa suits to the Saint Stupid's Day parade or all the facepainters out to the faire.

We are all of us still learning to collaborate with each other in new ways; some of us never played well with others in the conventional ways and places, such as the office or church picnic or family gatherings, but there are new playing fields of group activity and new etiquettes to be discovered. If we're not good at this yet, give us time. And we should watch the kids. They'll figure it out.

First Person, Confessional

As a medium for writing, the Internet favors the confessional. There's something about the quasi-informality, the semi-anonymity of the Web that brings out personal storytelling, first-person points-of-view, and that quiet voice almost whispered into the amplified microphone that can fill up a room. The Web is reshaping the boundaries between public and private, creating a gray area or hybrid area between those two spheres, or at least forcing—for those who venture into publishing their own creative work and ideas online—a re-examination of the borders between what is held close to the chest and what is shared with the world.

Well before the explosion of weblogs as the dominant form of communication on the Web, there was a thriving subculture of online journalers, who didn't necessarily include a lot of links in their sites, who weren't necessarily logging their web-finds each day, but who were instead using the pseudo-privacy of the web medium to broadcast their innermost thoughts to the entire planet. On first discovering online journals, most people find them puzzling, a paradox. Who would put their private diary online? Do you want people to read it or not? Omigod, my mother read my blog! Indeed, there are countless stories of people who misjudged the effects of putting their thoughts and ideas into the public domain and who lived to regret the confidences broken, the parties offended by their snarky comments, their exposed secrets.

In time, though, anyone who continues the exhilarating tightrope walk of online self-examination will manage to cultivate that gray area between public and private that seems just personal and revealing enough to draw in readers and invite scrutiny but that still holds back what truly belongs out of public view entirely.

The old rule of thumb used to be, don't post anything to Usenet (or send any email) that you would mind seeing on the front page of *The New York Times*. Don't expect that obscurity will always protect you. Once people decide to start looking for you, they will find you.

One way of dealing with the public/private identity issue is to create a new identity or to employ some form of anonymity in order to avoid exposure in your real life. Even people who don't create fictional personas for their online presence still find themselves experimenting with their identity. You construct a self online if you start to put bits of yourself out there. If you have a blog, for many people you may never meet in person, you are writing yourself into existence.

Another person who grasped the intimate storytelling potential of the Web early on was Derek Powazek, who created the San Francisco Stories website, as well as the {fray}—which features first-person memoirs open to comments—and the now-defunct kvetch site, which was dedicated to complaints. With a great instinct for what it takes to cultivate a community, Powazek early on started holding reading/open-mic events called {fray day}, which have been running annually now for seven years and have taken place in cities all over the planet. Similarly, Powazek's San Francisco Stories website has spawned a series of sites dedicated to stories that revolve around other cities and locations.

Fray Days have taken place at the annual South by Southwest (SXSW) conference, which began as a showcase for up-and-coming independent musical acts but has expanded to include a web-geek track as well. Like other conferences and conventions, SXSW provides an opportunity to get people who may know each other only through each other's online writing or via email signatures and blog comments into the same rooms at the same time for panels, hallway conversations, and parties. Inevitably, the real-world interactions filter back to their online relationships once the parties are over and people scatter back to their home ports.

Fandom as Contemporary Folk Culture

The television shows (and advertisements) of your childhood are sometimes the only shared cultural reference points with other members of your generation.

People like myself who grew up in the '70s have always bonded over shared memories of *Scooby Doo, Gilligan's Island,* and the *Groovie Ghoulies* (pardon my flashback).

I first read about K/S—Kirk/Spock—fan fiction when I was in college. There was already a scholarly book on this subject, hardbound in the stacks of that library. (This was the mid '80s; I used to wander around a lot and try to find random stuff.) These were stories, usually published in printed 'zines, starting in the 1970s, featuring the characters from the original *Star Trek* television show. The typical plot involved Kirk and Spock stranded somewhere just as the Vulcan's "pon farr" seven-year mating cycle is coming to its peak. The authors of these homo-erotic reimaginings seem to enjoy telling a story in which their favorite male protagonists bond deeply.

From the slash symbol K/S indicating that the storyline was a Kirk/Spock love affair, the fan fiction (or fanfic) genre, particularly this prurient-yet-strangely-soft-core subgenre, has come to be called *slash fiction.*

Slash fiction isn't limited to *Star Trek* and other science-fiction and fantasy television shows, but it did inherit a lot of its jargon and online naming conventions from the overlap with the science fiction communities. Just as science fiction fans attend conventions (usually abbreviated as "cons" as in Something-Con), so do fanfic and slash writers.

The point of fan fiction is that the audience becomes involved in a creative process, derivative though it may be. The Internet has expanded the reach of fanfic and slash, but the interaction among writers and readers—or more generally between artists and audiences—isn't limited to remote digital online exchanges of drafts and feedback.

When I interviewed U.C. Berkeley researcher danah boyd, she told me that people create their strongest attachments to identities associated with "the axes along which they have been marginalized." At some point, I felt compelled to make myself vulnerable to her judgment by confessing that the two online communities in which I myself had most fully participated were the Grateful Dead newsgroup in the mid-to-late '90s and the recent Dean online meta-organization. I can't be sure what her wry smile meant but of course I hoped that I hadn't pigeonholed myself in her mind by signing on to those two allegiances (filter under Dea?).

Deadheads have populated the Internet since it was the Arpanet and Usenet. They used it as a grapevine. Early on, they discovered a truism of organizational email lists: you need one for announcements (shows, tickets, dates), and a separate one for discussion. The first had to stay low-traffic, high signal-to-noise ratio. The second could ramble more, but the people who prefer only one of those styles of communication need to be protected from each other, like certain fish that will tear each other apart if put in the same tank.

Deadheads had real-world events to go to: Dead shows. Their online life was in many ways subordinated to the actual real-world experience of following or caring about or listening to the music of the Dead. In the wake of the demise of band leader Jerry Garcia and the formal retirement of the original band in its final configuration, the online community was left without its central focus (not unlike the way the Dean community found itself without a candidate in early 2004). Deadheads had to do some searching to look for commonalities. For some, fragmentation ensued when the flywheel went off the handle. Others found commonalities that transcended personalities or even specific shared experiences.

Now that the Dead has reconstituted itself, more or less, the diffuse community, with its physical and virtual manifestations, has proven resilient enough to enable newcomers to tap in and once again make plans to meet up at show. Who's bringing the hacky sack and who's bringing the juggling sticks? Remember, at a Dead concert, you aren't just part of an audience. You're part of the show.

Temporary Autonomous Zones

One of the most famous collaborative art happenings is the annual Burning Man festival that takes place in the desert every year around Labor Day. The motto of the festival is "No Spectators." If you go to Burning Man, you are a participant. You may not have designed one of the art installations destined to be burned down in the playa at the end of the weekend, but you'd better at least be part of a crew helping to build it.

In danah boyd's writings on Friendster, she often cites the Burning Man subculture there, and their creation of a Burning Man "fakester" identity to approximate the tribe-community group node they wanted to be able to use as a badge of belonging. Meanwhile, she says, Friendster's founder sees the sub-cultures as subverting the more all-American bottom line: dating. But the Burn-ing Man community both in the Bay Area and more widely has always used mailing lists and, more recently, websites and other online collaborative tech-niques to plan the now-year-round festival schedule. The Burning Man project for a long while grew more or less organically among an (admittedly early-adopter wired) community of adventurous artists looking for something to do.

No less a countercultural saint than Grateful Dead lyricist and EFF spokesmodel John Perry Barlow said this about the collective but anti-activist nature of the Burning Man community:

> If someone like Karl Rove had wanted to neutralize the most creative, intel-ligent, and passionate members of his opposition, he'd have a hard time coming up with a better tool than Burning Man. Exile them to the wilder-ness, give them a culture in which alpha status requires months of focus and resource-consumptive preparation, provide them with metric tons of psy-chotropic confusicants, and then…ignore them. It's a pretty safe bet that they won't be out registering voters—or doing anything that might actu-ally threaten electoral change—when they have an art car to build.

Community Creativity

As an editor of Enterzone, I once published a work-in-progress by digital artist Mark Napier, an exploration of Barbie dolls and female body images called The Distorted Barbie. To make a long story short, Mattel threatened to sue us to take the artwork off the Web. We publicized the threat, and numerous people volunteered to mirror and host the art to prevent it from being squelched.

At the time, I remember thinking that having Mattel threaten to sue us could quite possibly be the big break that most artists and creative people hope for. A lot of people responded by trying to help, so it felt like the online com-munity of artists was willing to knit together and fight back against an unrea-sonable assault. In addition, there was for a while a drumbeat of mainstream and crossover news coverage that made me feel we had struck a nerve. But even in the absence of controversy, the experience of working together to produce art online was an exhilarating one.

A friend once asked me why I hadn't started off like most people with a personal home page or website but had instead started a webzine to publish other people. In trying to answer him, I realized that I found it more satisfying to give other people a leg up into the new medium. Inviting people to collaborate and to produce art and writing was better than any one of us were capable of on our own. I felt that I was managing to tap into a kind of dynamic that—at least for me—was more inspiring and motivating than the inherited image of the lone artist working away in solitude. Being each other's audience and co-creators and advisors led to a community form of creativity.

The same one-step-ahead-of-the-lawyers approach used for The Distorted Barbie has been used by other "illegal" art such as DJ Dangermouse's *The Grey Album* (a remix of Jay-Z's *The Black Album* using samples from the Beatles' *The White Album*). When the Beatles' music publisher, EMI, sent the DJ a cease-and-desist letter, the horse had already left the barn. Bloggers scheduled Grey Day in protest, where people would turn their websites grey and spread the word about where the many mirrors of the record were being hosted and how to obtain them. In addition to people voluntarily hosting the music (usually for a limited time) on their websites, the music is readily available on all the Napster-like P2P networks and can be downloaded very efficiently using BitTorrent.

Likewise, there are entire websites dedicated to archiving and making available suppressed digital art. Such works include the U2 remix by Negativland featuring Casey Kasem cursing off-the-air and an album of re-remixed Beck songs shut down by his management.

I met Mark Napier through a mailing list for web artists called antiweb. While antiwebbers were scattered all over the world, there were a few clusters of us, mainly in the San Francisco and New York areas. Thus any time one of us traveled to the Bay Area or to New York, we'd notify the list and an impromptu dinner party or get-together would inevitably ensue. Through one of these events, I met Napier's partner Liza Sabater, an artist and writer, who is now one of the co-authors of my Radio Free Blogistan blog.

Today, Sabater and Napier are working on an open-source art project, and Sabater is setting up blogs for artists and cultural critics at her CultureKitchen.com website. She is connected with a number of active artist email lists and online communities such as Rhizome.org (which is based in Los Angeles), thingist, and nettime-1.

During the SARS outbreak last year, the Rhizome artists launched the SARS Art Project, in which artists all over the world contributed artworks inspired by the disease and the media panic it engendered. This led eventually to an installation and a gallery show in Los Angeles.

Ultimately, this kind of community artmaking has the potential to open up to a much wider audience the stories, songs, and artwork of the online communities.

Even for those who are not particularly interested in art or music, this creative process offers yet another model for a form of organization not structured particularly around profit. Of course, financial sustainability is the key to any enterprise "growing up and leaving home."

The Oldest Established Permanent Floating Flash Mob in New York

In the wake of Howard Rheingold's book (and weblog) *Smart Mobs*, which talks about the ways that people are using digital technology such as cell phones and instant messaging to coordinate collective actions, the fad of *flash mobs* waxed and waned in 2003. A flash mob is a sort of performance art stunt in which a group of people are alerted by email and text message to converge on a designated location, perform some pre-agreed-upon action or behavior, and then just as quickly disperse, before the "normals" get wind of what's going on.

A group in New York called MOB was sending out these alerts to a large set of recipients, and similar flash mob activities were scheduled all over the planet. At one point, the *Doonesbury* comic strip imagined a group of Dean activists planning a flash mob at the Space Needle in Seattle to build visibility for their preferred candidate. Naturally, once the cartoon appeared, the Deansters couldn't resist turning it into reality, and an actual Space Needle flash mob for Dean was quickly created.

Although the fad seems to have run its course, it appeared to get some of its juice from the exhilaration of bringing together large numbers of people to a single location in order to perform some pointless activity. Congregating itself was the point.

Still, one person's bonding experience is another's alienating clubbiness of people who happen to have geographical access to each other, often in Internet-glamorous locales such as New York, San Francisco, Los Angeles, London, Indianapolis, and so on. The ease of web publishing and self-expression online still favors the wealthy, the connected, the nontechnophobic, the experienced, the opportunistic, the better educated. Fortunately, it also favors people like writer Paul Ford, who strive toward a more humane voice in writing and sometimes can't resist poking fun at the pretensions of the so-called online "A-list." In Ford's short story *Flash,* he imagines a gory prank played on the digerati cool kids who are gathered together for one final, bloody, flash mob, where their love of their own cleverness and connectivity is used against them.

Aside from the potential of flash mobs (possibly inspired by the flash crowds described in Larry Niven's science fiction stories from the '60s) as a form of street theater or performance art, the lesson here may be the mundane need to schedule activities and get bodies together in one place at the same time.

When the artistic realm is expanded to include entertainment in all its many forms, then the manifestation of Internet-coordinated real-time activities comes down to the familiar issues of selling tickets and putting people in the seats.

Now Appearing

Not all artists are digital artists and not every form of creativity needs to be digitally mediated. Although every arts organization tends to have a website these days, or maybe even a blog, most don't do much with them. Still, every arts organization has shows, openers, fundraisers, and other events, and most use the Internet to promote them, to schedule them, and to get people to attend them.

Watchword Press, a nonprofit literary organization whose board I am on, has a minimal web presence. But they publish a great print magazine, and every time they release a new issue, they put together a release party to showcase some of the writers, to sell some copies, and to get their community of supporters in the same room at the same time. They use their mailing list primarily and their network of relationships with other small-press organizations in the Bay Area to promote these events.

Similarly, consider the Open Studios movement, in which the public is invited to visit artists in their studios, see their work, and possibly buy or patronize the artworks. Open Studios doesn't require the Internet to happen, but it benefits greatly from online listings, maps, and calendars.

Most of the arts groups that have something happening online (beyond informational sites, box office, and discussion forums) are either digital galleries or use it for volunteer sign-up. One example that goes further was posted by Gwen Harlow, who runs ofrenda.org in Oakland and has created and designed many artist-driven websites. In order to help the creative web community in Oakland get to know each other better, Harlow started an occasional series of large group meetings called "Ladies (and Gentlemen) Who Lunch."

As the Dean campaign made clear to so many, the people behind Meetup were onto something significant, adding an online networking capability to an existing bricks-and-mortar campaign structure. Dodgeball.com lets users who are connected as friends in any number of online ways find each other when their cell phones are proximate. The site also hosts a New York–based community-created guide to late-night spots and other venues.

I caught up with Andy Baio, a 27-year-old web programmer living and working in Santa Monica, and blogging at Waxy.org, who created upcoming.org, a community site that epitomizes how the living Web works.

Baio started working on the site originally to meet his own personal needs. "I was tired of losing track of the concerts I wanted to attend, and hearing about events from friends days or weeks after they happened."

> I was designing for multiple users from the beginning. I could've designed something for myself and my friends for L.A.-area concerts only, but that seemed like a colossal waste. With a little extra effort, I could make something that could be used for any event anywhere in the world. So I did that instead.

Upcoming.org is free, and Baio promises at the site that it will always remain so for its users. The first time I saw that, I wondered what he would do if his site became monstrously popular; he told me that things would get problematic only if it started approaching what he called "Friendster-like growth," at which point he said he could probably cover costs by charging venues for ads.

I think it's telling that some of the best and most useful sites like these are still created metaphorically in the garage, through woodshedding, often not timed directly to the rhythms of late capitalism. The twentieth century is dying hard, but the rust and the wheezing have set in, and these people working for free seem to be nimble, much less wasteful of time. There are other economies besides economies of scale and wage employment. Says Baio, "I'm already paying for a powerful colocated server for my other projects, so Upcoming.org runs on top of that. It doesn't cost me anything to maintain, except my time."

Baio says that while some have described Upcoming.org as "Evite meets Friendster," he didn't actually draw much inspiration from either of those sites. He was more inspired by Metafilter and Scenepoints.com, a calendar for the Los Angeles area, where only a few people were allowed to post events.

> I combined elements of that with the Metafilter ideal of letting anyone post. Anyone can create events, venues, cities, and so on. The social software aspect was a natural, so that you could view your friends' events. Instead of getting a comprehensive list of every crappy event, an event is only listed if at least one person is interested in it. The end result is a heavily moderated version of the local newspaper's Calendar section, with the good stuff floating to the top.

Beyond the "no one bothers to post crappy events" rule and the ability to view your friends' events, Baio expects to eventually add a recommendations feature as well. He's working on an recommendations algorithm with IRC regular Maciej Ceglowski. "I have something in beta now," says Baio, "but it's not very good."

Upcoming's primary unit of organization is user-created metros (meaning, roughly, metropolitan areas). Baio deliberately avoided using a term like *city* in order to encourage users to avoid balkanizing themselves by describing their location too narrowly.

"The site, fortunately, completely maintains itself," says Baio nonchalantly, as if perpetual motion were a simple matter of programming, "which is good, because I have very little time to work on it lately." Baio spends more time dealing with typographical errors in listings than with site malfunctions.

"Adding the ability for users to edit their own events helped with [user errors] dramatically."

To protect the community against inappropriate uses of their attention (he mentioned self-promotion and nefarious activities primarily), Baio built in "a nice banning system that silently hides bozo users from the rest of the community."

Upcoming.org's greatest success so far has come in New York, by far the most popular metro on the site. Baio mentions two New York sites that immediately adopted Upcoming for their events calendars and built their own visual interface to show their custom data feed from the Upcoming site. "Gothamist developed a beautiful calendar using the Upcoming.org feeds, and EverythingNY followed with a completely different interface. I love seeing how people are putting the events on their own sites, and as more people use the site in a metro, the better it gets for everyone."

Baio is wary of over-automating the event-adding process. He doesn't offer an API (application programming interface) that would enable others to write software for automatically listing events. He actually uses the inconvenience of posting as a sort of friction filter to raise the stakes for entering a particular event. "Plus," says the experienced programmer, "there'd be more duplicates and other garbage data to manage. So, for now, it's a community site with human intervention for adding events and venues."

Upcoming offers integration with blogs and other sites by exposing your data to you in the form of RSS, Atom, and iCal files (see the glossary for more on these formats). Each metro has its own XML feed, which can be consumed and displayed as either RSS or Atom (iCal is a synchronizable desktop calendar for Mac users). Gothamist and Baio worked out an upcoming namespace for Gothamist's full feed, in order to add venue information to the basic syndication standard, but Baio says that hasn't been documented yet. He has written a few tutorials and linked to them on the Upcoming.org homepage as well, to help people use other free tools to list their upcoming events.

Working in his spare time, Baio launched the site in about nine months. He relied on his experience doing database programming with Perl and PHP "often just for fun," and completed the work in a series of big bursts of productivity, first sketching out the database structure, functionality, and mockups "on my lunch breaks." The coding effort took relatively little time by comparison.

The next feature he plans to introduce is location-based searching (and, of course, webfeeds). "I have a postal code database for the U.S. and Canada, and can sort based on distance. I just need time to add it in."

Sources and Further Reading

Read these web pages for more detail on the ideas, events, and networks mentioned in this chapter.

David Plotz, "Luke Skywalker Is Gay? Fan Fiction Is America's Literature Of Obsession." *Slate*, April 14, 2000:
http://slate.msn.com/id/80225/

Archive of David Graper's PLATO writings, compiled by Brian Dear:
http://www.grapenotes.com

The story around DJ Dangermouse's *The Grey Album*, and some download options:
http://www.illegal-art.org/audio/grey.html

SITO online artist network collective:
http://sito.org

South by Southwest Interactive Festival:
http://www.sxsw.com/interactive/

Fray Days:
http://fray.com/events/

Derek Powazek's San Francisco Stories:
http://www.sfstories.com

The SARS Art Project:
http://www.sarsart.org/sars-stu.php

Paul Ford's short story "Flash":
http://www.ftrain.com/FlashMob.html

Online musician Yaniv Soha:
http://yanivsoha.com

Literary Kicks online salon:
http://www.litkicks.com

John Perry Barlow, "Surreality TV: From Burning Man To Running Man," *Disinformation*, October 29, 2003:
http://www.disinfo.com/site/displayarticle887.html

Gwen Harlow's "Ladies (and Gentlemen) Who Lunch," bringing web artists together:

http://ofrenda.org/lunch/

Upcoming.org, run by Andy Baio, is a collaborative event calendar that can help with scheduling and coordinating.

These sites present live, remixed, and mash art, and even arrange travelling exhibitions:

http://www.detritus.org

http://www.archive.org

http://www.illegal-art.org

The following are sites where you can find collaborative art, competitive art such as Photoshop Tennis, or forum-based discussion and critique of creative digital work:

http://www.designologue.com/v3/

http://www.digikitten.com

http://www.flashkit.com

http://www.worth1000.com

http://www.baseboard.net

http://www.were-here.com

http://www.twelvestone.com/forums/forumdisplay.php?forumid=7

http://www.corpse.org

http://www.were-over-there.com

http://www.graphic-forums.com

http://www.bd4d.com

http://www.coudal.com/index.php

http://yayhooray.com

http://www.newstoday.com

http://www.highend3d.com

http://www.graphics.com/modules.php?name=Gallery

http://birdhouse.org/birdhouse.html

Oh, and remember my mention at the start of this chapter of the toy called Spirograph? Yes, you can use the Web to draw those familiar swirly patterns:

http://www.wordsmith.org/~anu/java/spirograph.html

Chapter 7 Doing Business with Strangers

[Somebody please build a] special application (the developer can charge for it—I would easily fork over $50), which allows me to set up my own private Tribe.net, maintains the sanctity of my network, [and] insures the purity of the contacts. If I have something to sell, share or offer, I should profit from it, not some Sand Hill Road maharajah or some dot-commer who is getting a second chance.

—OM MALIK, "My Network, My Way!",
GigaOm

Despite its origins in the military-scientific-academic complex, the Internet has been a marketplace for over a decade now. Many people still prefer the world of landlines and faxes; they find the immediacy and informality of email and the other text-driven interfaces of the Net a bit too unbuttoned for business communication. But others have thrived in this environment, discovering new ways to cyberschmooze.

Beyond the innate connective aspects of the Internet, a raft of new social network software systems (SNSs) and services have arisen in the most recent cycle, some of them drawing venture capital and stirring up buzz among the early adopters and the influencers in blogs and business magazines. Basically, the Internet is a medium of communication and information exchange, so just about any application built on the Net can be adapted for business networking.

Meanwhile, the less glamorous workhorses of commerce, marketing, communications, and sales continue to quietly innovate online, as the 21st century equivalents of direct mail, telemarketing, call centers, and customer-relationship management migrate online and begin building dossiers on each and every one of us. This raises many questions:

- Who owns my information about me?

- Where is it stored?

- Who else can access it?

- What about the information about connections to and from me?

As with a credit report, can I dispute someone else's claim to know me, to vouch for me, or to have employed me in the past? Am I the same John Smith your profile claims to know?

Six Degrees of Hesitation

Most of these SNS tools—the ones that try to capture the information from your Rolodex to help you connect to other people—follow from the model of a startup called SixDegrees.com that was launched in the late '90s. As I recall, I got an invitation to join it from Scot Hacker, a friend from the antiweb mailing list whose birdhouse.org site I'd enjoyed for many years (Scot is now the webmaster for the Berkeley journalism school). I went in, signed up, looked around a little, found no one else I knew, and then never went back. At the time, the critical mass required to sustain such a site among online networkers wasn't present; the company went belly-up around the same time as a lot of too-early-for-their-time startups. But of course, nothing online ever really disappears completely. The company's assets were sold, and at least one social network tool that has appeared since then adapted some of the original code at the heart of SixDegrees.

The phrase "six degrees" is taken from Stanley Milham's 1967 hypothesis that everyone in the U.S. is connected to everyone else by no more than six interpersonal steps (I call them "handshakes"). I'm not sure this is true, but the idea persists, and to the extent that it is true, such relative closeness relies on the existence of superconnectors: hub people who know people from many different walks of life or circles of interest, and provide the bridges between islands of people.

Another Day, Another Social Network Software Launch

Google has a policy of allowing its employees to develop their own ideas using company servers in the interests of incubating innovations. A Google engineer named Orkut Buyyukkokten developed an SNS tool called Nexus while working on a Ph.D. at Stanford. He recently came up with a similar application—called Orkut—which Google agreed to release to the public as a beta test before its launch.

In order to limit the growth of the service during the testing period (at least), the system required an invitation from an existing user for a new user to join. At first, this meant that the site was populated mainly by Google engineers and personal friends of Orkut's. But as soon as the population began to include some of the superconnected people online, it naturally spilled over into the blogger A-list and other digerati, and from there to a much wider crowd.

This meant that quickly people started begging others for invitations. If, in the first week or so, you wrote something online about your experience playing around with Orkut in the first week or so, you'd get email or blog comments from strangers asking you to invite them into the service. Eventually, Orkut invitations were being traded on eBay—which is itself a kind of social network, at least in the sense that people rate each other's trustworthiness or karma based on past experiences transacting sales from person-to-person. (In fact, rating of buyers or sellers with letter grades, including facetious ratings such as "A+++++ I WOULD BUY AGAIN," has trickled over into humorous Amazon reviews and Orkut testimonials as a kind of out-of-context Internet gag.)

Another problem with the velvet-rope, invitation-only process of launching Orkut was that each invitation generated a fairly generic email message that looked to a lot of spam filters exactly like spam. So as a result, an invitation often got trapped in limbo and was never seen by the intended recipient (unless she happened to wonder what might be caught in her email's lint trap and waded through the endless Viagra ads and Nigerian scams looking for the occasional false positive). For that matter, the invitations look, act, and smell a lot like spam to some human beings as well.

Once the flurry of inviting people, seeing who you know on the system, and collecting quasi-"friendship" status with as many people as possible died down, it became clear that Orkut didn't actually do or offer much. There are some facilities for group formation, with message boards and event-scheduling features, but they lack the necessary stickiness required to help accrete a real community. Many of the groups ended up abandoned or bereft of activity—virtual ghost towns—soon after they were created.

Worse, there were some draconian terms of service and some sloppy security features, which led many people to feel like their information was too easily "scrapeable" (able to be identified and captured) or available for misuse. The messaging system built into Orkut also generates its own version of spam. You can send messages to all the friends of your friends, which includes a lot of people who have never heard of you and probably have very little in common with you.

Mary Hodder is a researcher doing interdisciplinary work related to information systems, journalism, and intellectual property; she's also a consultant to Technorati. She pointed out to me—in a long face-to-face discussion, I might add—that most online social interaction takes place in something of a vacuum, lacking most of the social cues that we rely on in face-to-face interactions. The bare bones "John Smith wants to be your friend. Is John Smith a friend of yours (Yes/No)?" style of interlocution can come across as particularly brusque and unfriendly.

I annoyed a few people early on by sending out silly joke messages to all my friends of friends. I also learned, to my chagrin, that messages sent only to my friends were in fact received by a wider group of people.

After this wave of Orkut activity died down, I noticed that I was getting no more invitations and recognizing no new people. Nobody was posting in any of the groups that I'd joined or created, and the whole thing was starting to wear off like a sugar high. So I sent around one last friends-of-friends message under the sardonic heading "Is Orkut Over?":

looks like everybody got bored. does anyone have tetris?

This resulted in an avalanche of replies. Many got the joke and kidded back ("Saying 'Orkut is over' is already over."). Others took it seriously and lamented that they'd only just got there. Still others sent me various working versions of Tetris, including one that I could have played on my cell phone if I could figure out how to load it and launch it there. Others, of course, begged me to stop spamming them (and I did).

It's still not clear what use there is for Orkut, if any. Some people, such as Yahoo! engineer Jeremy Zawodney, have speculated that Orkut is the kernel of a Google identity system that could be used to target advertisements or other services based on your interests or connections. Given that Google's competitors, from Yahoo! to MSN to AOL, all have membership and user bases, this theory seems plausible.

In its first incarnation, Orkut is being treated like a kind of game or recreation. But its eventual purpose might be something else, as Google figures out how to use different aspects of people's identities from Orkut, their new GMail email service, and their search habits to market targeted ads and services. It may be possible for Google to combine the information from these three services to develop sophisticated marketing techniques. This may or may not bother users, depending on how they feel about having these interactions combined, at least for targeted marketing campaigns.

Social networks used purely for socializing, for games, and for dating are something I'll talk about in the next chapter. But there is another characteristic of social networks: the different parts of a person's life can meet in one place, sometimes uncomfortably and sometimes even resulting in a painful or embarrassing shift in a person's employment or educational status.

One way this can happen with Orkut is through their profile system, which has three panels in it: general, professional, and personal. The professional profile is suitable for business networking, while the personal profile is geared toward dating. Mixing these two contexts together is potentially dangerous. Do you really want to know which of your business contacts is in an open marriage or "attached, but looking?" Do you want testimonials from people in one part of your life—who may tease you about something a little embarrassing—to be read by your boss, your students, or your customers? Probably not.

Services that blur the lines between work and play bring potential problems into the mix. On the other hand, even social networks systems with a business culture include personal aspects (after all, people do flirt at business mixers or find activity partners from among their work colleagues). LinkedIn, Spoke, and Ryze, for example, all foster a business climate. Ryze is the only SN out there yet that claims to be profitable (whatever that means).

Handshakes and Letters of Recommendation

Social network software comes in many procedural flavors. One business networking service, LinkedIn, allows you to claim connections only to people whose email addresses you know. If you find someone on the service by checking against their email address, LinkedIn enables you to send an invitation to ask that person to be one of your official connections. You can also use the service to search for people who meet some description (offering work, looking for work, have a special skill, profile matches a particular keyword) and the system calculates the path from you to that person.

If you wish to send a query, the intermediaries between you and the target are asked to pass along a recommendation. Your friend can vouch for you to her connection, and the connection can vouch for your friend, and so on, until the request reaches the target. That person can then either agree to entertain your idea in person or can turn you down from a distance.

LinkedIn is the only online SNS system (yet) that I've received any kind of work inquiries from. Its look and feel are more "grown up" than many of the more socially oriented services, and it gives the impression of not wasting your time and not devaluing the information in your network by exposing it willy nilly to every Tom, Dick, and Harry online.

Another business-oriented social network system that has some momentum and a fair amount of activity is Ryze. Anyone can join Ryze for free, but you can pay for a premium membership if you wish to join more than three tribes or use some of the extended features that Ryze offers.

Tribes can be organized around lines of business or any other affinity group. Other tribes relate to geographical areas *and* common business professions, such as the real estate groups in Nevada, Chicago, Cleveland, and the greater New York City "tri-state" area.

Tribes can form around the social media tools themselves, at least before the novelty wears off. For example, Ross Mayfield, the CEO of SocialText (a company that offers a hosted secure wiki service for businesses), started a blog tribe on Ryze in order to enable bloggers to find each other and to evangelize the benefits of blogging to the savvy Internet-connected business people congregating there.

Originally, Ryze's terms of service seemed onerous, claiming too much ownership of the information and contents supplied by users. This always comes up when an online service depends on contributed content to generate its usefulness. Who owns the information? Who else can see it? How can it be used? If the service can't reassure its users, it won't feel like a safe place to park your valuable information.

Once this wave of stand-alone, what-do-they-do-really social network systems plays out, I expect we'll start to see subsets of these functionalities embedded into existing products and services (Amazon or eBay social networking, blog social networking, Internet Movie Database social networking, iTunes social networking, and so on). Again, questions will arise about who gets to see and use the incredibly rich marketing data collected and whether people will feel safe enough to lodge some form of their personal identities there.

Ryze tries to keep you coming back to the site by alerting you when someone is sending you a message, signing your guestbook, or trying to add you to their list of contacts. The messages don't come through directly. You have to click back to the site to find out what was said (and while you're there, you'll see an ad or a solicitation to upgrade your membership). This is one way of dealing with the problem of sites that you sign up for or log into and then never see again.

Ryze also sends out weekly statistics showing you how many people have viewed your page and other traffic information, and comparing your numbers to the averages on the system so you have an incentive to keep up with the Joneses.

Ryze members also plan regular mixers and happy hours in the real world, so there's an opportunity—at least for the geographically cohesive tribes—to form face-to-face relationships that can strengthen the virtual connections. This means that Ryze has a touch of the aspect of Meetup in which virtual and physical groupings are blended, instead of the almost 100-percent-virtual nature of many other social networks.

There are so many SNSs that there are people managing lists of them (see the Glossary), and depending on how "SNS" is defined, the list is currently very long (40 and counting). But more strictly, there are about 10 serious systems right now, and I hear about a new launch nearly every week.

Before the best-of-breed practices emerge and get absorbed by Microsoft, Yahoo!, and other players in the web space, rapid Darwinian elimination will continue. When Evite announced its 2.0 version, for example, it cited "Friend-ster, Craigslist, Emode, Meetup, etc.," as its chief competitors. But on that same day, Emode merged with Ringo and changed its corporate name to Tickle. You can't tell the social-network players without a program, it seems.

Doing Deals without Meeting

So does anyone ever do any business over social networks? Isn't it more likely that you'll just pick up the phone when money is at stake? Sure, in most contexts. Then again, among other things, I do much of my work by email these days, and I have clients I consider friends whom I've never properly met.

I've gotten some inquiries via LinkedIn, and as I mentioned, it feels solid. I believe it could work. It has that "white-shoe" feel—it gives off the vibe that it's established and successful. Just as I was starting this book, a team of entrepreneurial writers, Scott Allen and David Teten, tracked me down through three different social networking contexts: They sent me a note via Ryze, found an intermediary to introduce themselves to me via LinkedIn, then saw me hanging out on the #joiito IRC channel and sent me a "whispered" IM pressing their pitch. Allen did most of that outreach.

Later, Allen wrote about the whole process in one of his websites, filing it under success stories, and demonstrating how he used his blog to help promote his ventures:

> I'm pleased to announce that Danielle Jatlow at Waterside Productions will
> be representing us for our second book, *The Virtual Handshake: Leveraging
> Online Social Networks to Grow Your Business.* ...

One of the most exciting things about working with Danielle is that, quite simply, "she gets it." It helps that our connection with her was through online social networking, rather than a traditional query letter. We had a couple of agents interested in representing us from earlier queries last year, but now that our first book is done, and we're really serious about pitching the second one to a major publisher, we decided to try to seek out an agent who was active on online social networking and would understand how important and timely this topic is, and be able to represent that to the publishers.

In the meantime, Allen and Teten have landed a book deal, and Allen points out that this networking experience itself demonstrates how such deals can be made entirely through remote telepresence. As he says, "My coauthor, David Teten, and I met online (and have yet to meet in person)." Many of the face-to-face cues we rely on in the analog world to feel comfortable with someone are still lacking on social networks to one degree or another. The digital presence is still too telegraphic, too semaphoric for most of us to read in the deeply intuitive way that we know how to interpret body language, tone of voice, eyes vs. mouth. But as these services evolve, and people become adept at using them to resolve issues and work together, the use of social network services will become more prevalent.

The Downsides of YASNs

Andrew Orlowski, a stringer for the UK-based *Register* in San Francisco, specializes in taking the piss out of the self-satisfied wisdoms emitting from the blogosphere. He straddles the line between the digerati and the mainstream technical press, passing judgment on the groupthink. As a gadfly, he serves a useful purpose, highlighting the shadowy downsides that lurk behind any hype. For example, he quoted a security expert named Roger Clarke extensively in an article that suggests that most social network services—or YASNs, for yet-another-social-network—are a security nightmare offering weak protection, if any, of your privacy.

TheSpoke (a Microsoft-owned portal for students) runs on ASP.NET technology and uses Microsoft's .NET Passport system for its login/user identity/authentication. I refused on principle to sign in. (I don't know about you, but of all the high-tech corporate monoliths that I don't trust with my personal information, Microsoft is at or near the top of the list.)

The real question is, why I would want to enter my Rolodex into a public repository? Who gets to see my data? How do you know who is seeing it and what they are doing with it? It seems reasonable to want to protect my own work and connections, as well as the personal information of my friends and colleagues. I risk angering them if they feel their information has been shared indiscriminately with people they don't know.

There's no doubt that we all need a personal network management system that's ubiquitous, fast, and interlinked with our communication devices, but so far, most people are just working on the edges of this. Phil Wolff writes:

> You may try to model me, but you can't define me. I'm larger than a tidy form.
>
> That's why God and evolution gave us the ability to lie. And posture. And pretend. And choose our words and body language.
>
> I am not my business card. Or my resumé. Or my orkut profile.
>
> They are merely shorthands, placeholders, for the real thing.
>
> And you never get the real thing.

Wolff ranks the various ways that one can try to capture a person's essence, starting with direct interaction, which he refers to as "self as black box"—because there is no annotation, no description, no metadata. Just behavior and perception. Next is "ethnographic observation" of real-life behavior, then the subject's own constructed narrative of self (if available), and finally a mechanical analysis of the subject's online behavior.

The problem with all of this, Wolff points out, is that human beings are not reducible to a single persona, demographic or otherwise: "I am many people in one skin, and we all change who's in charge with the ebb and flow of blood sugar, brain chemistry, and the damned cat that peed on the carpet and I'm one way in A's company, another in B's company, and some awkward way when in the company of both A & B, since I'm working with B, dating A, but had horribly bad sex with B, and I can't remember whose fault it was."

If it's that difficult to get a fix on a single person, imagine the problems involved in mapping the complex web of relationships between numerous individuals, all of whom themselves contain multitudes.

Despite the beta nature of most of these SNS systems, they produce an irresistible data set for researchers. Researcher and blogger danah boyd has already complained about how, as a participating researcher, she loses her anonymity—the ability to sit in a duck blind to just observe. She becomes one of the heavy connectors, one of the beneficiaries of the early-bird-gets-the-worm law that governs any emergent system. The galaxies clump together, the stars congeal. It's high school all over again. How to observe without interfering?

David Weinberger points to a problem inherent to social network software:

> [R]eal social networks are always implicit. The ones constructed explicitly are always—yes, always—infected with a heavy dose of social bullshit. It's like thinking that the invitation list for your wedding actually reflects your circle of friends and relatives. No, you had to invite Barry-the-Boozer because he's your cousin, and you couldn't invite Marsha because then you'd have to invite her husband Larry-the-Ass-Grabber and her daughter Erin-the-Snot-Flinger. Explicitly constructed social networks not only lack the differentiation that makes relationships real, they are falsehoods built to reinforce spectral relationships and to avoid ending shaky ones.

True as this is, mechanical approximations of human behavior and patterns inevitably feel crude, and they miss the point in their early stages. But they have a way of evolving, sometimes simply through trial and error, into simulacra with uncanny apparent insight into human social ways. I have little doubt that the social network software of today will eventually lead to tools that address many of the complaints made by observant users.

Privacy, Security, Terms of Service

In the meantime, the question remains why anyone should invest time and energy into supplying a third-party business with the details of their painstakingly accumulated social network when the reward or payoff seems so paltry. As Om

Malik wrote in an entry at his *GigaOm Broadband* blog, called "My Network, My Way:"

> The question I have is: why the F**K should I share my network of con-
> tacts with these commercial entities? They are like BlogSpot that does
> nothing for my brand equity and in many ways chews me out after making
> the network connections. Thus what I want is a "Movable Type" of social
> networking. Blogs took off because it was about one person—me. My social
> networks should be of my making for me. Let's figure out a way to cut out
> the middlemen.

Whether YASNs are truly a security nightmare or just a minefield in the realm of intellectual property and personal privacy, it behooves you to read any privacy declaration carefully and bear in mind that commercial services some-times change ownership and then change privacy rules without notice.

Turning the picture around for a moment, though, put yourself in the marketing/sales role. If you're the one trying to understand your customers, your potential customers, your constituency, or your base, then offering these people some useful SN services might be a good way to populate your database with their personal data. Just be sure you clearly disclose how you are going to pro-tect their privacy and what you will and won't do with any data entered so peo-ple feel comfortable trusting you with their data. (Or be Google.)

The existing customer relationship management (CRM) software mak-ers would do well to pay attention to any popular software format that induces users to fill out questionnaires describing themselves and all of their social rela-tionships and favorite consumer products (books, movies). Imagine what you could do with a rich database of your user's preferences, using the kinds of inference engines that go back to RINGO at MIT (which suggested music based on your five favorite bands); such engines are what help Amazon tell you that people who bought *Night Soldiers* by Alan Furst also bought *A Coffin for Demitrios* by Eric Ambler.

I like free content. I've done some of my best writing in the freedom of the Internet, scribbled publicly, but whenever I write something online, I think to myself, "Who owns this? Where is it stored? Will it last?" Sure, I want my words to be distributed widely, but when nobody but me is picking up the freight, I want to retain some control, some rights reserved, or a Creative Commons "derivative works OK but be sure to give me credit" license. On the WELL right now, in an independent conference that I cohost (blog.ind), people are debating whether Bloglines should really list the full content of RSS feeds and then perhaps eventually sell ads or other services built on this free content without compensating the webloggers themselves—let alone sharing any traffic information about the intercepted readers.

It's the same deal with your address book, only more so. Your address is far more personal. It's something a detective or identity thief would love to get their hands on. Does it make any sense to expose it, even partially, in the very public space of the Internet? (And frankly, I consider any privacy on the Internet to be purely temporary—anything I really want to keep private isn't stored unencrypted on a very open public internetwork, I hope.)

In fact, you owe it to the people who've given you their numbers and home addresses to provide some degree of stewardship to your personal collection. Would you give your friend's phone number to someone who didn't know them if that other person called you asking for it?

Add collaborative filtering or other ways for people to share preferences and opinions, as with Joshua Schacter's Delicious (http://del.icio.us) shared bookmarker or the fictional social network (imagined by Brian Dear in a satirical news release) "Pricekut," that enables Amazon shoppers to discuss what's in their shopping carts.

How long do you think it will be before a social network tool can tell you "People who like this person might also like that person."?

Other players in this area are find-your-old-high-school-friend services and alumni networks. Matcheroo, a service originally designed for alumni, now offers a product for use behind corporate firewalls, offering much more robust support for deliberate, regulated security.

Open Source Social Networks

People such as Marc Canter (he founded Macromind, which became Macromedia) don't see why all this social-network data must be stored in proprietary formats. Instead, just propagate standards and permit people to self-host and manage their own data and their own social networks. Naturally, of course, only a small percentage of the elite Internet users at this point are able to host all aspects of their online presence. This is why low-powered, high-ease-of-use sites such as GeoCities, Yahoo! Groups, and Blogger have been so successful. It's still not easy enough for most people to use a lot of these services, or even understand what is happening on the screen. It's intimidating, except perhaps for the geeks.

Even in this more open concept of social networking systems, there's still a potential business model in offering to host this type of information. Mark Pincus, the founder of Tribe Networks, specifically states that he sees Tribe as an interim solution for the time we're in, when the raw network itself doesn't simply "know" enough about us (from our own self-assertions and probably from other people's implicit connections to us) to offer us the information or services that we need.

Canter supports the FOAF (Friend of a Friend) format, an RDF (Resource Description Framework) language written in XML (Extensible Markup Language). There, I've lost you already, haven't I? Stay with me, it's actually simple.

Basically, a FOAF file is just a specially punctuated text file that registers a bunch of assertions about the person who owns or posted the file: name, some location information, addresses of other related Internet resources, and links to people "known" by the FOAFster.

There are problems with this approach too. If you can claim to know me, but I don't know you—what does that mean? Also, as with "friends" on Friendster or Orkut, what does it mean to be a friend online? Everyone defines it differently, situationally, and as a reflection of the different cultural environments we each grew up in.

As a joke, someone ran around a tech conference earlier this year yelling, "You are my friend! Yes or No?!" in people's faces, a parody of Orkut's confrontational confirmation dialogue.

People I call my friends may include family, friends, personal acquaintances, people I've corresponded with online, people I've worked with but never face-to-face, and strangers whose work I admire and vice versa. The contrast between the infinite variety of human relations and the finite definitions needed by computers became stark when Ian Davis and Eric Vitiello Jr. proposed just such a list of computer-readable definitions. Clay Shirky noted that such a list is "self-critiquing ... Human relations have the additional and curious property of changing the relationship through the act of labeling, [as] anyone who has ever said, 'I love you' can attest."

Although computer-defined relationships are hard to design, they can serve a purpose, and so people are still trying to design them. Canter's People-Aggregrator site promises to host FOAF for people and help them groom their information in a more pleasant visual environment. He is all about getting more media besides text into the online experience. He's all for pictures, movies, and sound, but we'll get back to that later.

Canter defends hosted, FOAF-speaking social network services against those who argue for a more distributed approach. But these two goals are not really at odds. The issue really is interoperability between hosted and distributed implementations.

The division between open source efforts and proprietary systems permeates a lot of the standards conflicts these days, because competing ideas of how to model this kind of data, distribute it, and make it machine readable have not yet played themselves entirely out (and may never).

A new company, Plink, gathers any FOAF that it can find on the Web and enables you to search for people and find out who they know. Software and services that emit FOAF automatically (TypePad, LiveJournal, PeopleAggregrator, DeanSpace/DeanLink) can generate your listing in a public repository like that without you even realizing it's happening.

When Phil Wolff pointed out the limitations involved in any social network trying to model human behavior, he made a few suggestions. Some deal with improving the subtlety of the data modeled by the networks to reflect more of our in-person experiences:

Model sociology. Not just nice stuff but all the icky horrible interactions we see in the office, in school, in gangs. Rites of passage. Flirting. Insults. Combat. Cliques. Authority. Power.

Model psychology. Squeeze in Maslow's hierarchy. Piaget or someone else who models childhood development, especially arrested development.

Let me do more. Solve real life problems virtually. Design tools for tasks I really need. Group formation. Group destruction. Group work. Better meetings. Prioritization of communication. Help people be useful to each other.

Do less. Email, texting, http, phone calls are all pretty dumb systems. They just move content, so the human content becomes paramount, richer, engaging. Find your core and strip away the rest.

But Wolff also advocated opening up these systems. This does not necessarily mean following the open source philosophy per se, but it does mean not trying to do everything and permitting the creativity and energy of your most advanced user base to add value to your network:

We need APIs so programmers can extend the models and tools.

I should be able to write an extension that lets you see a combined orkut profile and Google references.

Or find what the people in my virtual sub-community are buying on Amazon.

Or authenticate access to my calendar using friendship degrees.

Or sync my mobile phone behavior (who I text and who texts me) with my buddy list.

Or turn orkut into my smart phone's Caller ID system.

Or bounce new friends-of-friends against my interest profiles and nominate a few for acquaintanceship.

Or whatever. The world knows more than you do, so let them in.

Social Software versus Social Network Software

Questioning the value of dedicated social network systems, weblogger Dina Mehta wrote in her weblog, "My blog is ... my social network." This doesn't mean that her social life is limited to Internet-mediated interactions. Rather, it means that she doesn't need an additional service to manage or track her social network—her blog serves that purpose for her.

Most people who've invested time in any online system at all (think of your email addresses: Are you on mailing lists? Do you use filters to sort your mail?) hesitate before re-keying everything into a new system yet again. You have to ask, who is benefiting from my effort? And since when has almost any Internet software not been social software? Yahoo! Groups may not be "cool" like Orkut, but it represents a level of middleware that the ordinary person can understand. It's a better instant website than most people can otherwise build. There's a reason why Yahoo! Groups is phenomenally successful. A lot of press attention went to the custom tools that the Dean campaign developed (like DeanLink), but the vast majority of grassroots volunteers in that primary solved their online presence needs by starting Yahoo! Groups and using them primarily as mailing lists, but also as simple databases, calendars, and contact-management tools.

Comparing the explicit versus implicit ways of registering social relationship online, Lila Efimova writes

> My "reading distraction" turns into an urge to write when I see Dina's post, "My Blog is my Social Software and my Social Network." Dina passionately explains the feeling that I share as well, something that made me writing at my Ryze page "I'm not sure what to write here, because my main Internet identity is my blog."

> I guess many bloggers will share this feeling, but then why [do] YASNs manage to get us in? I'm thinking about differences between weblogs and on-line networking tools... Fuzzy and emotional vs. clear and square. Slow uncovering vs. instant visibility. Building relations vs. browsing them.

Tech Ronin writes about how blogging and connecting with others through a blog in effect becomes a commitment to others in your blog social media network:

> I've given most attention to Ryze (of which I've been a gold member since Mar-03), but have to admit that when I started blogging around the

beginning of May, most of my free *online networking* energy has been spent either blogging, perusing other blogs, or commenting on other blogs. Once you have a blog, you're committed in a way that being a member of these communities doesn't come close to unless perhaps you are the moderator of a network that is active.

Likewise, the most active social networking online is going on not within the boundaries of a venture capitalist's playground but around the edges as it always has: in email, on the phone, increasingly in instant messaging or chat, on Skype, across blogs, in peer-to-peer networks, on craigslist, at Meetups, and with organizations such as MoveOn.

Probably my most productive networking has been on the freenode IRC network. I've collaborated with people in political campaigns, done software development, and just bounced ideas off each other in the #joiito channel that I mentioned earlier. I turn on the chat (IRC) software only when I know that I can spare a little attention or need some relief. Even then, I let it log everything and don't try to keep up unless I get a break in what I'm doing. It can be fairly asynchronous, but when I'm there, it's probably the best way to get my full attention, if only briefly.

One key to remote presence and effective collaboration through limited communications tools is to be as present as possible in whichever media are available. If you call me on my cell phone, I will tell you right away whether it's a good time for me to talk. In fact, I'll probably pick up only if I can spare the attention. I will also let you know how much time I have. Then, in that time, I will give you my full attention just as if we were in the same room together.

Beyond telepresence or rich remote presence, there are also the channels of time-shifted media with application across a spectrum from communication to entertainment. No longer passive recipients of media streams, we are becoming empowered (from desktop publishing to moblogging) to rip, mix, and burn any of the sensory data we can capture. We are pushing and pulling media of our own generation, made by individuals and collectives, through these social networks.

Providing Presence

Given that so far only the ubergeeks have really even tried most social software networks, it's too early to write them off as a pointless data grab. Caterina Fake of Ludicorp (Flickr.com, GameNeverEnding.com) reminds the bleeding-edge crowd that the redundancies of social networks don't apply to people who haven't already cultivated a rich online presence (through blogging and participating in relevant online communities), when she says that they are missing the point of these networks. She agrees with the observations of Justin Hall (whose *Justin's Links from the Underground* journal was a popular blog a good five years before the word "blog" was coined and is still going strong), reported by a *Wired* article on social networks:

> Justin Hall, a veteran Net head and freelance writer, said the backlash seems to be limited only to those with an established online presence. To the vast majority of casual Internet users, especially those without personal Web pages, the services are a great way to establish an online identity.
>
> "They're great for people without a Web page," Hall said. "If you don't have a Web page, people can find out where you are and what you are up to. I have loads of non-Internet-savvy friends on Friendster, and they love it."

Fake decries the jaded elitism of experienced "digerati" who consider only the cream of each network to be of value, similar to the way people dismiss blogging as mostly chatter about what people ate that day or their loves and hates. Both criticisms miss the point that in the future (assuming we don't lose all this data) social scientists will be equally interested in what a teen did on their lunch break at school and the bloggings of a social-science theorist.

The value in these networks is both relative—at the individual level of people and their friends or contacts—and aggregated. The big question about the latter is who should have access and control over the data and who gets to mine the aggregated data. In other words, who owns it? There's no easy answer to that question, but it seems that the option of seceding from the Internet and withholding all information from it—while possibly a workable choice for a human being—simply doesn't make any sense for any enterprise that needs to be found and interacted with online and requires an aura of goodwill to encourage people to trust and do business with it.

Business Blogging

People have the choice of simply signing up for a social network system or launching their own idiosyncratic weblog as a way of creating an online presence that can be linked to other online presences. Businesses have more to do online than simply form connections with people. Corralling communities of people who wish to interact with the business, whether they are customers, employees, partners, suppliers, regulators, or so on, becomes a more important issue as the Internet continues to be adopted more fully as a platform for everyday interaction.

Some businesses thus are beginning to experiment with weblogging of one kind or another, if only because weblogs represent the current best practices for creating "living" content on the Web (in the sense of frequently updated content managed by and for the benefit of human beings).

In a business, weblogs can be used internally and externally. Internal weblogs can help with

- Logging project management milestones and stumbling blocks

- Internal reporting and review

- Any form of internal communications

- Aggregating the knowledge gained over the course of a project

An internal business blog doesn't have to be especially expressive or creative, as long as the salient parts of the author's workweek are being logged regularly and can be reviewed by whoever else in the organization has the right to keep track of that person's log.

Externally, weblogs can be used for marketing and communications outreach. In the same way that individuals can selectively expose personal information on the Internet and thus enable others to profile and respond to that information, business weblogs can help companies manage an online profile and generate the sort of reputation or aura of goodwill that enables strangers to trust each other and make commitments or transactions online.

The End of Mass-Market Advertising

Marketing guru Seth Godin, the author of *Ideavirus* and *Purple Cow*, suggests that we may be leaving behind the era of mass communication and mass advertising. "Maybe there is no mass market anymore," he told me. "Maybe just because a big company wants to reach everyone doesn't mean they have to have an economic right to do so."

I asked Godin how long he thought it would take for mass advertising to wither away. Without putting an exact timeline on it, he was willing to say, "I do think that over the next five years, fewer and fewer organizations will find that mass market advertising is cost effective."

The type of advertising that seems to work best online is targeted niche advertising. If someone is searching for a certain type of information, then providing that information, even as an advertisement, is not inherently offensive as long as paid placement is clearly marked as such and distinguished visibly from objective or editorially derived content.

In the gift economy of the Internet, a new form of advertising is unsolicited endorsements. If I love a new pen that I bought or if I discover a shareware application that I can no longer live without, I take it upon myself to advertise these products to my friends or to other people I believe will benefit from knowing about them. For example, when I fell in love with VoodooPad, a desktop wiki/whiteboard application for OS X, I immediately began blogging about it and insisting to all of my Macintosh-using friends that they immediately download it and share my joy. In the long run, these kinds of loyalty-inspired forms of promotion may prove more potent than any form of paid advertising. Influencers who are also early adopters may become the most potent form of marketing both online and offline, as people look for reliable filters for information and products.

At a recent conference in Berkeley looking at social network systems and journalism, someone pointed to Craig Newmark and told me that all the newspaper businesses were terrified of him because his little site was eating their lunch in the realm of classified ads. On a panel that morning, Mark Pincus from Tribe noted that people say they like craigslist because it has no ads, when in fact, as Pincus put it, "It's *all* ads." It's just that the ads or announcements are well categorized, and the social culture of craigslist frowns on people who spam or advertise inappropriately.

When Newmark was looking into ways to generate enough income to continue running the site, craigslist went to their users and asked what they should charge for. The wide consensus was that people listing jobs and apartment could be charged for their ads, because they were already directed toward a commercial transaction. So far, craigslist charges only for the employment ads but is thinking of taking the next step for real estate and housing as well.

Newmark told me that people generally welcome advertising as long as it's clearly marked as such. What they don't like, he said, is intrusive advertising.

Meanwhile, contrary to the conventional wisdom of many social network businesses that seem intent on gathering and owning as much data as possible, Newmark told me that craigslist keeps very little or no demographic info about its users. (Craigslist users do not have to sign in or create a username at the site to participate. In fact, craigslist has no login feature at all.) The site does no data mining and doesn't track users with cookies. What you see is what you get.

Permission Marketing

The same rules that apply to advertising online—be useful, be on topic, don't appear where not wanted—apply to marketing. In order to distinguish spamming from more accepted forms of marketing, the term "permission marketing" refers to contacting only people who have given explicit consent in advance. One technique is called "double opt-in." Double opt-in means that the subject must explicitly opt in (that is, not simply fail to notice and select the opt-out button on an online form) to a mailing list or other form of contact, and then must confirm the decision a second time, usually in response to an email sent to the submitted address. This prevents people from maliciously signing up others for unwanted marketing. If you receive the second part of a double opt-in without having completed the first part yourself, this tells you that a third party submitted your contact information to the marketer, probably without your consent. However, as long as you simply ignore the confirmation email request, you won't receive the marketing messages that you never signed up for in the first place.

Just as nonprofit organizations have learned to use these techniques and to exploit viral marketing—or what Godin calls "ideaviruses"—for-profit businesses can do so as well. It may be that the dynamic is different. A for-profit business may have a higher hurdle to climb to show that its message is not merely self-serving but also useful for the recipient. But the same methods for encouraging loyal customers to contact their trusted acquaintances to promote your product or service can work equally well when the product or service is perceived as a legitimate good.

Getting people to seek out your product—and even to seek out your marketing—is easier if you let them see that you're still looking out for customers' concerns:

- eBay must be considered as one of the most effective Internet social network businesses of all time. No inventory, no sales staff. Pure commissions based on connecting buyers with sellers and helping to secure the delivery (usually) of physical objects.

- Craigslist is an effective marketplace that doesn't keep track of its users at all.

- Monster and HotJobs, job search sites, already provide outsourced HR services, and Monster has just added Tickle, an SNS tool, to its basic service.

Before long, supply-chain management at the corporate level may include a social network aspect. Someone will have to federate all the data coming from multiple sources. New XML data exchange format dialects will emerge.

It often comes down to trust. To get the critical mass of people entrusting their information to a system requires a reliable brand, a track record, and an accessible CEO who blogs about the development of his product.

Real Customer Service

One of Craig Newmark's hobby horses is customer service. He has observed that traditional customer service is a dead-end job whose line employees are treated poorly and whose supervisors are being punished for something or other by being assigned to that field at all. Newmark turns these conventional notions on their heads, ascribing most of the success of craigslist to the attention to the customer's needs. Nearly half of the 14 or so employees of craigslist work in customer service, "and so do I," says Newmark, who makes that aspect his focus. They read all the feedback forms sent in to them, and they empower the customer service reps to gather ideas for improvement from users, usually waiting for a consensus to emerge. Then they relay that information to software engineers in the constant process of revamping and improving the site and its services.

"As far as we can tell," says Newmark, "we are much more responsive than anyone we've ever heard of. Much more so than the law requires. We hold ourselves more accountable than any entity that we know about." I asked him why it seems so difficult for other companies to imitate this ethos and its apparent success. "For most companies, in American corporate culture (which I only really know)," he told me, "customer service is not a priority. It gets a lot of lip service people don't follow.

"People have copied the site, but they haven't copied the obvious goodwill, the attention to customer service, [or even] the commitment to keeping the sites running."

Some have resorted to spamming Newmark's customers or scraping data from craigslist to populate their own deserted sites. They are constantly fighting the spammers in various ways. Recently, they have added a "captcha" step to the ad registration process: one of those distorted images of a word that machines and blind people have trouble using but most people do not.

I also asked Newmark how the site deals with people's dislike of spam and the craigslist email notification system, which originally started off as a mailing list and still sends out most of its information in the form of email to subscribers. He said that they err on the side of caution to avoid doing anything that could be considered spam. I asked him if this means that when in doubt they don't send the mail. He said that that's generally true, but that there are times when they have to send mail to the users whose emails they know, generally to get feedback, as when they were considering charging job posters in the L.A. and N.Y. markets (they already charge S.F. job posters). "We'll just send that to the job posters," he says.

Sources and Further Reading

Read these web pages and books for more detail on the ideas in this chapter.

Om Malik, "My Network, My Way!", *GigaOm,* December 30, 2003:
http://gigaom.com/archives/2003/12/my_network_my_way.html

A list of social networking sites and software:
http://www.typaldos.blogspot.com/#socialnetworkingsitesandsw

Links to several articles on Stanley Milham and others who have studied his "six degrees" or "small world" hypothesis:
http://x-pollen.com/many/2004/04/06/bogus_degrees_of_
separation.html

Lada A. Adamic, Orkut Buyukkokten, and Eytan Adar, "A social network caught in the Web," *First Monday: Peer-Reviewed Journal on the Internet*:
http://www.firstmonday.dk/issues/issue8_6/adamic/#a8

Brian Dear, "Amazon Launches New Social Network Called Pricekut," *Denounce,* January 27, 2004 (satire):
http://www.denounce.com/archives/000049.html

Andrew Orlowski, "Avoid Friendster and its clones, warns security expert," *The Register,* February 10, 2004:
http://www.theregister.co.uk/content/6/35443.html

Phil Wolff, "My YASNS riff: My orkut doesn't fit," *a klog apart,* February 1, 2004, on how people can't be shoehorned:
http://dijest.com/aka/2004/02/01.html#a2699

For the record, the ETech "You are my friend!" comic was Rael Dornfest, as reported by Doc Searls:
http://doc.weblogs.com/2004/02/13#submergingTechnologists

XFN, the XML Friends Network:
http://gmpg.org/xfn/

Scott Allen, "Waterside Productions to represent *The Virtual Handshake*," *Online Business Networks*, February 11, 2004:
http://www.onlinebusinessnetworks.com/blog/2004/2/11/waterside-productions-to-represent-ithe-virtual-handshakei

Paul Festa, "Friendster rivals merge; Evite enters," *cNet*, November 13, 2003, on the launch of Evite and the merger of Emode and Ringo into Tickle:
http://news.com.com/2100-1026-5106742.html?tag=nl

danah boyd, "venting my contempt for orkut," *apophenia*, January 30, 2004:
http://www.zephoria.org/thoughts/archives/2004/01/30/venting_my_contempt_for_orkut.html#004004

David Weinberger, "Does social software matter?", *Many-to-Many*, January 4, 2004:
http://www.corante.com/many/archives/2004/01/04/does_social_software_matter.php

David Weinberger, "The truth about why I hate Friendster," *JOHO the Blog*, March 26, 2004:
http://www.hyperorg.com/backissues/joho-mar26-04.html#friendster

Lila Efimova, "Networking: YASNs vs. blogs," *Mathemagenic*, January 27, 2004:
http://blog.mathemagenic.com/2004/01/27.html#a1021

Dina Mehta, "My Blog is my Social Software and my Social Network," *Conversations with Dina,* January 27, 2004:
http://radio.weblogs.com/0121664/2004/01/27.html#a356

Janet Tokerud, "Fragmented Social Networking Services," *Tech Ronin,* January 28, 2004:
http://tokerud.typepad.com/blog/2004/01/fragmented_onli.html

Caterina Fake, "Continued Enthusiasm for Social Networks," *Caterina.net,* January 28, 2004:
http://www.caterina.net/archive/000457.html

Leander Kahney, "Social Nets Not Making Friends," *Wired,* January 28, 2004:
http://www.wired.com/news/culture/0,1284,62070,00.html?tw=wn_cult head_3

Marc Canter, "Response to Fionas request," *Mark's Voice,* January 26, 2004, on hosted vs. distributed social-identity formats:
http://blogs.it/0100198/2004/01/26.html#a2199

"RELATIONSHIP: A vocabulary for describing relationships between people," a set of 33 terms to be used to describe human relations within databases and markup documents:
http://vocab.org/relationship

Clay Shirky's analysis of RELATIONSHIP, *Many-2-Many,* March 16, 2004:
http://www.corante.com/many/archives/2004/03/16/relationship_a_ vocabulary_for_describing_relationships_between_people.php

Cutting Through, a U.K. blog on business blogging:
http://www.infosential.com

Sébastien Paquet's wiki list of sites and blogs doing research on social software:
http://www2.iro.umontreal.ca/~paquetse/cgi-bin/om.cgi?Research_ Blogs/Social_Software

Chapter 8   Lonely Hearts' Club Bands

> It is my contention that managing identity online is a huge
> issue. At some point, a killer app will be developed to manage
> this interface between public identity, private identity, and
> anonymity.
>
> —CHRISTOPHER FILKINS

Dating services and personal ads for finding friends and activity partners are
nothing new. They predate the Internet and in fact have been around in one
form or another at least as long as there have been newspapers. (In the earliest
days, they may have been geared more toward arranged marriages, widows or
widowers needing a new spouse, lonely hearts' clubs, and the like.)

Internet dating adds a few additional twists to the technology of finding
a friend or a mate. A long questionnaire's worth of likes and dislikes can produce a unique data key that can then be matched against others, looking for the
most complementary fit. In principle, you can seek a mate anywhere on the
globe. However, in reality, most people continue to look for relationships within
their own geographical area.

When the Iron Curtain fell, some businesses sprang up (generally using
magazines) to bring women from former Communist countries to the U.S. as
potential wives. There have been analogous services originating in Asia as well;
unfortunately, these have often been fronts for smuggling and slavery. In fact, any
system that can be used to match two adults in a relationship can just as easily be
adapted to connect prostitutes (or "escorts," as they might prefer to be called) and
johns (or "hobbyists," as the readers of Redbook.com call themselves).

But Internet dating doesn't require any special software or apparatus. Off the top of my head, I can think of two married couples who met each other through Internet mailing lists that I participated in during the '90s. One list dissolved soon afterward for other reasons, but it almost seemed as if the primary purpose of the list was to enable these two people to meet and fall in love.

People used the now-primitive-seeming Usenet system for making their love connections all through the '80s and '90s and probably still do today. From that acronym-happy culture, we got MOTOS (member of the opposite sex), MOTSS (member of the same sex), and MOTAS (member of the appropriate sex).

People flirt using instant messaging. People get involved in the same discussion groups, discover common passions, and fall in love. Friendships can be developed and sustained online.

When I started researching this topic, I had a mind-expanding IM discussion with David Weinberger, quoted earlier in this book. At one point, he said,

> Obviously, there are advantages to the physical—body language, if nothing else. But there are also some things that virtual relationships do better than physical ones. ... I have more v[irtual] than p[hysical] relationships. The v's tend to be topic-based. They frequently last longer and occur more frequently. They encourage a type of wit I can't exhibit in p ones. I can switch personas more easily with v's. I expose different sides of myself in my v relationships. It's easier to be inconsistent. It's easier to be playful. It's easier to argue. So I'm not convinced that p is a superset of v, or v is a debased form of p.

At that point, I started thinking in terms of complementary realms—physical and virtual—and how more and more people are able to explore both and form social relationships in both.

David added, "Also, my v relationships tend to be better informed because I can open up a Google window right next door," to which I said, "Yeah, just wait till you can Google someone in real time as you meet them at a party. 'Hold on a sec... oh, you're that David Weinberger?!'"

Finding love, sex, and companionship will always rank high on the priority list of most people. "Flirting and gaming," says Rheingold, "will always be important. People love to play games, and people love to flirt." Once again, the fundamental difference that makes online dating possible is having a critical mass of participants available.

So it's no surprise that there are dedicated dating services such as Match.com, Yahoo! Personals, eHarmony, and Nerve Personals, as well as many services geared toward helping people find compatible sex partners. However, the latter are reputedly often seeded or even largely populated with fake female entries to make the largely male customer base believe that they will find someone readily through the service.

One source told me confidentially that Personals is Yahoo!'s most lucrative division. And Clay Shirky told me that the adoption curve for Match.com tracks very closely with the arrival of what we might call non-nerds or ordinary people. "As the chance of meeting someone who wasn't a C++ programmer went up," said Shirky, "the service got more useful for the newcomers."

There are social software network services (SNSs) designed for business networking (Ryze, LinkedIn) and there are others designed for friends and romance (Friendster). There are also those that blend the two (Tribe, Orkut), which can lead to some awkward contextual situations. (Do you really want to know that your business partner is in an open marriage?) However, even the sites designed to foster business connections tend to facilitate dating as well.

Even DeanLink, the Dean campaign's social network tool designed to help people organize grassroots events locally, provides a space for your picture. During the peak of Deanmania, I noticed a lot of attractive younger folk signing up. At the time, I joked that, after the campaign, win or lose, DeanLink could be turned into a dating site. Of course, people have always met partners through such outside-the-house activities as volunteering and work.

Christopher Filkins has an idea for a new kind of online dating service that would combine a nonproprietary (open-source) XML vocabulary with a trusted repository of information that could help match people as well as keep one's sexual proclivities and preferences confidential, to be revealed only on a need-to-know basis.

Filkins tells me that the "choke point" through which dating services make money is in keeping control of the user's information. Filkins envisions (and has been planning the architecture for) this open-source, private, secure

XML standard, not particularly to make money but to take the profit motive out of the current market. Filkins told me that the most financially successful dating service—AdultFriendFinder (AFF)—primarily features pinup photos like a barker to get shills to come in and pay for adult access to more images of the imaginary date.

Missed Connections

As discussed in earlier chapters, craigslist is a kind of all-purpose community bulletin board. It helps people find housing and roommates, learn about upcoming events, discuss issues, and so on. But one of the most active sections of the site is the personals, broken into an ever-increasing set of categories. The current categories are

- strictly platonic
- women seek women
- women seeking men
- men seeking women
- men seeking men
- misc romance
- casual encounters
- missed connections
- rants and raves

As with most taxonomies, the new sections (most recently, "strictly platonic" and "misc romance") grow out of the existing sections, when a new type of posting is overwhelming the primary ones. "Rants and raves," for example, arose to give people a place to complain or crow about the matchmaking possibilities and to keep those non-ads out of the other sections. (Escorts or other pros posting to the personals section are redirected to a commercial section of the site called "erotic services.")

Any section of craigslist can be subscribed to as an RSS feed.

Many of these sections can be read for their entertainment value, even if you are not shopping for a mate. Some people post humorous entries that comment on the craigslist culture or stereotypes. These are often flagged by enough readers to be added to a "best of craigslist" section.

"Missed connections" is the most poignant. In it, people recount brief encounters ("Saw you on Muni"), glimpses across crowded rooms, and so on. They identify themselves ("I was the guy with the funny hat") and hope that their lost object of infatuation happens also to be a craigslist junkie, sees the ad, responds, and manages to connect, redeeming the missed opportunity. It probably doesn't work most of the time, but it makes for fascinating reading and gives you a voyeuristic glimpse into the workings of other people's minds, as well as a kind of catalogue of shyness.

Naturally, the craigslist approach doesn't rely on automation or even profiling, aside from some classification by desire. Some categories have arisen from the actual usage: "missed connections" has also run in the local papers so it's nothing new, and "rants and raves" provides a place for the often entertaining commentary by regular users of the service that is less intrusive than if it was interspersed with actual ads. Not that a witty or observant post to that category isn't itself an ad. It was Norman Mailer who wrote "Advertisements for Myself" back in the '50s, right?

Some dating services charge thousands of dollars for very personalized service, and there's a middle level as well in the hundreds-of-dollars range. Newmark still doesn't charge anything for the personals services, although he says he has considered hosting images and charging for that. I asked him whether the service would likely be popular with professionals. "We figure we'll donate the proceeds to the St. James Infirmary [a health organization that ministers to sex workers]; they never get a break…if they want to contribute to their own health."

I asked Newmark how a community like craigslist develops a communal sense of ethics. He pointed to common sense and reasonable morality, saying, "Most people are moderate. Most people want to get on with their lives and give other people a break."

The community also has a mechanism for dealing with the inevitable antisocial visitors: the user-driven flagging system tends to weed the garden pretty well. Again Newmark reminded me, "It's the job of customer service to work with tech to improve the service." "Is that the genius part?" I asked him, "Well, I don't know about genius," was his reply, "but it's the beauty part, isn't it?" That thing of paying attention to what customers ask for and what line workers say they need to do their job better—that magic of systems that learn just through transparent accountability.

Open-Source Dating

One open-source approach to mapping relationships that has caught on is called FOAF (for "Friend of a Friend"). It uses a resource description framework (RDF) vocabulary to enable individuals to make assertions about who they know and the nature of their relationship to each person in the form of an XML file that can be maintained on one's own server (or along with a blog, for example) or hosted in a central location by a third-party service.

Six Apart's TypePad-hosted weblog service automatically generates a FOAF file from the blogger's About page and from their links to other people. Some have complained that this dumbs down the potential of FOAF, but others are glad to see it adopted, even in a rudimentary form, by a software developer, because even the perfect standard is useless if it doesn't become, well, standard.

The current dating services are very expensive on a per-contact basis. Only eHarmony offers any degree of granularity of detail (and the jury is out on how well self-classification works), and eHarmony is the most expensive of the popular services. As Christopher Filkins put it, "The cost is really heavy when you consider the number of initial contacts needed to get a good taste of what is out there."

Filkins isn't trying to reinvent the wheel. He's "simply building a new namespace" for FOAF (an RDF dialect of XML—that's probably more than you wanted to know already—don't get me started on LOAF):

> The current methodology for dating services is that the point of contact between the profiles is the boogie for the business model. I want to turn that on its head and make that point of contact free. This should produce some very interesting results and may even produce an ecosystem of developers and apps around the core namespace.

(Filkins kindly explained to me that *boogie* is "a very old medical term for a device used to hold open a slit in the skin to allow the work of leeches on the blood. In other words, the current business model relies upon control of that single point of contact. Take that away and the current business model for dating services on the Web simply disappears.")

Would anyone be able to make money in the kind of revamped, open-source-driven dating market Filkins envisions his Dating Syndicate bringing about? He sees a business model in managing privacy for a fee. The namespace anticipates this, but, as he says, "I don't see a very large margin. I am specifically trying to cut out all the profit from online dating. I know that a slice will be available for profit once the costs of running the service are factored in. But to be honest, I haven't explored what the actual pricing would be. I imagine it will be something like $1 to $5 a month. Of course, if one is willing to make your dating syndicate FOAF file on a public server, the system is free."

Mark Pincus, the founder of Tribe Network (Tribe.net) thinks his kind of site is an interim solution until people get comfortable with the idea of exposing more (non-secret) information about themselves to the Internet, simply because it turns out to be rewarding. In a nutshell, people and things and activities that you want find their way to you more easily. Filkins agrees, "It is my contention that managing identity online is a huge issue. At some point, a killer app will be developed to manage this interface between public identity, private identity, and anonymity."

Marc Canter of BroadBand Mechanics, another prolific blogger, is working on a web application called PeopleAggregrator that is built around the FOAF standard. The service offers an open-source platform for creating one's online identity. Filkins suggested that the Dating Syndicate's FOAF namespace extension could share information with services like PeopleAggregrator, noting however that "any system would have to work under the license and make its data available to other tools." PeopleAggregrator uses FOAF as its glue but provides a convenient graphical interface for anyone to create their own profile and connect to other people in the system. The XML framework is kept hidden.

There's already a search engine called Plink (for "people link") that harvests available FOAF information from public websites to map relationships. If you search for a person and they're in the database, Plink shows you who else that person knows (or claims to know, via FOAF). One criticism of FOAF is that there is, as of yet, no way to verify reciprocal relationships, so I can claim that I am a friend of Justin Timberlake, even if he doesn't know me from Adam.

It can also be disconcerting for people who don't know that their Type-Pad blog or DeanLink entry has automatically generated FOAF information for them and is now populating a third-party database.

One other open-source approach to friends and relationships is called XFN, which stands for XHTML Friends Network. XFN relies on users inserting metadata tags into the headers of their personal web pages to declare machine-readable relationships with the owners of the other sites.

Although he is working with FOAF, Filkins doesn't hesitate to criticize how both FOAF and XFN are currently oriented:

> Both FOAF and XFN, as they are currently designed, seem to go in the opposite direction of what is needed for dating. As someone looking for a date, I'm not so interested in whether you know person A or person B. Certainly if you approach dating from a perspective that you, knowing person A or B, would be willing to set me up with one of them, then these are viable approaches. Maybe this speaks to my world view, but I don't want friends or acquaintances setting me up on dates. The politics involved in things not working out can be difficult for all involved. Not to mention, actively seeking dates through people you know seems to be a way to get friends intimately involved in your life in a way that doesn't always seem that healthy for the friendship.

As the air gets thick with three- and four-letter acronyms, we are once again reminded that we are still in a realm subject to the decisions of geeks. As the Web's pervasiveness continues a change more of quality than scale, the online demographics continue to approach those of the real world.

How thoroughly it penetrates (American, primarily, at first) well-to-do culture is still up in the air, but at the moment the wires are still showing and the alienness of engineer-designed social interfaces and vocabularies is still hampering development. Fortunately, we have people like Craig Newmark, who speak for those who have felt left out. (Maybe it's clearer to refer to the ham-radio techie personality as "geekiness" and reserve the word *nerd* for the social nebbish connotation?)

Dating is, of course, just one form of face-to-face socializing, if a rather urgent one at various times in our lives. Services such as Meetup.com and Dodgeball.com provide many other contexts for social interaction attached to activities and shared interests that can as easily lead to friendship as to romance.

Parsing Human Relations: A Simple Matter of Programming

The term *computer dating* has been around at least since the time of *The Bob Newhart Show*. The stereotype persists to this day: a refuge for losers and misfits. *Mad TV*'s "Lowered Expectations" comedy sketches are a more recent example. People respond to these jokes because we all feel instinctively that no computer program is going to capture the essence of friendship, let alone love.

University of California graduate student danah boyd is a hands-on sociological researcher who participates in online environments unreservedly (and who attends Burning Man); she has also consulted with Tribe Networks on their social network model. As she pointed out to me, it is primarily marginalized people who pioneer digital social network systems. "The utopian view is everybody wants to meet people," she says, but in fact, high school jocks (to make just one generalization) aren't going to look for friends online because they don't need to.

Teens, says boyd, prepopulate all the successful network sites, going back to Usenet, whose old flavor is now more fully embodied by Yahoo! Groups. Something similar may be going on with LiveJournal.

Friendster was one of the first SNSs to appear that was designed for friendship and dating as opposed to business networking. While still in beta as of this writing, it's already considered "over" by a lot of the people who originally signed up for it enthusiastically. One complaint about Friendster is that the terms of service are too strict. If you try to use the network for anything not in its charter, you can be banned. Such a reaction may miss the point of a beta stage; when developing new kinds of software, it's often a good idea to notice what your actual users really want to do and how they are manipulating the system to get what they want. This can be a clue to the direction that your software's feature set should take.

For example, a number of people set up fake Friendster identities, commonly referred to as Fakesters, usually fictional or historical characters. You might log in to Friendster to learn that "Jesus Christ" would like to be your friend. Most participants found these fake entities amusing. For one thing, they provided a kind of neutral bridge to other people you might not otherwise meet. Anyone unamused by such characters could simply decline to become friends with them. But the management of Friendster didn't like the Fakesters and eliminated them from the system. This led some Friendster users to protest and even set up an entirely new network for Fakesters (which, unfortunately, outside of the original context, didn't offer the same amusement value).

Each new SNS that emerges tends to pick and choose from the palette of successes and failures of its predecessors. Friendster, for example, makes you identify yourself as male or female; Tribe.net gives a third option, "I would prefer not to say;" and Flickr offers the choices of male, female, and other. Then again, Orkut came after Friendster and Tribe but reverted to the binary gender identification that some people object to, either because they don't want you to know their gender when encountering their online presence or because they identify with some kind of fluid concept of gender that doesn't fit into the traditional scheme.

Generally, there's some new twist introduced with each new system to justify its existence. For example, Tribe's fundamental organizing structure is based on the concept of people with related interests (tribes). Ryze, the business networking tool, also uses the tribe terminology to describe interest or affinity groups.

Orkut has a "crush" feature in which you can register the fact that you are attracted to another person within the system. This does nothing beyond putting the person on your crush list, *unless* they also admit to having a crush on you. In that case, Orkut notifies both people of the mutual attraction. I was told by danah boyd that, as a general rule, men initiate the vast majority of contacts on most social network systems. (I happen to know that none of my many crushes are reciprocated!)

People still disagree strongly on whether dating, friendship, and business networking should be done in the same context or segregated somehow. Most services focus in one or more areas (although some, such as Orkut or People-Aggregrator, deliberately blur the line), but that doesn't stop people from doing deals on Friendster or dating someone they met at a local Ryze business networking event.

When I discussed this with boyd, she reminded me that 1970s-era second-wave feminism made the case that sexualizing the workplace or the business networking environment is something that most women don't want or don't feel is appropriate. I don't know what third-wave feminists might have to tell me about this.

The Awkwardness of Ranking Your Friends and Lovers

Many social network systems provide interfaces for rating your friends in a number of areas. For example, Orkut lets you grant one, two, or three symbols representing trustworthiness, coolness, and sexiness (sounds scientific, eh?). Orkut also allows you to declare yourself a "fan" of any of your friends. For the more subjective minded, there's also a way to write testimonials that don't have any numerical value but can be used to explain in plain English why you think someone else is nice or cool or whatever.

Any system that asks you to explicitly rate your friends in a number of areas—whether they use numerical grades or silly little icons—is asking you to quantify something that, in real life, is rarely ever put in those terms. (Isn't that what Harriet the Spy got in trouble for doing in her private notebooks when they were discovered by her friends?)

Yes, people—usually children—do sometimes rank their friends, but even then the relationships are generally fluid and rapidly changing. Is there any way a computerized system can keep up with the changing nature of relationships, let alone even get a single snapshot of the current state of the system correct?

Considering how subjective these things are, it seems that there would always be gross distortions in any one person's database. Perhaps that would smooth out somewhat in the longer view and add some kind of value to the entire data repository, but it's hard to know. At this point, it seems unlikely to me that you could capture all the dimensions and nuances of human relationships through a series of rankings and assertions.

Yahoo! engineer Jeremy Zawodny speculated in his weblog about the possible uses for a "FriendRank" concept, a way of quantifying influential "friend nodes" in a social network. He imagines a politician seeking his vote and trying to find the shortest path to him through a social network:

> Social networks don't always use the shortest path—at least not in the "six degrees of Kevin Bacon" sense. Often times they use the most well-lubricated path. Or the path that may result in reaching the greatest number of people who are "close" to me. Or those that have more influence with me in matters of politics, as opposed to something completely unrelated like cat grooming.

Nothing is that simple, really. When I first read about the RELATIONSHIP vocabulary mentioned in Chapter 7, "Doing Business with Strangers," I honestly thought it was a joke. Sadly, it is not. A recent visit to the specification for the vocabulary revealed that its creators are still adding to the list such terms as lostContactWith and apprenticeTo. They now have exactly 33 possible relations that can exist between two people; I'm sure the job of fully limiting human interaction will be tidied up soon. Fortunately, the vocabulary *is* RDF- and FOAF-friendly. Clay Shirky nails the whole project dead to rights:

> The whole list is like that—we get friendOf, then for a semantic richness bonus, closeFriendOf. But if we're going that route, where's veryCloseFriendOf? sleepsWith? usedToSleepWith? Where's wentToHighSchoolWith? … [O]nce we go the route of disallowing certain characterizations, we are destroying real-world meaning in the name of controlled vocabulary, a strategy that is internally consistent but useless. …

> The RELATIONSHIP list should make it obvious that explicit linguistic clarity in human relations is a pipe dream. It probably won't though—the madness of the age is to assume that people can spell out, in explicit detail, the messiest aspects of their lives, and that they will eagerly do so in order to provide better inputs to cool new software.

Shirky points out that mapping out relationships with linguistic clarity is "a pipe dream." I'm reminded of all the attempts, which I studied as a philosophy major, to derive language from logical or algebraic principles, all incomplete, inherently. In the meantime, entrepreneurs are investing in schemes that rely on people eagerly spelling out, "in explicit detail, the messiest aspects of their lives…to provide better inputs to cool new software."

Mark Pincus, the founder of Tribe.net, says that people will slowly learn that giving the network—whether they think of it as the Internet, or as some instantiation of Google, or as a SN interface—more (nonsecret) information about themselves results in the network being better able to provide you with what it discovers you need. This is not to say that people are wrong to be wary of sharing their private information with strangers. We need safeguards that address how information is disseminated and used, but the fact remains that those who offer a robust online presence will tend to be "found" more easily.

A recent job interviewer told me that he doesn't look at resumes anymore. "I just Google the person," he said. "If they've been doing anything, it should be out there."

Karma and Reputation Management

One of the benefits of large groups of people congregating online is that they can collaborate on such things as filtering the news, rating products and services, or vouching for each other. Services like eBay have a facility for rating a person based on how well your transaction went and how responsive they were. Before you agree to buy or sell with someone, you can look at their karma and see how others have rated them.

Similarly, news/discussion sites such as Slashdot and kuro5hin have features that enable people to rate each other's entries. You can set your view of the site to exclude any entries whose ratings are below the threshold you set, which means that you rely on others to determine what is worth reading. In some of these systems, people with high karma can attain a trusted user status that enables them to play more of an administrative role at the site.

As social network software matures, it will need to have some way to manage people's reputations.

A Great Way to Collect Marketing Data

Dating and making friends can be an end in itself, but one criticism often voiced about today's online social network tools is that they don't actually do anything. After the initial buzz of signing up, finding people you already know, and adding them to your network wears off, it's not clear what you can actually do at many of these sites.

Yes, you can set up your own group, community, or tribe or join existing ones. Then you can do the sorts of things that people have always done online, post to message boards and notify each other of upcoming events. But beyond that, there's still little to be gained, and with each new service offering its own proprietary interface, you are faced with the prospect of once again entering your likes and dislikes or coming up with yet another online persona. I've noticed on Orkut, for example, that profiles will often start with a disclaimer along the lines of "Pasted from Friendster," because the participant didn't feel like generating an entirely new set of original and clever self-descriptions.

One thing that's missing from these systemts is a public, distributed, portable online identity. If I want to comment on your weblog, I have to enter a name and usually an email address or website. Your blog may remember who I am the next time I come back (if I have cookies enabled, if you offer that feature, and if I opt into it), but when I show up at someone else's blog, the process starts over, unless both of you happen to be using the same backend service to manage your comments.

Why can't I instead register my identity information in one secure trusted place and then when I need to log in to a new site to comment or participate, why can't I just point to the identity server and have it supply my bona fides? This would make it much easier to join multiple social networks using the same identifying information. If the services aren't willing to interoperate smoothly out of fear of losing their lock on your data, then third-party developers can just make up common standards and route around the discontinuities.

A lot of venture capital money is going into social network systems these days. Already people are talking about another Internet bubble like the one that ended in 2000, because it isn't clear what the business model is going to be. Sites such as Ryze enable you to sign up for free (it's hard to get critical mass in any system without enabling people to join for free), but then offer additional services for paid members.

One speculation I had was that the kind of functionalities being tested now in SNSs will end up trickling over into other sites that already serve another purpose. If people could incorporate social networking with their other online activities as a way of finding out "who else is on," that might make sense.

Flickr.com is a social network site that ties together the networking aspect (you can rate people as acquaintances, friends, best buddies, or soul mates, but you can't escalate to the next level unless the other person has already reciprocated at the lower echelon) with instant messaging and a service geared toward image exchange.

Mediachest.com enables its users to organize their media collection (books, CDs, DVDs, video games) and then loan them to other people in their social network.

Regardless of what the benefit is for the user, one clear benefit for anyone creating and hosting a social network is the huge amount of self-described data that can be harvested from the network. If you can mine that information to discern trends or commonalities of interest (the way Amazon tells you that people who bought this book also bought that book), then there could be a number of sales and marketing applications for that information.

Perhaps I'm paranoid. I still refuse to accept those grocery store discount cards, because I can't be sure it is a fair exchange for giving the corporation a running account of my purchases.

Many people fear a too-intrusive government, and others worry about corporate interests as well. Perhaps most disturbing for people is the fear of losing control over what you reveal and when. Julie Cohen, a professor at Georgetown Law Center and a privacy expert, says that people have a right to partial disclosure and should not be forced to reveal—for example—personal information at work (which is why there are laws preventing an interviewer from requiring you to state your age or political or religious affiliations). This right is backed up in our case law, and yet the Internet—and particularly the YASNs—are getting around this check on intrusions into our existing privacy rights.

Indeed, as the government privatizes and outsources its data-collection (such as the voter roll management process that led to widespread disenfranchisement in Florida in the 2000 presidential election), the strictures that prevent governments from misusing such data are evaded and the information potentially enters the commercial marketplace.

Because the world of romance and dating involves issues of privacy and information you might not want everyone to know, services that can offer some form of anonymity or that can keep your social or sexual preferences private have advantages over those that create the equivalent of a public want ad that anyone can read. The opponents of a journalist who is also a popular blogger discovered an explicit relationship ad he had posted at a site for gay men with HIV. Although he removed his ad soon afterward, his enemies made backups and still point to it in order to shame him. And about a year ago, a political consultant was drummed out of D.C. when his online swinger ads were made public. Although there may be no shame in seeking sexual relationships, almost everyone can think of some people in their lives or in the world whom they would not want studying their erotic desires.

I asked Christopher Filkins how his open-source Dating Syndicates architecture model would protect privacy. He said, "Everyone who is a contributor to the network will have full access to every other profile which fits the viewer's profile." Filkins is aware that he has to design the system so that it defends itself against people trying to harvest contact or personal or identity information from the system:

> That is one of the problems. Ultimately the system is designed to make it very difficult to game, but anyone with an overwhelming desire to do so, the patience, and the skills will surely be able to. For instance, I could go into the system and create a new profile which was all about S&M so that I could peruse folks who are into that, even if I am not. I am exploring several different options for dissuading this type of behavior. I'm not sure what the answer is.

Filkins anticipates a system of federated access, something like what Six Apart—a popular blogging software maker—seems to be doing with its TypeKey authentication standard (which will tie in with both TypePad and Movable Type 3.0, as well as with anyone else who wants to work with the format).

Says Filkins, "The idea here is that in order to access the full contents namespace (all the files in the network, both public and private), the tool maker will have to make their files available to other tool makers while at the same time ensuring that members' files are only revealed through matching." He's still working on the central "widget" that can do the matching.

At first, Filkins thought that the problems he's addressing are unique to dating. But when pressed, he conceded that, "This would work very well for job searches as well. But I don't know enough about that space or the needs of employers to really know for sure." As with dating, any successful implementation would need to achieve a critical mass whose size is not determined yet.

At the same time, the popularity of online dating has spawned the two-headed hound from hell known as dating spam. Hardly a day passes that my spam filters don't trap yet another come-on to explore a dating service, couched in the form of a fake notification that someone has set me up on a date or someone is searching for me on their network. Inevitably, if you click through to the site, you are asked to sign up and start exploring, and the cyberhotty who wants you never shows up.

As spam strategies go, it's a fairly good one; who doesn't want to learn they have a secret admirer? By pretending that you can passively plug in and immediately hook up with someone, the spammers lure you into participating in their business. In the long run, it doesn't seem sustainable, and any business that markets itself through spam is suspect.

It's also possible that such entire sites are fake, with no real entries in them at all. As with any other kind of service, it's important to know who you're dealing with, and known brands provide that kind of reassurance. This is probably one of the reasons why Yahoo! Personals is a leader in that marketplace. People trust Yahoo! and may not have heard of reputable sites such as Nerve, eHarmony, or Match.com.

In the future, we may all be engaged in actively grooming whitelists and blacklists of accepted and banned IP addresses, domains, identities, and brands in order to filter out both spam and lower-quality information. At the same time, people living online implicitly associate themselves with others through links to information about other people in their representations of selves online. Right now, a link is viewed by Google or Technorati as an endorsement for the linked resource, but some have proposed more nuanced linking systems (sometimes called "vote links") that would enable a person to spin a link as explicitly positive, neutral, or negative—enabling someone, for example, to link to an objectionable view while at the same time disavowing it.

Already, the karma system at sites such as Slashdot enables people to publicly vote on each other's worth or value. Mary Hodder imagines a future in which vote links are used

> to filter people, or particular qualities, or whatever. I think the greatest fear we have regarding privacy is that fear we have over each other, access we give to others to sensitive information about ourselves. And I'm guessing, but I think it is a tacit, under-the-rug fear, not articulated but very prevalent in what is behind our decision making on the Web and in our associations online. In the U.S., we have very little protection, versus in the EU, where for now they have tremendous blanket protections in comparison.

> In the loss of privacy, the control we lose is over information we have given to other people.

> Privacy is a double-edged sword. The withering away of privacy may help catch some evildoers, but human dignity will always requires a private realm of conscience. Still, the Internet is hell on secrets.

Sources and Further Reading

Read these web pages and books for more detail on the ideas in this chapter. Also, see the "Sources and Further Reading" section at the end of Chapter 7, because the two topics—business networking and social circles—share many common ideas and tools.

> One list of social networking sites and software:
> http://www.typaldos.blogspot.com/#socialnetworkingsitesandsw

> Jeremy Zawodny, "FriendRank," *Jeremy Zawodny's blog*:
> http://jeremy.zawodny.com/blog/archives/001324.html

Michael Fitzgerald, "Call It the Dead E-Mail Office," *Wired*, June 7, 2004, on how Lawrence Lessig declared "e-mail bankruptcy":
http://www.wired.com/news/culture/0,1284,63733,00.html?tw=wn_tophead_7

"RELATIONSHIP: A vocabulary for describing relationships between people," a set of 33 terms to be used to describe human relations within databases and markup documents:
http://vocab.org/relationship

Clay Shirky's analysis of RELATIONSHIP, *Many-2-Many*, March 16, 2004:
http://www.corante.com/many/archives/2004/03/16/relationship_a_vocabulary_for_describing_relationships_between_people.php

Chapter 9   Tom Sawyer Whitewashes a Fence

> I think the Internet, the blogging, is the closest we've come in a long time to the history of the American media in the beginning. You know, in the 1820s, 1830s, all you needed to be a journalist was to buy a press. That's why they called them inkstained wretches: because they operated their own hand presses. For a little bit of money, like Tom Payne and others, you could have your own press. … After the revolution, independent journalists—printers, they called themselves—sprung up all over the country. … They were partisan by the way, vociferously. They attacked the others' politics, but it was a healthy period of bombast in America in which people could sort out the information. I think the bloggers, then the websites, come closest to the spirit of cacophony, to that democratic expression, that we had in the early part of this country's history.
>
> —BILL MOYERS, in an interview on
> National Public Radio's *Fresh Air*

It started with a conference call I missed. I heard about it on my answering machine. On the line were two of my friends, a publisher and an editor, respectively, at a publishing house with whom I've had a long and fruitful relationship. They had an idea for a book, and they wanted me to hear them out before turning it down.

I'm a writer. Any time a publisher calls me up to convince me to do a book, I'm all ears. I called them back the same day. They were following the Dean Internet effort, and they had also noticed the Internet being used more widely by charities and by neighborhood organizations. They wondered whether there was a "bigger picture" there. Was there a trend, and if so, was there a book about it? Perhaps something about digital civic organizing or online nonprofit efforts. They were close, but they didn't know it. I pointed out that the same kinds of things were happening in commercial endeavors—business networking, dating services, knowledge management, and many other areas.

I had lived in discussions like these for years, through my research and reporting on blogging and other online phenomena, so I knew that "digital organizing" (their original, clumsy phrase) wasn't limited to politics, to activism, or to organizing large groups of people to get things done. I knew there was a "there" there—something new is changing everything. We kicked the idea around for another week while I tried to determine whether there was any way that I could write a book in time to catch the wave.

There was one way.

I'd have to accelerate my research and start interviewing and writing, all at the same time, and hope that by the time the book was finished, it would all add up. Even more important, I was going to need all the help I could get from my personal online network of friends, acquaintances, and colleagues assembled over the course of the last decade.

Many Hands Make Light Work

In fact, it occurred to me, the only way to make this book work would be to engage fully in whatever social media or communications tools were at my disposal to enlist the aid of all the people who knew so much more about this topic than I did. This was going to be a publishing project and a communications project, one that would involve telephone, email, instant messaging, and YASNs left and right. I would need to track down memes from the blogosphere and somehow freeze them into some marketable package that could be published, informative, and relevant in time for the upcoming presidential election, without going instantly stale in six months.

I think it was physicist Niels Bohr who said, "Prediction is difficult, especially about the future." I was going out on some limbs, so I went looking for some sturdy ones with a bunch of people already out there testing the tensile strength.

There are currently over 60 people in the links sidebar of this book's blog—the core of an XFN-based social network. There is also the Orkut group, which turned mainly into a feeble broadcast email system for telling people when a new chapter is ready for feedback and for soliciting advice and suggestions, but with no way of letting me know who wasn't checking their messages or having them forwarded into their mail anymore.

I interviewed dozens of people by a half dozen different means. Many others volunteered to review one or more chapters just to help out. (I name all the names in the acknowledgments and on the book's blog. Everyone deserves more thanks than I can give them there or anywhere else.)

Completing this project in an incredibly short period of time was possible because of today's technology. Increased collaboration is only one of the effects that digital technologies have had on the publishing industry—or more broadly speaking, the media industry, or even more broadly speaking, the information business.

From Hot Lead to Hot Wax to Hot Links (in One Generation, or One Century?)

In the beginning, the Web was viewed by many people as a publishing medium, a cheaper, easier, and more democratic way of making public written (and other) materials. Academics used it to share their research quickly while waiting to be published in peer-reviewed journals. Zine publishers saw it as an extension of the desktop-publishing-plus-copy-machine revolution of the '80s.

The metaphor for the Web's publishing revolution is Gutenberg's printing press of the 15th century. Of course Gutenberg didn't invent printing. I think the Chinese did. But up to that time printing meant impressing entire pages one at a time, which meant carving blocks to represent (in reverse) the entire content of each page. Gutenberg's innovation was to create elements to represent whole words or even individual characters that could be arranged manually in rows in any combination. In a sense, this was the first step in digitizing publishing: breaking something down into its smaller component parts for easier manipulation.

When I was born in the early '60s, it was still not uncommon for printers to use hot lead, a mechanical process not too far removed from Gutenberg's blocks of text. My father worked in the printing business and used to bring home print dummies for his children to draw in as well as books on typography and type design—thus began my fascination with publishing and communication. In this period, phototypesetting began to come into play. The letterforms created by exposing bits of film through letter-shaped stencils were much sharper than those created by stamping ink on paper with hot lead. Furthermore, through the use of lenses, a single-font strip could be used to generate a wide range of type sizes. These innovations changed the nature of publishing fundamentally, altering the economics and the skill sets involved. They also brought an end to the manual process of assembling lines of type and began a trend of greater reliance on technological automation, including dedicated computer technology.

In the late '70s I edited my high school's weekly paper. We typed our articles on an old CompuGraphic machine that had a single line of display, something like an old stock ticker with no editing function beyond the ability to backspace before each line was entered and set. The photographic output had to be developed with caustic chemicals and then run through a waxer and pasted directly onto bluelined layout pages. Eventually, the school upgraded to a newer CompuGraphic machine that had *memory*! It could store files on 9-inch floppy disks! It could display a good 20 or so lines of text at once! Ah, the breakthroughs that look so quaint now.

In college I edited another weekly paper and presided over the upgrade to digital technology. As soon as we determined that the new Macintosh machine was capable of generating digitized type that was close enough in quality to the phototypeset copy, we raised money and made the switch, going from a dedicated technology to the multipurpose world of personal computers. The digitized type was inferior to the phototypeset type, but of course printing presses were undergoing their own digitization revolution during the same period.

Around this time, most of the professional publishing world was grappling with the transition to digital.

Out of college, I eventually found work in the book publishing world and watched its processes evolve as well. The entire editorial staff shared one portable (or rather "luggable") computer, and we did all our editing in red pencil on typescript. A staff of word processors entered our changes; there was a separate department of expert typesetters. The page designers and layout artists used the exact same kind of waxer I had used in high school and college to make up news pages.

The publisher (the same one publishing this book) specialized in covering technology, so it was hard for us editors and authors not to notice the changes occurring around us. I used to sit in the office of a colleague and we'd talk about a not-too-distant future in which publishing would become an ever-more electronic affair, and where virtual publishing collectives might prove more nimble than a dedicated in-house staff.

Disrupting the Darkroom

Photography has experienced the same kind of revolution as publishing. In the early '90s, the industry argued about whether digital images would *ever* completely replace film; by the mid '90s, most in the industry assumed that film would be dead within five years. Well, the truth lay in the middle: film will be edged aside, but at a pace and in ways that nobody expected. Most technological innovations—especially those that can be demonstrated easily, such as those used to capture and record information (such as cameras and tape recorders)—have boosters who underestimate and opponents who over-estimate the time it will take for the change to ripple through the old way of doing things.

Similarly, back in the publishing world, there was what I like to call "the great e-book scare of '99," when I kept hearing that the book as we know it is doomed, to be replaced, real soon now, by electronic books (or e-books). The advantages seemed obvious: no trees killed, all the flexibility of digital content, and so on. The disadvantages were equally obvious, usually summed up in terms of "You can't read them in the bathtub or at the beach."

As with many of the utopian visions that came to the fore in the mid '90s, the idea that conventional publishing was obsolete and that new forms of digitally mediated publishing will take over was probably correct, but they tended to vastly understate the transitional period involved in making such a change. At least one generation will probably pass before the type of book you are holding in your hands is no longer the most common way to obtain and consume written information.

What the e-book visionaries got right is that the printing business forces publishing into a small range of forms, and excludes materials that do not fit the book or magazine format. If a piece of writing is longer than a magazine article and shorter than a book, there is no commercial way to sell it (at least not without bundling it into something like a collection of essays). An e-publication, by contrast, can be any length, removing the need for gratuitous cutting or padding just to suit a sales-channel niche.

The e-book scare came and went and—aside from the consolidation over a decade of mergers and acquisitions—the great book publishing houses remain standing. They all continue to experiment with other ways of repurposing their content in electronic forms, and no doubt some form of electronic smart paper—flexible, browsable, and easy in the hands—will come along and make e-books a reality.

In Usenet parlance, this story would be titled, "Imminent Death of Publishing Predicted, Film at Eleven." Of course it's much more likely that publishing will evolve. At the margins, some new players (nanopublishers?) will emerge, and perhaps some older ones will fail to make the transition. In the meantime, I don't expect paper books to ever disappear. More likely, their use will be reserved for long-lasting, high-quality material and for more precious art books and the like. Ephemeral information is more appropriately published in an electronic medium. And who would begrudge a schoolchild the opportunity to lug around a single e-book or tablet reader as opposed to the 20 pounds of hardcover textbooks injuring their lower backs these days?

The idea of what is a book has changed before. The ancient words for *book* (such as *liber* in Latin) referred to scrolls, the then-dominant long form for publishing. What we call a *book* today—cut-up pieces of paper stacked atop each other—was referred to until the Middle Ages as a *codex*. We will know the e-book revolution has occurred when the word *e-book* goes away and good old *book* is used simply to refer to handheld electronic information bundles. A new word will have to be coined for paper books.

Don't believe me? You differentiate between a "guitar" and an "acoustic guitar," don't you?

Technology evolves, and we will create digital phenomena to provide us with new channels for accessing and consuming information. However, the more radical evolution in publishing is not so much in the form and production methods and pricing models, but in the nature of authorship and the author.

Shifting the Value Proposition

One of the promises of syndication (or webfeeds, or pubsub, or RSS, or whatever you want to call the whole enchilada) is that it represents an entirely different business model from publishing, e-publishing, or nanopublishing. By publishing microcontent or notifications in an RSS feed, a business is selling, among other things, time savings.

For the writer of a weblog or the creator of content for any form of nanopublishing or niche publishing, the value is still the ideas contained in the wrapper. It's very hard to sell content, though. It's much easier to sell time savings, with metadata and syndication. As the penetration of RSS-type news- or feed-readers reaches a majority of people online, the model of counting page clicks will start making less sense.

In the long run, though, the syndication model can give books a run for their money. People will still want books to take to the beach, but these books might be MP3s on an iPod, something downloaded last night onto a tablet, or maybe even something flexible and waterproof!

As members of communities and social networks collaboratively filter information sources and direct traffic on a huge scale, the economics of information flow will be turned inside out. In the disruption, some large companies will find that their slice of the pie isn't where it's at anymore. Some will adjust. Inevitably new intermediaries will sell services around the new information flows, much the same way that Technorati.com is right now looking for ways to mine the data of millions of bloggers and offer something useful enough to bring in revenues some day.

Participatory Journalism

In the beginning (we imagine) people sat around camp fires telling each other stories. Some people were better at this than others, and perhaps they became the bards or shamans who could spellbind the tribe with their words, but there was nothing stopping anyone from speaking up.

We are all naturally storytellers and narrators when we construct our memories and ideas of ourselves. It's how our minds work. We may be more comfortable ceding the floor to the expert storytellers and master narrators, but we all possess those same skills to some degree, and in fact we are each the most knowledgeable, most expert, best-prepared person to speak about one topic or another, if only reporting on our own internal states.

In many ways, the Web provides a global "open mic," where anyone can speak and be heard. Of course, this doesn't guarantee an audience. Not everyone wants the attention, the audience, the scrutiny. Some people really are more talented communicators than others. But on the Web, we can tell any story we like, no matter our level of skill or our access to an audience.

The Web is challenging the monopoly on expression that large corporate publishing entities have held for the last few centuries. Although not everyone is guaranteed an audience, just about anybody can get up on the Web soapbox and tell their version of reality. Some of the people who might otherwise never have been heard now have a forum in which to speak. A good example of this is a site called Correspondences.org, whose motto is "News by the people for the people."

San Jose Mercury News technology columnist Dan Gillmor publishes a daily weblog and a weekly print column, usually culled from the topics he has blogged about. Anyone interested in seeing his stories or perspectives developing can follow his blog. He also uses the blog as an interactive medium, seeking insight, corrections, and expertise from his readers. Gillmor has often remarked, "My readers know more than I do." He explains that there is no way he can be the ultimate authority on everything he writes about. Inevitably, somebody out there knows more about whatever the subject of the day is. Although a journalist's job is to track down experts and convey their insights, Dan also invites those people to come forward of their own accord and share their knowledge with him, giving them the media access they might not otherwise be able to obtain, while at the same time strengthening his sources and his conclusions.

Gillmor is working on his own book on the effects of blogging on journalism. True to form, he published his book proposal, outline, and even drafts of his chapters in progress on his weblog as a way of soliciting advance feedback from readers:

> My editors and I are most interested in your immediate feedback on:
>
> - What's missing—that is, a topic or perfect anecdote that absolutely has to be included.
>
> - More important, what's wrong? If there's a factual error I want to fix it before the book is published.
>
> In both cases I'll ask that you send me e-mail ... and please include your phone number in case I need to contact you. Otherwise, feel free to comment on and discuss (or ignore) what you've read in the comment-posting area.

One of the great buzzwords of the Internet age is "disintermediation," which means removing the monopoly of a media elite class over the interpretation of information. The Internet cuts out the middleman in any number of ways, not just in terms of information. However, the truth is that new middlemen arise—those who can provide guidance, aggregation, filtering, or other methods of enabling ordinary readers to sort through the surfeit of information and opinions proliferating online.

Buying a Press

Freelance journalist Dave Neiwert wrote, "Journalism is kind of like the weather. We all like to complain about it, but none of us ever do anything about it." He has gone on to do something about it ... and now most of us can too.

In the last century in the United States, one had freedom of the press as long as one owned a printing press. In this day and age, one needs only a free or cheap blog account with hosting to get in on the public conversation. (Then again, I prefer to run my own server and host my own data for exactly the reason that I feel freer knowing that no one else can unilaterally turn off my spigot.)

Nanopublishing entrepreneur Nick Denton, whose Gawker media publishes a series of niche-oriented, blog-driven, ad-supported publications, explains the revolution in these terms:

> The only time, in traditional media, when you get to express yourself is when you're 60 and no longer have any opinions that speak to the person you once were. Blogs allow those types of writers to circumvent the usual journalistic training program. It allows them to have the voice they have when they're young, without having it knocked out of them.

The blogging world has gone around and around on blogging and journalism. Is blogging journalism? Should journalists blog? The fact is that blogging can be journalism and is in some ways much closer to American ("yellow") journalism, in exactly the sense that Bill Moyers pointed out in the interview on *Fresh Air* quoted at the head of this chapter.

Blog-evangelist Dave Winer believes that journalists acting as middlemen between experts and readers can be crossed out of the equation entirely. He would prefer that experts report on their own knowledge (in weblogs) and let the readers sort it out for themselves.

But few people believe that blogging spells the end of journalism in the traditional sense. In fact, it's commonplace to note that most of the news-oriented commentary found on weblogs can be traced back to commercial media sources. It's not so much that the disintermediation vanquishes corporate media, but rather that between the two existing poles of publishers and readers, there is now a nearly infinite series of gradients that expand the public conversation at its fringes.

On the other hand, it must be somewhat disconcerting to people who've made their career in the writing and publishing business to find themselves competing with people doing nearly the same thing for free in their spare time.

In some ways, a bigger threat to the traditional newspaper is craigslist, because its classified-ads structure threatens the profit base of most newspapers. At a recent media conference in Berkeley, one news professional remarked that craigslist is "eating our lunch." During the lunchtime schmoozing that is the most interesting part of any conference, another journalist pointed to Craig Newmark and said, "They're all terrified of him." I asked, "Why don't they just copy what he's doing?" but nobody had a solid answer besides pointing to inertia. As Newmark drifted over to join the group, I said, "The twentieth century is dying hard."

Some papers invest in multimedia widgets in order to inject "interactivity" into their online properties. But, says former AOL executive and consultant Susan Mernit, "These things aren't interactive. Clicking to vote in a poll isn't interactive. Plus, AOL and others digest the news, and people want that. Blog items are short; people want headlines and short excerpts, so they can decide which to read further."

As Mary Hodder put it to me,

> Think of this as a situation where people are navigating info, like driving down the freeway; they glance at exit signs, read three words, until they get to their exit. Then they get off and stay. Blogs and RSS are exit signs, pointing the way to specific and longer material.

At the same time, blogs undermine some of the traditional touchstones of journalistic standards and ethics. Many bloggers frankly reject the call for objectivity in most newspapers' guidelines, questioning whether such a thing is at all possible and suggesting that honest partisanship may yield better aggregated results/information than warmed-over "on-the-other-hand"-ism.

David Neiwert has made a specialty of studying proto-fascist movements in the United States. Neiwert feels comfortable pointing the finger at the political right in this country as fellow travelers of some of the more unsavory fringe groups. He complains that the major media have abdicated their watchdog role, and in May 2004, he published a manifesto on his weblog calling for a partisan form of citizen journalism to take on that role. The independence of the news is gone; the filter that journalism used to provide—helping us find out what was important to know—has become instead a bottleneck, where powerful interests prevent us from finding out what really matters.

In fact, no one-size-fits-all service will ever be able to know enough about us to help us that much. It's only through the weighted, aggregated, sifted, and filtered opinions of those whom we trust in our social net that we'll ever be able to find what we're looking for.

> The blogosphere is a direct result of those bottlenecks. Information is now flowing around them through the networks of dissemination that blogs have become.

For Neiwert, blogs serve the traditional journalistic goal of "keeping the public duly and properly informed." They take a wider range of stories to a mass audience than a print-limited or broadcast-limited medium can do. In addition, they provide information relevant to very small niche audiences that wouldn't be profitable for larger outlets to target. As Vin Crosbie recently put it, news of an earthquake in Peru is usually too small for an American paper's morning edition, but it's extremely valuable to the few in the U.S. who have relatives in Peru.

Neiwert points out that this form of reporting is a specific extension of the more general power of many:

> Blogs can also be terrific means for organizing, particularly for putting together a concerted response to political and media atrocities. One need only survey the ability of blogs to affect real-world politics—their role in bringing about the fall of Trent Lott was just a start—to understand that their power can readily extend to reshaping the media, since they represent in themselves a kind of citizens' solution to needed reforms in the media.

> To bring that about, two things are needed: 1) A recognition that this power exists, and 2) Organizing in a thoughtful and effective fashion to wield it.

Eyewitness News

Blogging is only part of the story. In fact, writing and text are only part of the story. The Web is rapidly becoming a multimedia platform. Other digital tools, such as mobile phones with built-in cameras, are enabling on-the-spot citizen reportage that is still very new. The neighbor who videotaped Rodney King's beating in Los Angeles ensured that the police would at least be taken to trial.

Antiwar protesters with camera phones have documented events that would otherwise go unreported, such as their own numbers or the actions of the police.

This is still a fringe activity—most people don't *take* such pictures—but it's already having an impact. More and more police cars are equipped with dashboard video cameras—the better to document arrests. Broadcast of such tapes has helped demystify the policing process, though it has also fed the television audience's hunger for "You are there" coverage of crime.

As this book was going to press, the American military, intelligence, and government infrastructure has been rocked by a prisoner-abuse scandal emanating from Saddam Hussein's former torture chambers at Abu Ghraib. Ironically, the story seems to have come to light because soldiers who are themselves allegedly complicit in the abuse took digital photos in order to further humiliate or threaten the inmates or perhaps simply to amuse themselves and their friends.

When soldiers can take digital snapshots on the battlefield or in the midst of ordinarily classified actions; when military prisons feature Internet cafes where soldiers can maintain weblogs or email photos to their families; when the ability to burn a CD full of photos has become ubiquitous, the so-called "fog of war" begins to lift. This extends the trend of ever-more-ubiquitous, ever-more transparent battlefield reportage that started with photographs of the American Civil War and continued through daily news camera coverage of the Vietnam war.

Internet theorist Clay Shirky also relates Abu Ghraib to the analogy of the Protestant Reformation, in the sense that the end of an information monopoly has begun. Ironically, the initial reaction of the Pentagon chain of command has been to ban the possession of digital camera phones in the war theater. This seems like a futile attempt to lock the barn door after the horse has already escaped. If authoritarian governments have been unable to crack down on text messaging, faxes, cell phones, and the like, what makes military leaders think that a democratic republic will be able to do so more effectively?

The Decentralization of Expertise

So if everyone can be an author, is this the end of expertise? Not really. There is a broadening, a democratization of expertise, but there will always be people who are better informed or better trained in one subject area or another than the rest. What has changed is that these people can tell their own stories and gather their own niche audiences rather than hope to be contacted by the booking agent for a television news show.

At a recent publishing conference, I sat on a panel about the power of many and the impact of Internet organizing on everything from politics to business with SocialText CEO Ross Mayfield, who discussed a book on Internet politics to which he contributed. His company hosted a wiki for the authors, and the book was—last time I checked—being assembled collaboratively in part through the enabling technology of that wiki. Ross suggested to the audience (which consisted mainly of technology writers and publishers) that a new model for reference books might be emerging, in which open source–style collaborations among volunteer collectives of people might outperform any single author or author team or even commercial enterprise. He pointed to the Wikipedia as an example. Already that site is one of the most detailed encyclopedias in the world, and the entire thing is created by its readers and distributed for free under the GNU license.

Some in the audience found this challenge threatening to their role as experts or expert-proxies. Others, such as author Molly Holzschlag, saw it as simply a new entrepreneurial opportunity for publishing professionals. This is the dual nature of any disruptive change. For some, it's an opportunity, but for others, it undermines the whole competitive advantage on which their livelihood is based.

We may be a long way off from group-written novels (although Ken Kesey attempted this with a creative writing class, publishing a book under the group name A.U. Levon). But there's really no reason why certain types of references and other nonfiction information shouldn't be assembled by teams—or at least by one or a few people with the contributions of many. J. D. Lasica has been posting chapters of his forthcoming book on the digital media revolution, *Darknet,* to a wiki for what he calls "group editing."

Similarly, Dan Gillmor's been posting nearly final drafts of his chapters in his eJournal weblog at the *San Jose Mercury News* site, in order to solicit feedback. Each author seems to find a different way to peel the onion, inviting a range of feedback from the members of a limited social network to the entire wired public at large, with their prose in various stages of undress.

Brian Dear has been working on a book about the history of PLATO (which was profiled in Chapter 6, "CultureJamming the Hollywood Monolith") for more than eight years now. To start, he simply posted a web page calling for information about the instructional program and waited for people to find the page in their daily browsing. He wrote on Orkut recently,

> They did. Hundreds of them. Thousands of them. And many of them emailed me, and many did phone interviews. … And in the past two years, on the same website, I've been blogging the progress of the book, now that so many people know about it and want to know how it's going. That too has led to more contacts with folks, and more good material for the book.

Of course, the truth is that publishing (like moviemaking) has nearly always been done by teams of people. One or more of them get their name on the cover and take ultimate responsibility for the authorship and authority embodied in the book, but editors craft the language and structure, reviewers check the facts, contributors supply missing bits of information and insight, and readers submit corrections destined for future revisions.

In the case of this book, my name is on the cover, but the ideas in it largely come from other people, whom I've attempted to credit as completely as possible. My role in this book, in some ways, is to be the person who knows which questions to ask and to whom. The course of contacting sources for this book involved every form of networking I'm capable of, from email and the phone to letter writing and even reaching back through family and college contacts. Some people are still easier to reach than others. Some are online and available for any reasonable communication. Others are famous and employ intermediaries to sift through interview requests and determine how to spend their scarce time.

Blogging a Book in Progress

Still, my name is on the cover of this book, and I do take responsibility for its contents. Also, neither myself nor my publisher is so sanguine about collaboration or so free that we've been willing to expose drafts-in-progress to the public for feedback. Instead, I've asked the people who've agreed to participate as interviewees, reviewers, or advisers to read chapters for me and give me feedback. I've also invited them to participate in several web-based entities, some fully public and others out of sight. As one aspect of this project, I can't imagine writing this book now without the help of The Power of Many blog.

The moment I started writing this book, I also began blogging my notes, largely as a web-accessible way of keeping the relevant hyperlinks available. At the outset, the site was cloaked: it required a password for access, and it didn't notify the world when it was updated. I also invited my editor to post to the weblog, and in the long run, he has provided much of the most compelling content—especially when I've been neck-deep in deadlines. Whenever I interviewed somebody, I gave them the blog's password and invited them to read and comment on it.

When I worked on a chapter, whether the first draft or any of the subsequent rewrites or reviews, I visited the blog (which went public once the book was closer to being done), sorted the entries by chapter, and made sure that I incorporated any leads or insights that had accumulated since the previous draft.

There are two schools of thought about blogging while writing a book, perhaps best exemplified by two popular science fiction writers. William Gibson, probably the best-known writer in the subgenre commonly known as cyberpunk, started a weblog in 2002 and immediately garnered a huge online audience (which is still heavily overrepresented by science-fiction fans). However, when the time came to begin work on his next project, he folded up his blog and stopped posting to it, explaining that he needed privacy in which to incubate his ideas and that blogging about his thoughts removed the urgency that he needed to harness to create his fiction.

By contrast, Cory Doctorow is one of the primary contributors to the massively popular Boing Boing weblog. Doctorow asserts that keeping track of his ideas, thoughts, and links in the site he often refers to as his "outboard brain" only helps in his fiction writing. The difference may be generational, or it may be a matter of temperament.

A Wiki? Are You Xerious?

A high school student named Taylor House, who has a website called Imperious (imp.erio.us), found my experimental literary weblog after I bought an ad (sort of) on Ftrain, Paul Ford's magnum opus. (Actually what I did was send Paul $51 by PayPal, and he deemed that worth two links to my site, *A Supposedly Stagger-ing Infinite Work of Heartbreaking Illumination I'll Never Read.* Paul's secret iden-tity is as a freelance ad copywriter, and both of his text ads drove quite a bit of traffic to my site, essentially sharing an adventurous portion of his own reader base—a fraction of them clicked through, a smaller fraction stayed to read, and an even smaller fraction began coming back to the site whenever anything new was posted.)

Taylor had asked Paul to contribute to a project in which he asked many of the most prominent web writers to tell him what they were writing when they were 16 (House was 16 at the time) or to otherwise offer advice to a writer at 16. Taylor started reading *Infinite Work* and occasionally commenting on the entries there. I got notified of his comments and ventured back by clicking his name to see his Imperious website (which looked at the time a lot like Paul's and had a URL somewhat like Joshua Schachter's deli.cio.us site—so I wasn't really sure who Taylor was or if he was connected with either of those guys). I found his wiki where he was soliciting advice on colleges to apply to, and I offered my two cents.

He came back and found the blog for this book and noticed an entry where I complained that I was having trouble getting wiki software up and running for the book. (My plan is to publish the book's glossary in wiki form and solicit help adding new entries and grooming the existing ones.) House quickly whipped me up a wiki using phpwiki on his server; we had it set up at http://x.erio.us after just a few days of back-and-forth email and IM conversations, working out some passwords and permissions issues and debugging a few problems.

Why did Taylor help me? I asked him that because it occurred to me that we were a de facto publishing network and no money was changing hands, but suddenly a precocious talented intern was, in answer to my prayers, solving some of my technical problems. He told me about wandering from one blog to the next and how he appreciated my advice about college and that it wasn't difficult for him to help me, so why not? This is the Internet gift economy at work.

After we got the wiki going, I sent out a few invitations to people inter-ested in this book to come by and check it out. J. D. Lasica mentioned it on his blog, and another San *Jose Mercury News* reporter, Michael Bazeley, contacted me to explore this idea of writers using wikis to introduce some of the transparency and bug-fixing used by the open-source process into the editorial routine. He reminded me that most writers are very protective of their embryonic writings and hesitant to expose them to the sunlight too soon.

This is true. I let people review these chapters in progress but I didn't post them on the Internet. Maybe someday I will trust this ethos of transparency and the hygienic properties of sunlight, but it's a slow dialectical process as the culture of the solitary writer gives way to the power of many.

Email Is Still King

Today—months before publication—there are 537 email messages in the mailbox I set up for this book, from brainstorming chapter topics and candidates to review content to ideas for titles and subtitles to updates on who has agreed to talk to me about this book and who wants to review chapters.

I submitted draft chapters via email and FTP. When I was stuck, I sent messages begging for help to my editor, who replied with suggestions. Many of the people I asked for help with the book I first contacted via email; even some of the very busy, high-powered executives and media people were accessible this way or through common acquaintances.

I sent messages to various mailing lists I'm on, writers from my old school, a bunch of web artists, and people who've contributed to other books I've worked on, looking for contacts, suggestions, and ideas. Amidst all the newfangled digital communication techniques—from blogs to social network system tools—email continues to be the mainstay of my online network.

Some believe that syndication formats (or *webfeeds*) popularized by weblogs (namely RSS and its close variant Atom) represent a way out of the spam-clogged email inboxes that plague us today. Because webfeeds follow a publish-and-subscribe model, you receive updates only if you have deliberately opted in by subscribing. It's therefore impossible for anyone to spam you with RSS unless they've somehow hijacked an existing site.

Email may not be king forever. It's been the Internet's killer app since the system was Arpanet, but all things must pass. Still, it's currently a much more open system, with people's addresses easily discoverable, than IM or even RSS webfeeds, which aren't indexed or catalogued comprehensively anywhere and probably couldn't really ever be. For the moment, email still feels relatively private, although that is generally an illusion, because it's easy enough to see and it gets archived just about everywhere.

IM, UR, We Is

In conducting interviews, I tried to use every available medium. I did some interviews on the phone, typing as fast as I could to take notes and capture key phrases and ideas. I did some interviews face to face when people were in the San Francisco Bay Area (where I live) or when I was traveling, scribbling in the notebook that I always carry and transcribing them later.

I did many interviews and follow-ups via email, and I did some via instant messaging. David Weinberger and I had a great IM conversation that I was tempted to reproduce in full, because it proved how warm the medium can be in the hands of experienced users. One nice thing about instant messaging software is that it's easy to log the conversation—everything (as with email) is already in written form, if not yet consistent with *The Chicago Manual of Style*.

This Social Software Stuff Is Tricky

While I was writing the book, Google launched a beta test of a social software network system (SNS)—Orkut—and many of the people I was talking to were playing around with it. It occurred to me that I should set up a tribe or community or group for the book in one of these systems and see whether it was useful for organizing a group of people (what we call "eating our own dog food" in the tech business). I chose Orkut because it was the "it girl" SNS of the moment, even though a backlash against it had already begun, and some people I invited to my group, such as blogger Halley Suitt, politely refused to be sucked into yet another SNS.

One of the people I invited to be my online "friend" in Orkut and to join The Power of Many community was Berkeley researcher danah boyd. I knew her mainly by reputation, but we had met in person once at an impromptu dinner of people who knew each other's names or online handles from Internet

Relay Chat). I liked danah and wanted an excuse to get to know her better, and the book project suddenly made me something like a colleague and not just some random person at a cocktail party.

At the time, Orkut listed one's friends in order of popularity (this has since been changed), and the top nine would appear on one's Orkut home page. Of my top nine faces, eight were men and the other was danah. However, as other people climbed the list, danah eventually dropped off my first nine, leaving me with nine male faces. This prompted me to send out a careless little joke via Orkut's friends-of-friends messaging system:

Warning to males

ok, you guys have now knocked danah off my top-nine friends view on my dashboard (why can't we order and sort other ways?), so now it's nine guys. i may have to drop one of you guys, no hard feelings, just to improve the scenery on my orkut home page.

The problem was, I was thinking in terms of the sort of joke that I might make with my close friends, where things can be subtle or nuanced or one can use unsafe language without fear of offending people. By trying to mock the sexism of the geek networking world, I ended up describing boyd—someone I barely knew but falsely felt already familiar with—as "scenery".

boyd posted about how my message made her feel bad at misbehaving.net, a group weblog about women in technology. She didn't name names, but she made it clear that she had been hurt, and she dropped me from her friends list. Someone pointed out her post to me the next day, and I realized I had crossed a line without being aware of it.

My immediate impulse was to "out" myself and apologize. It was kind of boyd not to tell her readers that I was the rude culprit, but enough people had seen the comment that I felt I ought to come clean. (I sent it just to friends, but a bug in Orkut's system passed it along to my friends of friends—a list of thousands of people, mostly strangers.) Frankly, I didn't want to lose boyd as a source either. This was no way to go about cultivating a network of colleagues and contributors!

I posted an entry to my Radio Free Blogistan site in which I took responsibility for my gaffe and apologized profusely. Immediately, some people—

mostly men—leapt to my defense and accused boyd of overreacting and having no sense of humor. (These always seem to be the charges against women when they speak up for themselves.) I had to disagree. I wasn't trolling for support. I was saying I was sorry.

Reactions—to my original message, to my apology, and to the entire affair—were colored by the lack, in the online environment, of social cues that we've evolved for face-to-face interaction. Further, social software networks, blogging, and wikis take relationships out of their former contexts, so even the social cues that a system *can* deliver are dependent on the context of the interaction and the messy nature of relationships.

Launching an Ideavirus

> Here's a big idea: Ideas are driving the economy. Here's a bigger idea: Ideas
> that spread fastest win.
>
> —subtitle to a Seth Godin article in *Fast Company*

As we've noticed in other contexts, the online networking environment benefits hugely from the intelligent use of real-world face-to-face meetings and activities. Just as there comes a time in many email exchanges when it makes sense for everyone to pick up the phone and deal with issues in real time while listening to the timbre of each other's voices, so there comes a time in many book projects when the head of sales and marketing needs to take the author and editors out to lunch at a fancy restaurant, make the author feel special, and talk about how they're going to promote the book.

Let's plan a conference, I suggested, visions of an unlimited PR budget dancing in my head. Let's throw a series of parties coast to coast.

Let's have a website that announces news and updates related to the book, suggested the sales exec. Let's use the Internet as a marketing and customer relations tool to promote the book. Let's build a buzz among the influentials online. Let's start a viral email marketing campaign.

And so we did. Or we will. I'm still writing this book, after all, but we're planning to. You may have seen this book mentioned in email or on the Web before you saw the printed book. In fact, I proposed a rather lame email signature virus on my weblog and very quickly one of my contributors, Phil Wolff, posted about four or five that were much better, catchier. I'm using them now instead of my original idea. Thus Tom Sawyer whitewashes the fence with the help of his friends.

You may have heard me talking about this book on the radio. Or maybe we just did a good job of getting shelved in the right part of the bookstore or indexed properly on Amazon. Whatever we did must have worked, or you wouldn't be here now, right?

The Nonphysical Interpersonal World

Howard Rheingold wrote,

> It has taken 10 years of talk about 'new media' for a critical mass to under-
> stand that every computer desktop, and now every pocket, is a worldwide
> printing press, broadcasting station, place of assembly, and organizing
> tool—and to learn how to use that infrastructure to affect change.

Convergence is shrinking journalism, reviving the town square, and pro-ducing political miniparties.

And yet, as Rheingold told us even earlier, the critical mass and new media aren't cure-alls. "There is no market for solving social problems," he wrote. "Throwing technology at problems can be helpful, but the fundamental prob-lems are political and economic and rooted in human nature. ... A tool is not the task."

Rheingold also made another observation when I interviewed him that startled me a bit out of my complacency about the newness of the virtual world. "There has been a nonphysical world for a very long time," he pointed out. "There wouldn't have been a U.S. Revolution without committees of corre-spondence." Rheingold also noted that "the Protestant Reformation was a vir-tual world in many ways, built around the printing press," because Gutenberg's Bible ushered in the era that devolved control over that ancient text and dis-tributed it, opening up the realm of discussion and interpretation to literate people in all the written languages of Europe and eventually the world. For the history of nonphysical worlds, Rheingold even pointed to the Sufi concept of an imaginal realm—the world you're thinking about when you're meditating or dreaming.

But fantasy, meditation, and dreaming are inherently private experiences, only sharable through forms of communication.

Let's get busy dreaming up a new world together.

Sources and Further Reading

This book is just a snapshot around the time of the second major turning point on the Internet, the moment in which the living Web has reached critical mass and is starting to have a significant impact on the real world. We're still at the very beginning of something—a veritable dawning of the age of Aquarius, so to speak—and there are sure to be many exciting new developments to come. Tune in to our website to keep up with the continuing story of the power of many and the might of the living Web.

First and foremost, for more information and discussion on all the topics in this book, visit The Power of Many site:

http://thepowerofmany.com

Then, read these web pages and books for more detail on the ideas in this specific chapter:

Bill Moyers interview on National Public Radio's *Fresh Air*, May 13, 2004:
http://freshair.npr.org/day_fa.jhtml?display=day&todayDate=05/13/2004

Just for fun, how about a biography of Niels Bohr?:
http://www.nobel.se/physics/laureates/1922/bohr-bio.html

Dan Gillmor's eJournal:
http://weblog.siliconvalley.com/column/dangillmor

James Fallow, "The Twilight of the Information Middlemen," *The New York Times*, May 16, 2004:
http://www.nytimes.com/2004/05/16/business/yourmoney/16tech.html?ex=1400040000&en=5cc6f0f89e819a14&ei=5007

Jay Rosen, "Brain Food for BloggerCon: Journalism and Weblogging in Their Corrected Fullness," *PressThink* (introduction to a BloggerCon session); and Dave Winer's response:
http://journalism.nyu.edu/pubzone/weblogs/pressthink/2004/04/16/con_prelude.html

http://blogs.law.harvard.edu/bloggerCon/2004/04/16#a1227

Brian Dear, "Topic: community for a book?", e-mail to the "Power of Many" Orkut group:
http://www.orkut.com/CommMsgs.aspx?cmm=3196&tid=1

"PRWEEK.COM Q&A: Nick Denton, Gawker Media," May 20, 2004:
http://www.prweek.com/news/news_story_free.cfm?ID=211404&site=3

Dave Neiwert, "Media Revolt: A Manifesto," *Orcinus,* May 7, 2004:
http://dneiwert.blogspot.com/2004_05_02_dneiwert_archive.html#108390182327224560

Vin Crosbie, "What Newspapers and Their Web Sites Must Do to Survive," USC Annenberg School *Online Journalism Review,* March 4, 2004:
http://www.ojr.org/ojr/business/1078349998.php

"Rumsfeld bans camera phones," News.com.au, May 23, 2004:
http://news.com.au/common/story_page/0,4057,9643950%255E401,00.html

Wikipedia, a free, open-source encyclopedia:
http://wikipedia.com

William Gibson, "Last Postcard from Costa Del Blog," September 12, 2003:
http://www.williamgibsonbooks.com/blog/2003_09_01_archive.asp#106337201260041604

Boing Boing blog, where Cory Doctorow is a contributor:
http://boingboing.net

danah boyd, "Sexist Jokes and Orkut Invites," *misbehaving,* February 4, 2004, and the follow-ups on my blog and hers:
http://www.misbehaving.net/2004/02/sexist_jokes_an.html

http://radiofreeblogistan.com/2004/02/04/this_social_software_stuff_is_tricky.html

http://www.zephoria.org/thoughts/archives/2004/02/05/publicly_processing_hurt.html

Seth Godin, "Unleash Your Ideavirus," *Fast Company,* August 2000:
http://www.fastcompany.com/magazine/37/ideavirus.html

Howard Rheingold, "From the Screen to the Streets," *In These Times,* October 28, 2003:
http://inthesetimes.com/comments.php?id=414_0_1_0_M

Howard Rheingold, "Why can't we use technology to solve social problems?" Edge.org's *The World Question Center 2001: What Questions Have Disappeared?*:
http://www.edge.org/documents/questions/q2001.2.html#rheingold

Glossary

This section defines and explains many of the technologies, standards, formats, services, and philosophies—as well as a few products and organizations—that are mentioned throughout this book. It also defines a few of the key jargon terms that you'll encounter. (If you can't find the term you're looking for here, see the online version of this glossary at http://x.erio.us/index.php?Glossary. The term that you're looking for may be there and if it isn't you can request it.)

Italicized terms serve as cross-references to other glossary entries.

accountability

For a *learning system* to succeed, what are required are open channels of communication in a group and a culture of taking responsibility, owning up to mistakes, and fixing what needs to be fixed, along with *transparency* and *listening*.

action alert

A message sent to signed-up members of a website or organization suggesting that they take a specific action in the near future.

aggregator

A software application or web service used to collect and read a list of subscribed *syndicated* newsfeeds all in one location.

AIM

AOL Instant Messenger. One of several common *IM* applications.

Apache

An *open-source* web server application designed originally for Unix and its variants. Apache now also runs on Windows and Macintosh computers and is the most popular web server application on the Internet. The name is based on a pun: "a patchy web server." Apache is part of the *LAMP* software development platform.

ARM

Activist relationship management: an acronym I've coined (though I am probably not the first to have done so) to describe a class of software analogous to *CRM* software but geared toward activists instead of toward customers.

astroturfing

A term intended to suggest fake grassroots movements: the practice of setting up progressive-sounding organizations and using them to stir up the appearance of an independent public constituency. Also, the practice of organizing volunteers to send essentially the same message, usually to independent outlets, such as the letters columns of local newspapers, in order to get talking points into wide distribution.

Atom

A format for *weblog syndication* and remote administration designed to build and improve upon the *RSS* syndication format and the *MetaWeblog API*. At press time, Atom is in pre-beta format, version 0.3, and is about to be turned over to an IETF working group. *Google*'s *Blogger* software and Six Apart's *Movable Type* and *TypePad* applications now support Atom as their default format for putting out blog information, with reduced support for *RSS*. Nonetheless, RSS is much more widely adopted as a format at this time.

http://www.mnot.net/drafts/draft-nottingham-atom-format-02.html

blog

See *weblog*.

Blogger

A commercial *weblog* product originally developed by Pyra Labs and now a product of *Google*.

blogger

A person who maintains, reads, or comments on blogs.

Bloglines

A hosted web service (Bloglines.com) used to *aggregrate syndicated* feeds.

http://www.bloglines.com

blogosphere

The collected words of all webloggers everywhere. The term is also sometimes applied to a smaller "galaxy" of writers clustered around a topic or genre or theme or some other affinity.

blogroll

A list of recommended sites, usually other weblogs. Managing them isn't a core feature yet in most popular weblog tools, so they tend to grow stale. The coinage may be safely attributed to Doc Searls, who modeled it on logrolling, the practice of recommending one another's books that I sincerely hope all my writer friends will honor in the coming months. (See also *XFN*.)

BlogSpot

A *weblog* hosting service owned by *Google* that provides free (advertising-supported) or paid hosting for *Blogger* weblogs.

http://blogspot.com

Blosxom

A *weblog* application developed by Rael Dornfest of O'Reilly; originally for OS X, hence the name, pronounced "blossom."

Channel Z

An experimental blog/knowledge-management application being developed, at press time, by Dave Winer. Channel Z enables hierarchical classification of *weblog* entries (much like *Blosxom*).

chat

Real-time (synchronous) written communication over the Internet.

CivicSpace

An open source version of Drupal, inheriting characteristics from DeanSpace and developed by Zack Rosen and Neil Drumm, who led the DeanSpace effort. CivicSpace, like the software it is based on, is open-source, and CivicSpace Labs is underwritten by the same venture activist who has underwritten the Music for America startup.

CMS

Content management system, a back-end administrative system for updating the content at a website. Often retrofitted as an afterthought from 6 to 12 months after a website build, when the content bottlenecks have clearly presented themselves.

Any website that needs frequent updating requires a CMS. A *weblog* application is a form of streamlined CMS designed for rapid updating.

Convio

A company that makes *CMS* and *CRM* software for nonprofits and other progressive activist organizations.

craigslist

A community bulletin-board service founded originally as a mailing list, then as a series of mailing lists, and finally as a website hosted by Craig Newmark. craigslist continues to grow in popularity and has expanded to many cities beyond its original San Francisco location by paying close attention to the wishes of its users.

http://www.craigslist.org

CRM

Customer relationship management (CRM) refers to the practice of centralizing all the customer-facing services in one workflow or enterprise software application. For most businesses this involves sales, customer service, billing, and marketing at a minimum. Often seen as "CRM software" or eCRM.

DeanLink

A social network system (*SNS*) developed by the Dean for America (DFA) campaign as a way of enabling volunteers to find people geographically nearby who share the same priorities or who know the same people.

DeanSpace

Pro-Dean campaign website software package developed by Zack Rosen and Neil Drumm, originally as Hack4Dean, and a host of volunteers as an open-source project based on Drupal—which is itself an open-source Slashcode clone that refers to itself as "community plumbing." (See also *CivicSpace, Drupal.*)

disruption, disruptive change

A (usually technological) change that yields new economies of practice or scale and threatens to upend the locked-in advantage of business interests built on the existing technologies. Incumbents find it difficult to co-opt the change successfully because they have more to lose from it than upstarts do.

For example, peer-to-peer music sharing, as first exemplified by *Napster*, is a disruptive threat to music companies whose advantages in the marketplace are tied to distribution channels that are quickly becoming obsolete.

Dodgeball.com

A social network service (*SNS*) for people and events in New York City, involving phones and other handheld devices.

Drupal

An *open-source* content management system (*CMS*) used as the basis for *DeanSpace* and a number of other campaign and cause websites, including http://eb4democracy.com, http://musicforamerica.com, and http://civicspacelabs.com. Drupal's feature set is similar to that of Slashcode, *Scoop*, and the various flavors of Nuke.

eCRM

Electronic CRM. A synonym for *CRM* used to distinguish current types of CRM from pre-Web forms of customer care.

eHarmony

A commercial online dating service.

http://www.eharmony.com

eRoom

A hosted, secure web application used to facilitate remote group collaboration by providing a persistent repository for collaborative documents and for tracking project milestones. One of the few successful social collaboration business tools of the last five years.

ESF

Event Share Framework. A format for sharing event information built as an extension to *RSS* 2.0.

http://www.esfstandard.org

Evite

A web service that automates the process of inviting people to parties and other occasions. Late deciders can see who's going to be there and who isn't before responding to an Evite invitation.

http://www.evite.com

Feedster

A search engine that searches *RSS* (and *Atom*) feeds instead of HTML pages, providing more fine-grained results, particularly when searching *weblogs*.

http://www.feedster.com

Findory

A collaboratively filtered custom news service that learns what kinds of stories you like to read and finds them for you.

http://www.Findory.com

Flash

A rich application (and animation) development format for the Web from Macromedia, used as the basis for *GNE*.

Flickr

A social network system (*SNS*) application created by Ludicorp and designed for sharing images. It includes a chat feature and is built on the *GNE* codebase.

http://www.flickr.com

FOAF

"Friend of a friend." A concept describing a set of relationships and a format based on *RDF* used to indicate these relationships between people. The file generated in RDF is built automatically by *TypePad*, *PeopleAggregrator*, and *LiveJournal*.

http://xmlns.com/foaf/0.1

Friendster

A social network service (*SNS*) designed to allow people to meet friends of their friends for friendship and dating.

http://www.friendster.com

Frontier

A scripting platform written with *UserTalk*, originally designed for the Macintosh platform and used as the basis for UserLand's Manila and *Radio* products, as well as Dave Winer's *Channel Z* product. The kernel of Frontier was made *open-source* in 2004.

GNE

Game Neverending. An online multiuser game built from *Flash* and providing the GNE codebase used in *Flickr*.

Google

The most popular search engine on the Internet; also the owner of *Blogger* (and BlogSpot) and *Orkut*. Seems to favor *Atom* over *RSS* 2.0 (new Google groups have Atom feeds; compare with *Yahoo! Groups* and their *RSS* 2.0 feeds).

grassroots

Locally based ("rooted") volunteer activists, nominally desired by both parties but at times neglected in favor of fundraising and television advertising. Even the Dean campaign, which presented a vigorous grassroots phenomenon, had problems coordinating the centralized official campaign with the numerous volunteer cells. (See also *astroturfing*.)

homeostasis, homeostatic

A self-correcting way for a system to keep its environmental variables within an acceptable range. For example, a human body sheds heat when the temperature is too high, because the body can function properly only within a certain range of temperatures.

hosted

A service whose data is maintained by a remote entity.

ideavirus

A marketing concept that is spread "virally" from person to person instead of through the mass media. The idea was coined, or at least spread virally, by Seth Godin.

IM

Instant messaging is both an application and an activity. The application is installed on users' computers or hosted remotely. The use of that service allows users to create a conversation in an IM box that is faster and often more conversational and shorter than conversations in email.

IRC

Internet Relay Chat. An open, multiuser chat format used as an alternative to proprietary commercial chat formats such as *AIM* and *Y!M*.

Java

A programming language designed at Sun Microsystems to be cross-platform; originally intended as a controller for household applications.

karma

A measurement of a community member's status used at *Slashdot* and other community sites. People award merits and demerits to each other based on their participation in the group. The opinions of higher-status people are generally weighted more highly as well, but there is no single dominant algorithm for ranking people yet.

KM

Knowledge management, a concept modeled on document management and content management that primarily deals with capturing explicit and implicit knowledge from workers so that an entire enterprise can learn as a whole. Many cumbersome KM systems have been implemented in large corporations with varying levels of success. Some business blog advocates believe that the time-stamped log is the most natural KM input device and that a good search engine or a wiki would solve the problems of grooming and retrieval of information.

LAMP

The *open-source* Linux, Apache, MySQL, PHP platform, popularly used as an alternative to commercial and proprietary web-application development platforms such as *.NET* and ColdFusion.

learning system

A process that isn't locked into a static set of procedural rules but has the capacity to improve through feedback from customers (or users) and the people in the system deputized to listen to and meet customers' needs. When Craig Newmark explained how this works at craigslist, I concluded that the essential elements of a learning system are *transparency*, *listening*, and *accountability*.

LinkedIn

A social network system (*SNS*) system designed for business networking (see Chapter 8, "Lonely Hearts' Club Band").

https://www.linkedin.com

Linux

An *open-source* Unix clone designed to run on systems designed for Windows.

list server

A mailing-list management application, for example, ListServ, Majordomo, or Mailman.

listening

To improve the processes in a service, both the users and the customer service employees must be heard, because they can tell you what isn't working as well as it should be. Craig Newmark has a lot to say about empowering people to improve their own environments and enabling people to take pride in their work. Along with *transparency* and *accountability*, listening is a pillar of any *learning system*.

Phil Wolff has promised to explain to me some day how listening doesn't scale. Look for it in this book's blog.

LiveJournal

An *open-source*–hosted *weblog*/diary service with some social network system (*SNS*) elements, such as friends' groups and communities based on shared declared interests.

https://www.livejournal.com

LOAF

Originally a humorous takeoff on *FOAF*, LOAF is now an actual method of encoding your whitelist (approved email addresses) in a hash appended to each outgoing email message.

Longhorn

Microsoft's next-generation operating system, currently scheduled for 2005 or 2006, rumored to incorporate *RSS* syndication and *aggregation*.

Manila

A content *CMS* from UserLand that runs on *Frontier* and is written in *UserTalk*. Many of the *weblog* concepts found in *Radio* and other blog applications originated with Manila.

Match.com

An online dating service, one of the two largest dating services on the Web.

http://www.match.com

Meetup

An online service used to schedule monthly meetings of interest groups in real-time and real space.

http://www.meetup.com

meme

An imitatible idea; memes "replicate" by copying from one person's mind to the next. The term was coined by Richard Dawkins in his book *The Selfish Gene*, originally intended as a metaphorical analogy to the gene as a unit or subject of evolution. Dawkins was arguing that you could apply Darwinistic principles to the evolution of genes themselves, as opposed to organisms or entire species.

Meme is therefore a jargon or cant word of a subset of geeks and intellectuals, and can often be translated simply as "idea" or "fad" or "something everybody's posting on their blogs today."

metacrap

Metadata that is entered inaccurately, inconsistently, or haphazardly; often caused by inhumane or unreasonable interfaces or workflow models. People who refer to the metacrap argument are generally advocating "letting the software sort it out" instead of asking people to explicitly tag everything before making any contribution. The term was coined by science fiction writer and BoingBoing blogger Cory Doctorow in his essay, "Metacrap: Putting the torch to seven straw-men of the meta-utopia":

http://www.well.com/~doctorow/metacrap.htm

metadata

Descriptive information about the data in a database, usually tracked for sorting or filtering purposes. Some metadata can be generated and tracked automatically. Other metadata must be entered explicitly by the user, creating a barrier to contribution often referred to as the "*metacrap* problem." Common metadata fields include author, publication date, and data such as category or geographical region.

MetaWeblog API

An application programming interface (API) for remotely posting to a *weblog*, based on the *Blogger* API, extended by UserLand to incorporate elements necessary for *Radio*, and then extended further by Six Apart to incorporate elements necessary for *Movable Type*. The *Atom* API is intended as an alternative.

Movable Type (MT)

A free *weblog* application made by Six Apart that requires that the user have access to one's own server (that is, it is not hosted), some skill with web servers and scripting, or the ability to locate someone who has those skills to initially set it up. *TypePad* is similar to MT but hosted and not free.

MySQL

A free version of SQL (structured query language), a database-management format, part of the *LAMP* platform.

Napster

The breakthrough peer-to-peer (decentralized) music filesharing service that upended the traditional economies of the music distribution business. It was sued out of existence and then resurrected by Roxio as a fully-licensed service.

Nerve Personals

A dating service that is syndicated at such web publications as Nerve and Salon.

.NET

Microsoft's platform for rich web application development. It contains an abstraction layer that enables data exchange via *XML*. It is intended as an alternative to *Java*.

netroots

Jerome Armstrong's term for web-aided grassroots activists. Armstrong and Markos Zuniga (nicknamed "Kos") advised the Dean campaign to use a blog and to use Meetup to aid local organizing. Joe Trippi, Dean's former campaign manager, has adopted this term as well.

OML

Outline Markup Language. An alternative to *OPML* based on *RDF* but not widely adopted.

http://oml.sourceforge.net/cgi-bin/blosxom.cgi/specification

open-source

A philosophy of software development in which the source code is not kept secret and the combined efforts of many volunteer programmers work to eliminate bugs and add features. At one time this was called "Free Software," until Tim O'Reilly suggested re-branding it for PR purposes.

For more information on open-source philosophy, see Eric Raymond's seminal "The Cathedral and the Bazaar":

http://www.firstmonday.dk/issues/issue3_3/raymond

OPML

Outline Processor Markup Language. A format invented by Dave Winer to express outline relationships in *XML* and most commonly used to express *RSS* subscription lists.

http://www.opml.org

Orkut

A social network service (*SNS*) invented by a *Google* engineer and at press time still in beta testing. To join, one must be invited by somebody already in the system. (See also Chapter 7, "Doing Business with Strangers.")

http://www.orkut.com

PeopleAggregrator

An *open-source* social network service (*SNS*) created by Marc Canter of BroadbandMechanics.com. It is a hosted service based on *FOAF*.

http://peopleaggregator.com

Perl

A programming language popular among Unix-oriented web developers. *Movable Type* is written in Perl.

permalink

A link to a specific entry in a *weblog*, invented by Paul Bausch at Pyra Labs for the *Blogger* product as a way of dealing with the fact that weblog entries eventually scroll off a weblog's main page and can then only be found in their archive location.

permission marketing

A spam-free philosophy of marketing that requires participants to consciously opt in before they are sent messages, promoted by Seth Godin in his book of the same name.

petition

A technique used by online organizers to promote a cause and gather email contact information.

PHP

Hypertext Preprocessor. A server-side scripting language embedded into HTML documents to add dynamic elements to web pages; part of the *LAMP* platform.

Plaxo

A *CMS* that is trying to incorporate some social networking features for users. (See also *YASNS*.)

pMachine

A free *weblog* application that requires users to have their own hosting and enough savvy to set up an application for their web server; written in *PHP*.

PubSub

An abbreviation for publication/subscription, a proposed alternative name for *RSS*. Also, an *aggregator* website.

http://www.pubsub.com

Python

An *open-source* programming language popular among web developers.

Radio

A *weblog* and *aggregator* product made by UserLand, based on *Frontier* and written in *UserTalk*. Savvy users can take advantage of its scriptability to extend it, and there are many add-ons created by its user community.

RDF

Resource Description Framework. An *XML* dialect that expresses relationships in terms of triplets (think: subject, verb, object). RDF is considered to be a building block of an eventual *semantic web*.

http://www.w3.org/TR/REC-rdf-syntax

REST

Representational State Transfer. A philosophy of web application development that favors simplicity, elegance, and the proper use of the four main HTTP verbs: POST, PUT, GET, and DELETE. (*Atom* is a RESTful format.)

Ringo

A now-ended research project at MIT in the mid '90s that asked people to list their music preferences and then drew inferences and made recommendations from its data set; a precursor to Amazon's recommendations and other similar services today.

RSS

Originally known as RDF Site Summary, a news-headline syndication format invented at Netscape for its portal service and intended to compete with Microsoft's CDF format. The first version was RSS 0.9. Netscape then came out with RSS 0.91 and dropped the *RDF* support, renaming the format Rich Site Summary. UserLand then came out with an alternative RSS 0.91 format that was a merger of Netscape's RSS and UserLand's ScriptingNews format. This branch was subsequently updated as 0.91, 0.92, and 0.93. An 0.94 version was eventually renamed RSS 2.0, which is the recommended version of RSS today. The RSS 2.0 specification is now hosted at Harvard's Berkman Center, has been frozen, and is said to stand for Really Simple Syndication.

http://www.reallysimplesyndication.com

RDF supporters created a version of RSS, called RSS 1.0, that reintroduced the RDF support. This version is also still widely used, particularly among *semantic web* enthusiasts and users of products that generate the format automatically (such as *Movable Type* and, formerly, *Blogger*).

The *Atom* format is similar to RSS but is not backward-compatible with it.

http://blogs.law.harvard.edu/tech/rss

Ryze

A social network service (*SNS*) intended for business networking.

http://www.ryze.com

Scoop

An *open-source CMS* written in *Perl* mostly by Rusty Foster, the founder of Kuro5hin ("corrosion") and a partner in Armstrong Zuniga LLC.

Scoop is designed for collaborative media filtering and community moderation of each other's contributions. It powered the official Clark campaign blog community, and it replaced *Movable Type* as the basis for DailyKos.com when the level of participation from comments began to present scaling strains. Scoop and *Drupal* seem to be the leading open-source Slashcode-style solutions, although Bricolage—a full-featured open-source CMS—represents yet another alternative.

semantic web

A dream of the web's creator, Tim Berners-Lee, of a second-generation Web that would incorporate semantic information ("meaning") into its links and relationships among objects, enabling automated machine manipulation of statements (or "triplets") in subject-verb-object form: Jason Kottke/writes/a blog, Jason Kottke/is linked to in the blogrolls of/many people, Jason Kottke/reviewed/*The Matrix*, Jason Kottke's blog/has/comments, and so on.

RDF (Resource Description Framework) is an *XML* format designed to help build the semantic web.

Detractors consider the semantic web to be a pipe dream at best or entirely wrongheaded at worst.

SenseCam

A Microsoft gadget that lets you spy on your own life. SenseCam, touted as a visual diary of sorts by Microsoft, is designed to be worn around the neck. The prototype responds to changes such as bright lights and sudden movements and can take up to 2,000 images in a 12-hour day without the wearer doing a thing.

Shrook

An *RSS* news *aggregator* for Mac OS X.

http://www.fondantfancies.com/shrook

SixDegrees.com

A seminal social network system (*SNS*) that failed because there wasn't a sufficient critical mass of potential users when it launched. Its source code lives on in some of the *YASNS*s of today.

http://www.sixdegrees.com

Slashdot

One of the first successful media/community sites (their slogan is "News for Nerds. Stuff that matters."), whose mechanisms enable the readership of the multiauthor weblog to work together to filter the best comments to the fore.

The *open-source* code of Slashdot, Slashcode, is said to be somewhat tangled. This has inspired a number of alternative clones (each has their proponents and detractors), including a family of applications called somethingNuke, as well as *Drupal* and *Scoop*.

SNS

A social network system or service, meaning a service explicitly offering social-networking tools and ideally (if rarely) facilitating social media exchange or offering useful communication or collaboration facilities (as opposed to sites with other purposes that inadvertently function as better social networks than the overt SNS).

SocialText

A hosted *wiki* application designed to make wikis secure and easier for business types to work with.

http://www.socialtext.com

syndication

On the Web, usually refers to distribution of the headlines of news articles (in the form of clickable links) or to freely distributed full-text entries or excerpts from *weblogs* in an *XML* format such as *RSS* or *Atom*. Also used as a general term for the whole publication-and-subscription (pub-sub) model that is neither push nor pull precisely.

Syndication Studio 2004

A commercial software product; the first desktop application allowing the creation of feeds in all *syndication* formats.

http://www.howdev.com/products/syndicationstudio2004

Technorati

A website that tracks links among *weblogs* and other frequently updated websites. Technorati identifies the stories that are most often commented on at any given time and can be used for ego-surfing in the sense of discovering who out there is linking to your site or blog.

http://www.technorati.com

Tickle

A social network service (*SNS*) purchased by Monster.com to incorporate networking more directly into the online job search experience. Now, when you forward a job lead to a friend, the software prompts you by pointing out that what you were doing was networking and asks if you would like to do some more.

http://web.tickle.com

transparency

The web fosters transparency. Nothing you want to be kept private should be posted to the Web at all, even in a locked or password protected or otherwise secured location. My theory is that anything that's gone out over the Internet will eventually see the light of day. However, the Web rewards openness, and light and air are antiseptic. Together with *listening* and *accountability*, transparency is a pillar of a *learning system*.

Tribe

A social network system (*SNS*) at Tribe.net organized around "tribes" of likeminded people who share one or more interests.

http://www.tribe.net

tribe

A group of likeminded people at *Ryze*. Free users of Ryze can belong to up to three tribes.

two-way web

A term coined by Dave Winer to describe the way the Web is supposed to work, as a two-way, many-to-many medium in which readers can also be writers. Sometimes referred to as the "writable web," the "read-write web," the "world live web," or the "living web." Another shorthand for the entire phenomenon is *RSS* (as framed by http://www.reallysimplesyndication.com).

TypeKey

A hosted authentication system for *weblog* comments (but conveniently generating a profile page, the stub of any *SNS*) from Six Apart. Free, released at first during the alpha review of *Movable Type* 3.0, and one of the first signs that the *blogosphere* was getting over its crush on the founders of Six Apart, once viewed as immune to criticism, like (in the words of Shelley Powers) "baby squirrels":

http://weblog.burningbird.net/archives/2003/06/24/kicking-the-baby-squirrels-again

TypePad

A hosted commercial *weblog* service Six Apart, similar to *Movable Type* but much easier for non-techies to use.

http://www.typepad.com

Upcoming.org

A free shared-event calendar service created by Andy Baio. It can generate *syndicated RSS* feeds listing upcoming events that can then be inserted into any web page.

http://www.upcoming.org

UserTalk

A scripting language originally intended for the Apple Macintosh platform as an alternative to AppleTalk; used as the basis for *Frontier*, *Manila*, and *Radio*.

VoodooPad

A desktop *wiki*-like tool (for Mac OS X only) from Flying Meat. VoodooPad works more like my brain than any other computer tool I've ever used. At heart, it is simply a notepad that uses hyperlinks and some wiki-style shortcuts as a way of connecting one scrap of paper to others. It's a completely unstructured database evading all the *metacrap* problems inherent with Palm, iCal, Outlook, Entourage, Word, and so on. As a desktop wiki, it's also not dependent on the whims of a web browser (but you can synch it with a public web-driven wiki). The best $19.95 I've ever spent.

http://www.flyingmeat.com/voodoopad.html

weblog

Literally, a web-based log of entries, often written in a personal voice, frequently including links to interesting found resources on the Web, generally updated frequently, even daily or several times a day, and most commonly organized in reverse chronological order. The primary platform for personal expression on the Web today.

The Well

The Whole Earth 'Lectronic Link (WELL) is one of the earlier Internet communities. It was launched by the people doing the Whole Earth Catalogue with Stewart Brand, and they actively cultivated journalists, writers, and people besides just techies. Howard Rheingold is probably the foremost virtual-community thinker to emerge from the early days of The Well. The Well is now web-accessible and is owned by Salon.com.

http://www.well.com

wiki

A website containing a single document or set of documents that can be edited by anyone (or by any authorized user) in the browser. Used to assemble collaborative websites with a minimal threshold for participation. Also *wiki wiki*, from the Hawaiian word for quick.

XFN

XML Friends Network. A proposed open standard for social networking that involves simply incorporating "rel" attributes in one's links to people, such as in the *blogroll* of a *weblog* or list of participants or attendees for some event. The links with attributes are just a bit longer—for example,

<a href="http://joe.blogs.com/" rel="friend">

XHTML

Extensible Hypertext Markup Language. A form of HTML that is also valid XML.

http://www.w3.org/TR/xhtml1

XML

Extensible Markup Language. A machine-readable form of markup intended to facilitate data interchange over the Internet.

http://www.w3.org/TR/REC-xml

YASNS

"Yet Another Social Network System," a facetious term used by experts in the social-software field to describe the proliferation of these services.

Y!M

Yahoo! Messenger. A proprietary *IM* application.

Yahoo! Groups

Yahoo!'s free (advertising-supported) mailing list and group-formation service that permits anyone to easily create a group with a mailing list, a data repository, a list of links, a set of files, and other features. One of the most common forms of social groupings online. Potentially threatened by *Google* groups (and a thus far minimal blogging play). On the other hand, Yahoo! has embraced *RSS* rather effectively.

http://groups.yahoo.com

Yahoo! Personals

Yahoo!'s dating service—the most profitable part of Yahoo!, according to some sources, and one of the two largest dating services on the Web.

Index